The United Nations and
Human Rights in Iraq

# The Untold Story of
# Camp Ashraf

## Tahar Boumedra

*Main Entrance to Camp Ashraf in Diyala Province*

I dedicate this testimony to my father who died as a martyr during the war of national liberation; to my mother who continued the battle as a mujahedah till Algeria recovered its independence and to Idris, my son, for his support.

# Acknowledgement

My thanks and gratitude to Dr Davina Miller, from Peace Studies, University of Bradford, who devoted her precious time to correct the manuscript and put it in the present shape. My thanks also go to all those colleagues and friends, who are too many to name, who motivated me to put on record what I experienced and witnessed while monitoring the situation of Camp Ashraf residents and related issues.

# Contents

# Forward

This monograph is very timely. The "untold story" is not about a tragedy or misconduct in the past, but about current failure of the international community to take the necessary measures to protect over 3000 Iranian dissidents residing in Camp Ashraf and Camp Liberty in Iraq.

The facts are stark. The Unite States, in writing, guaranteed these people safety when they handed over to the US Army their only means of defending themselves, and they are now dying at the hands of America's erstwhile allies, the Iraqi Government, goaded by Baghdad's new best friends, the Government of Iran. This is certainly a political and moral failure.

Simultaneously, the UN has proved completely incapable and disingenuous in attempting to protect the refugees, constantly siding with the Iraqi government. The UN Mission in Iraq has been remarkably not only ineffective, but counterproductive, always offering excuses about why this is someone else's fault, and by providing misleading information to justify its failure. The UNHCR has also failed to uphold its obligations and take full responsibility for protecting and assisting these refugees, in accordance to its mandate.

The book highlights how lack of knowledge, prejudice and misguided policy coupled with bad intentions and outright misconduct in some cases resulted in so much pain, and the loss of so many lives.

**John Bolton**
Former United States Ambassador to the United Nations

# Preface

As Chief of the Human Rights Office of United Nations Assistance Mission for Iraq (UNAMI), and Adviser to the Special Representative of the Secretary-General (SRSG) on Camp Ashraf related issues from 2009 until 2012, I was urged by a number of diplomats, parliamentarians, NGO representatives and by my civilian and military colleagues at different UN agencies to write my memoirs for the period I was the UN lead person on the question of Camp Ashraf, where 3400 members of Mujahedin-e Khalq (MEK) lived for over 26 years. For some time, I resisted the idea of writing as my job at the United Nations requires confidentiality and the internal reporting mechanism restricted my ability to freely express myself. The UN reporting mechanism is severely hampered by checks and balances that often shade the truth and dilute responsibilities for political expediency.

In the fall of autumn 2011, new developments took place. A new SRSG arrived to the mission in Iraq and made it a priority to close Camp Ashraf. Ashraf residents were evicted from their 26 years place of residence and transferred to a new location in Iraq called Camp Liberty. The legality of this eviction and the transfer process were highly contested. A number of crimes against the inhabitants of Camp Ashraf were committed in both locations. Some of these crimes could amount to crimes against humanity. UNAMI mandated by the UN Security

Council to assist Iraq in reconciliation and reconstruction based on the rule of law and respect of human rights had failed to uphold the rule of law and protect human rights in Iraq. It had at times covered up for certain unlawful conduct of the Government. In order to distance myself from what UNAMI and the SRSG concocted with the Government of Iraq against Ashraf population and be able to speak out without censorship, I had to give up my UN job and its privileges and immunities.

Now from outside the UN system, I could avail myself to speak out to reveal the untold story. I do it to combat the silence observed towards the cruel, inhumane and degrading treatment inflicted on a defenceless population in Camp Ashraf and the extra-judicial killing committed against them in total impunity. I also do it as a therapy for myself from the stress and frustrations I experienced during the three and half years I was in charge of monitoring the situation of this population. Of course I assume full responsibility for what I publish in this testimony.

The story will be an account of what I had observed and witnessed on the ground. It will be put across in a chronological order but events are interconnected, sometimes overlapping and sometimes repetitive and might not always appear chronologically sound. All allegations in my statements are documented and most of them are extracts from notes to the file or from my personal diary. I will try as much as possible to refrain from making value judgements and will leave it to the reader to draw conclusions. The story will focus on the Iraqi policy towards Ashraf residents since the beginning of the drawdown and eventual departure of the United States Forces in Iraq and how the Iraqi government implemented such a policy on the ground and the ensuing consequences. I will shed some light on the embargo imposed on the Camp in order to break its residents resolve; the fact finding missions I conducted after two deadly attacks by the Iraqi army against Ashraf residents. I will address the passivity and indifference, sometime complicity of the United Nations. I will attempt to give elements of reply to the often raised question on the UN biased conduct towards the MEK and its members in Ashraf; how the UN made arrangements with the Iraqi Prime Minister to transfer the Ashrafis to a detention centre ironically called Camp Liberty. How reports were doctored to mislead the international community and to perpetuate the terrorist stigma against the Ashrafis. In a final chapter I will present to the readers accounts of judicial proceedings conducted before different jurisdictions under diverse legal systems that cleared the MEK from accusations of terrorism and led to its removal from the European and American Foreign Terrorist Organizations lists.

I will supply few pictures of significant events and append some documents readers would be curious to examine while going through the story.

# Introduction

Before joining the United Nations Assistance Mission for Iraq (UNAMI), I was the Regional Director of *Penal Reform International* (PRI) for the Middle East and North Africa (MENA), based in Amman, Jordan. I was working with the MENA governments to introduce human rights based reforms in the penal and prison systems in the region. In November 2008, I was offered the position of Chief of UNAMI Human Rights Office who also represents the United Nations High Commissioner for Human Rights (HCHR) in Iraq.

UNAMI Human Rights Office, conducts activities as mandated by the Security Council resolution 1546 of June 2004 and expanded by resolutions 1770 (2007) and 2061 (2012) to "promote the protection of human rights, national reconciliation, and judicial and legal reform in order to strengthen the rule of law in Iraq". The latter resolution expanded the mandate "… to take all feasible steps and to develop modalities to ensure the protection of affected civilians, including children, women and members of religious and ethnic minority groups". It urges "all those concerned, as set forth in international humanitarian law, including the Geneva Conventions and the Hague Regulations, to allow full unimpeded access by humanitarian personnel to all people in need of assistance, and to make available, as far as possible, all necessary facilities for their operations…".

UNAMI Human Rights Office works with the Government of Iraq as well as members of Iraqi Civil Society to support the promotion, respect and protection of human rights of all without discrimination. UNAMI Human Rights Office also works closely with other United Nations Funds and Agencies to ensure that respect, promotion and protection of human rights are integrated in their programmes and activities.

My job was focused in particular on the protection of civilians from the effects of armed conflict and violence, the rule of law and the protection of the rights of those who are detained or are being tried before the courts, the rights and protection of children, promotion of empowerment of women, the rights of persons with disabilities, the rights and protection of minorities, and the protection of freedom of expression. My office also focused on economic, social and cultural rights, including access to healthcare, education, housing, employment, and a reasonable standard of living for all. My Office, in collaboration with its partners, undertakes a number of specific activities all of which are aimed at promoting and protecting human rights in Iraq. These activities include: monitoring the human rights situation in the country and reporting on it publicly and to the United Nations; advocacy with the Government of Iraq and other actors who have the obligation to promote and protect human rights in Iraq; training of government officials, security forces, judiciary and members of civil society organisations on human rights law, awareness raising and education on human rights.

I arrived in Baghdad on 19 March 2009 to take up the above described position. This was nearly three months after the expiry of the mandate of the Multinational Forces in Iraq (MNF-I) and the entry into force of the Agreement between the United States of America and Iraq on the Withdrawal of United States Forces (USF-I) from Iraq and the Organization of their Activities during their Temporary Presence in Iraq, commonly referred to as the Status of Forces Agreement (SOFA).

UN missions operating in dangerous and conflict-ridden areas are designated, for security reasons, as "non-family missions". UNAMI is one of these non-family duty stations classified as a high security risk location. Staff members are not allowed to bring in their families and celibacy life is the rule in the mission. Before travelling to Iraq, UN personnel are required to take four days mandatory Security Awareness Induction Training (S.A.I.T) designed to equip staff with skills to operate in hostile and hazardous environments. The course is provided by a profit-driven security company, run by former army officers from different countries. Some of the trainers were survivors of kidnapping in Somalia, signs of post-traumatic stress disorder syndrome still apparent in their conduct. Although part of the training covered general cultural issues, local manners and how to interact with Iraqis, in practice, it was an expensive exercise completely detached from the realities of Iraq.

The regulations require taking draconian security measures before meeting Iraqis. In Baghdad, on my first visit to the Minister of Justice in the red zone, my heavily armed escort occupied the whole of the 4th floor of the ministry's building where the Minister's office was located. Before we started the discussion, the Minister told me this was not a dignified way for one Arab to visit another Arab. I apologised. My mind took me straight back to the ill conceived SAIT course specifically designed to prevent such situations. A smile imposed itself on my face, and I said to myself that indeed it was shameful to talk to the Minister while four American soldiers are standing in each corner of the room in their combat gear, fingers on triggers and a personal security detail (PSD) standing at the door ready to grab me by the scruff of my neck and run away. Those who designed the SAIT failed to take into consideration the Iraqi cultural sensitivities and failed to implement the appropriate measures to the appropriate circumstances. In contrast, the International Committee of the Red Cross (ICRC) has more outreach in Iraq and interacts with the Iraqis more efficiently than the UN simply because they keep low profile and they blend harmoniously with the local population. The UN pays one thousand

US dollars per trainee per day to the company that runs the course on a continuous rolling basis; it is a lucrative business for some.

On my first visit to Camp Ashraf[1], I went to pay a visit to the USF-I commanding officer in the Forward Operations Base (FOB) Grizzly, north of the Camp. Before entering the commandment office, my PSDs stubbornly insisted on searching the place. They were at first challenged but after a long argument, the American officer gave in. He was stunned, standing there with his arms folded across his chest watching the UN security staff searching his office for improvised explosive devices (IED). The UN Department of Safety and Security (DSS)

---

[1] Camp Ashraf is a small, self-contained, well maintained city, situated 27.6 km north east of the Iraqi town of al-Khalis, about 80 kilometers west of the Iranian border and 40 kilometers north of Baghdad, in the Diyala province where a population of about 3,400 Iranians, members of an opposition organization called the Mojahedin e-Khalq (MEK), also referred to as the People's Mojahedin Organization of Iran (PMOI), had lived since 1986. For some Iraqis, they are considered honourable guests of Iraq, to be protected as refugees; for others, they are unwanted foreigners, a source of tension in Iran-Iraq relations. After the US invasion of Iraq in April 2003, the residents of Camp Ashraf were interned and granted "protected person status" under the Fourth Geneva Convention. Ashraf officially passed to the control of the Iraqi army on 1 January 2009. As Chief of UNAMI Human Rights Section, monitoring the human rights and humanitarian situation of Ashraf residents came under my responsibility. It was one of the issues that had shaped my perception of the United Nations.

policy on security matters is zero tolerance. The PSDs mechanically implemented the rule. They took no account of the fact that we were in the office of the commanding officer of the USF-I, the force which protects the entire UN mission in Iraq and who had facilitated the visit to Ashraf. Once again I had to apologise.

It was already dark on Thursday, 19 March, when the UN flight arriving from Marka Airport in Amman landed in Baghdad International Airport (BIAP). The UN/US terminal at the Airport is separate from the commercial side of BIAP. It is a designated high security area controlled by the USF-I. There were no passport checks, no customs, and no evidence of any Iraqi sovereignty over that part of the airport. I was confused. I thought Iraq had regained its sovereignty in 2004. Outside the arrival hall on the way to the restroom a notice attracted my attention. It points to a little cubic shelter built with sand bags where it was written "AMNESTY: if you have any weapons or bombs drop them here, there will be no prosecution". Interesting enough, drugs were not mentioned.

That evening, the weather was not favourable for the helicopters to take off so I was taken to a transit hotel used by the USF-I for senior officers. It was one of Saddam's palaces. I was put in the Kirkuk Room, next to the Mosul Room and opposite the al-Ramadi Room. It was so serene and as silent as a night in a cemetery. I could not sleep, feeling like a trespasser in Saddam's house. This is something for which the

SAIT training had not prepared me. However, I should have been grateful not to have had to spend the night at the 'Stables', the transit facility in BIAP where soldiers and UN staff stay overnight to await their onward journey to Baghdad or other destinations. The name of the facility reveals a lot about the conditions of the accommodation. It is a conglomeration of open tents where UN civilians (males and females) mix with USF-I soldiers, each one equipped with a blanket to protect against the cold of the night and the sandstorms. The real discomfort was not the weather or the sandstorms; it was the closeness of heavily armed, exhausted and nervous young men and women.

The next day, UNAMI Movement Control (MOVCON) came to collect me. They put me on a USF-I Black Hawk and five minutes later I was in Washington. 'Washington' is the name of the helipad in the heart of the Green Zone known as the international zone (IZ) three minutes away from UNAMI life base compound, codenamed 'Uniform Charlie'. Here the US army jargon is dominant and one has to get used to it. All roads in the Green Zone are lined by a curtain of T-walls rising on both sides. The T-walls also known as Bremer walls are portable, steel-reinforced concrete walls used to protect against blasts, direct or indirect small arms fire, mortars, rockets and shrapnel. They are twelve-foot-high (3.7 m) in the shape of an inverted letter T. A wall of this shape does not need a foundation; gravity and weight keep it stable. It requires no time installing or removing. It turns the road into a tunnel only open from above to the sky. Nothing in the surrounding is visible until one arrives at destination. I checked in at 'Uniform Charlie'. I was allocated room 34A opening on a little plaza in front of the dining facility. It was a room of the lowest standard. I spent more than a year in there before I came to learn that higher standard rooms are allocated to those with the wit to provide a gift, preferably a bottle of whisky, to the appropriate staff at UNAMI mission support. In spite of the declaratory position of the UN about corruption, it is, in fact, endemic at UNAMI.

Accommodation was in trailers arranged in rows and columns forming a complex labyrinth. Exits are impossible to find if one does not familiarise oneself with its endless alleys and narrow passages. Some call them 'the containers', others 'the bunkers'. Layers and layers of sand bags cover all sides of the containers. The roofs are covered in layers of sand bags and steel sheets for protection against incoming projectiles. No daylight penetrates the rooms and power cuts are part of the daily routine.

I sat down on the edge of my bed trying to make sense of the surrealistic scenes I had seen since leaving Marka Airport the previous day. Suddenly the sound of a blast came through the half-open door, followed by a distant terrified voice shouting in panic, "Incoming, incoming; take cover, take cover, put on your PPE (personal protection equipment), stay away from the windows". The tone is meant to make you react instantly and decisively. Instead, I froze in the darkness and deafening silence which followed the order. I did not put my PPE or run to take cover. I counted: One, two, three explosions. This is my welcome to Baghdad. The explosions seemed to be at a far distance, to the east across the Tigris. A few minutes later, a more relaxed voice announced, "Stand down; all clear". I took a deep breath and ventured outside to familiarize myself with my new environment. "Incoming" and "Stand down; all clear" alerts would now become part of my life in Baghdad. I quickly learned that patience and resilience are essential survival skills in the new Iraq.

Seven years after the fall of Baghdad in April 2003, nature had claimed parts of it. Shrubs and hardies have found their way to the destroyed palaces. Cranes used for constructing edifices during Saddam's ruling are still standing up with their tops submissively bent down under the effect of the bombardments they endured. They seem to be waiting for Saladin (Salah Eddine al Ayoubi) to one day resurrect and come to their rescue as the new Iraq leadership are too busy settling score with one another. Aerial views of Baghdad reminded me of a television programme "life after people". A science fiction film, showing New York after the disappearance of mankind and how gradually, year after year, nature claimed back the city and turned it into a jungle. So had nature done to Baghdad after the American invasion.

# Myths and Realities of the MEK in Camp Ashraf

The situation in Camp Ashraf was very tense by the time I arrived in Baghdad. The Iraqi Government's public rhetoric had hardened with statements from the National Security Adviser, Muwaffaq al-Rubaie, vowing to close the camp by the end of March 2009 and the announcement from Prime Minister al-Maleki that Iraq was determined to put an end to the MEK's presence because it was affecting Iraq's relations with its neighbour Iran. On the other side, the al-Iraqiya coalition leadership including Ayad Allawi, Iraq's interim Prime Minister 2004-2005; the Vice-President, Tariq al-Hashemi, and, Saleh Mutlaq who later became Deputy Prime Minister, repeatedly declared that the presence of the MEK in Iraq was perfectly legal under both Iraqi and international law.

The Iraqi forces assumed responsibility for Camp Ashraf on 1 January 2009 under the SOFA agreement, while the handover took place on 22 February 2009. My colleagues in the human rights office visited Ashraf on 19 March. They briefed me on the security arrangements in and around Camp Ashraf. The Iraqi Army (IA) controlled access to the camp, while the MNF-I Task Force 134 observed the situation from the Forward Operating Base (FOB) 'Grizzly' to the north of the Camp. By a show of a disproportionate force, the Iraqi Army had seized the check-points surrounding the Camp from the

Ashrafis as well as one of the buildings in the vicinity of the Lions' Gate, the main entrance into Ashraf, which became the HQ of the Iraqi police at Ashraf. The Ashrafi community, who built this small city (named after one of the senior members of the MEK/PMOI killed by Khomeini's Revolutionary Guards in 1982) and continuously developed it over 25 years as friends of the Iraqi people, are now to be blockaded and treated as terrorists. Muwaffaq Al-Rubaie, the then National Security Advisor (NSA), vowed that the lives of the Ashrafis would soon become "unbearable", forcing their departure from Iraq. This was, and is, Iraq's policy towards Camp Ashraf.

*Positions of the Iraqi Army and Police around Camp Ashraf after March 2009*

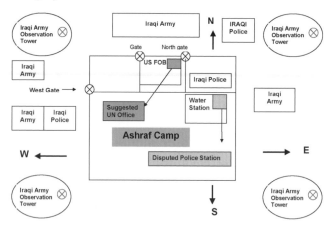

By the spring of 2009, Camp Ashraf had been searched by the Iraqi security forces (ISF) twice. Earlier searches were undertaken by the MNF-I/USF-I. During the last search, the ISF used sniffer dogs. All searches concluded that there were no weapons in the Camp. The Iraqi Ministry of the Interior issued a statement to that effect. UNAMI, influenced by politically expedient unverified speculations never believed that all weapons were handed over to the MNF-I in 2003.

On 21 April, the Ministry of Human Rights (MoHR) invited me to visit its team stationed outside Ashraf. For more than a month, they had been interviewing and recording the wishes of Ashraf residents. By the time of my visit, they had completed 3144 interviews of the 3418 residents. The MoHR team informed me that the interview forms showed that only four individuals wanted to return to Iran, and only 13 had opted for an exit to a third country (the interview forms did not offer remaining in Iraq as an option). I was not shown any evidence to confirm the four individuals' wishes of a return to Iran. The United Nations High Commission for Refugees (UNHCR), the International Committee of the Red Cross (ICRC) and UNAMI would not take these results as representing the genuine desires of the Ashrafis, asserting that, as long as Ashraf residents are under control of the MEK they are unable to express their true wishes. On the other hand, the same organizations seem to be too lenient in accepting the information/disinformation provided over the years by the Iranian regime and some Iraqi officials designed to settle scores with the only Iranian fearsome and popular opposition movement.

In May 2009, a delegation of Ashrafis came to see me in my office at Diwan (the UNAMI administrative HQ in Baghdad). I was expecting some tough warmongering terrorists to turn up in my office. I called my deputy in charge of the protection component of HRO, to join me. He had already spent one year in Iraq and had been interim Chief of the Human Rights Office between the departure of my predecessor and my arrival. Like me, he had an NGO background, having previously worked for Human Rights Watch (HRW). At the time I was not aware of the controversial HRW report of 2005[2] on Ashraf

---

[2] Human Rights Watch, a prominent US based NGO issued on 18 May 2005 a 28-page report, based on 12 hours of telephone interviews with 12 individuals who claim to have been mistreated while they were in the MEK/PMOI camps in Iraq. This report's allegations were refuted by another report of a delegation of MEPs who conducted a mission to Camp Ashraf in Iraq, held face-to-face private interviews with PMOI members and officials and randomly talked to over one hundred residents of Camp Ashraf and conducted impromptu inspections of the sites in search whether or not there was any evidence to corroborate the allegations in the said HRW report. The mission was conducted by MEPs André Brie and Paulo Casaca assisted by Azadeh Zabeti. In their report, made public on 21 September 2005, the MEPs delegation concluded that the allegations contained in the HRW report published in May 2005 were

and he had never mentioned it to me. All I knew about Camp Ashraf and the Ashrafis was from my colleagues' briefings and the speculative stories I heard in 'Uniform Charlie'. The Ashrafis, Behzad Safari and Shahriar Kiamanesh, arrived. I found myself in front of two men who looked like CEOs and spoke with both humility and eloquence. After the usual courtesies, we entered into the subject.

Behzad briefed me on the current situation in Ashraf: the effects of the blockade imposed by the Prime Minister's Office impeded access to food, fuel, water and medical services while a number of items judged by the Iraqi army as having potential military use were totally banned. He explained how the Iraqi officers had broken all commitments the GoI made to the Americans at the time of the handover. Behzad asserted that the Ashrafis no longer had a credible interlocutor with whom to address their difficulties. He told me that the Ashrafis were ready to leave Iraq for third countries, but they needed to establish a dialogue with the Iraqis in order to ensure a dignified exit from Iraq.

In reply, I told my visitors that I had been informed that interviews conducted by UNAMI and UNHCR with individuals who have left the Camp had consistently asserted that they were misled into

---

unfounded, devoid of any truth, were procedurally flawed and substantively inaccurate.

17

joining the organisation, often in the belief that they would be assisted to travel and live in third countries. Once under the control of the MEK they found themselves subject to extreme psychological and physical pressure to remain. Intensive ideological indoctrination, extreme isolation, and the strict requirement that they renounce all personal and family ties, had taken their toll on the psychological health of many individuals within the Camp making them extremely fragile and vulnerable. The MEK leadership, at the Camp and in third countries were described by defectors as exerting a powerful influence over members and actively preventing their defection and departure from the Camp. Out of respect, I stopped short of saying to my visitors that they were representatives of a criminal cult.

In retrospect, I could see that Behzad gave me great latitude as a newcomer, containing his outrage and contempt at my remarks. The enormous task of monitoring, protecting and promoting human rights in Iraq made Ashraf, at the time, a secondary priority for my office. Post-conflict Iraq was facing titanic human rights challenges. I was at the stage of setting the priorities for the human rights office. Behzad's answer to my remarks was, "Come to the Camp, talk directly to the residents, and find out their wishes for yourself. You will be welcome anytime and without any restriction". We ended our meeting with my promise to do that.

Months later, I realized that my statement to Behzad was ill-founded. I had been influenced by information provided to me based on the controversial HRW report of 2005. I also later discovered that the substance of the interviews my colleagues claimed to have had with "defectors" were based on allegations lifted from the HRW report and supplemented with hearsay from UNHCR officers. During the period 2010-11, I personally interviewed nine individuals presented to me as "defectors" by Iraqi security officials. None of them expressed the wish to go back to Iran, none of them said they were lured to Ashraf and none of them said they were ill-treated at Ashraf.

I, later on, came across a letter from Brigadier General David Phillips[3] ''Griffin-6'' of the 89th

---

[3] BG David Phillips assumed duty as the Commander of the 89th Military Police Brigade and the Installation Provost Marshal in 2002. He deployed to the brigade combat in support of Operation Iraqi Freedom-II. While in Iraq, the brigade provided military police combat support across the theatre including joint operations with the Iraqi Police. In addition, the brigade ran the Iraq National Police Academy producing over 6000 new police officers. The brigade also provided custody and control for the high value Iraqi detainees including Saddam Hussein. The brigade provided protective custody for the members of the Mujahedin-e Khalq (MeK) at Camp Ashraf. Following brigade command, BG Phillips assumed duties as the Deputy Commanding Officer of the United States Army Criminal Investigation Command at Fort Belvoir, Virginia. In April 2006, BG Phillips was promoted to Brigadier General and assumed

Military Police Brigade, sent on May 27, 2005, to Mr. Kenneth Roth, Executive Director of Human Rights Watch, regarding Human Rights Watch's 2005 report on alleged human rights abuses by the Mujahedin-e Khalq (MEK). He wrote: "I am the commander of the 89th Military Police Brigade and in that role was responsible for the safety and security of Camp Ashraf from January-December 2004. Over the year long period I was apprised of numerous reports of torture, concealed weapons and people being held against their will by the leadership of the Mujahedin-e Khalq. I directed my subordinate units to investigate each allegation. In many cases I personally led inspection teams on unannounced visits to the MeK/PMOI facilities where the alleged abuses were reported to occur. At no time over the 12 month period did we ever discover any credible evidence supporting the allegations raised in your recent report. I would not have tolerated the abuses outlined in your report, nor would I have sanctioned any acts on the part of the MeK/PMOI to hold people against their will. Each report of torture, kidnapping and psychological depravation turned out to be unsubstantiated. The MeK/PMOI in fact notified us on a routine basis of people who desired to leave the organization and then transported them to our gate. At your request, I can explain in detail

---

duties as the Deputy Provost Marshal General of the Army. He later on returned to Iraq as the Deputy Commanding General of the Civilian Police Assistance Training Team. He was the senior military policeman in theatre.

specific allegations and the subsequent investigation by my units. To my knowledge, as the senior officer responsible for safe-guarding and securing Camp Ashraf through-out 2004, there was never a single substantiated incident as outlined in your report". The former residents of Ashraf I interviewed in 2010 and 2011 confirmed this statement.

I gradually came to understand how the stigma of terrorism had been attached to Ashraf and its residents and how the UN contributed to the dissemination of the perception of the MEK as a terrorist organization, holding people in Camp Ashraf against their will and committing human rights abuses inside the Camp.

Those newly posted in Baghdad among UN staff, get their informal induction to Iraqi affairs and Camp Ashraf at the UNAMI undercover bar or in the plaza at 'Uniform Charlie' in front of the dining facility. If one is in Baghdad, has read the controversial HRW and the RAND reports, visited some related websites and gossiped in the 'Uniform Charlie' plaza or the undercover bar, then one is considered quite the expert on Ashraf and the MEK. Civilian personnel, security officers, military advisors, who have nowhere to go outside of office hours spend their time in the plaza or the undercover bar of the compound spicing up stories and spreading myths and rumours about the Mujahedin e-Khalq. Fueled by the allegation that Camp Ashraf shelters a group of "protected terrorists", the story became the favourite subject of discussion at all gatherings. It was also the only "training" UNAMI officers receive before they visited Ashraf. Staff of the diplomatic missions and the US Department of State also frequented the UN undercover bar. They too have their own stories to tell. The stories of such 'experts' will undoubtedly be echoed in reports of the diplomatic missions and will shape up the policies of their respective governments. Strange enough, no one in UNAMI would mention that a delegation of Members of the European Parliament had verified the allegations on the ground and concluded that the 2005 HRW report was unfounded[4] and devoid of any truth. Nor would they mention the statements of BG David Phillips and other US high officers who served in the military police brigade protecting Ashraf and who testified that they investigated the allegations against the MEK in Camp Ashraf and found it groundless.

On 23 November 2011, I interviewed in Hotel al-Zohoor in Baghdad four former residents of Camp Ashraf and two couples with relatives living in Ashraf. The meeting was at the request of the Iranian Ambassador in Baghdad, Hassan Danaifar. The four individuals were not willing to meet at the Iranian Embassy. Although UNAMI had been informed by the Iranian Embassy that the former residents spoke English, it transpired that this was not the case and interpretation was provided by Massoud Khodabandeh, a renowned activist,

---

[4] Supra note 2

lobbying for the closure of the Camp and the "release" of its residents. He travelled from the United Kingdom to arrange this meeting in collaboration with the Iranian Embassy. Notably, despite being in the presence of Khodabandeh and the meeting having been arranged at the request of the Iranian Embassy, each of the interviewees said they had not been subjected to abuse by the Camp's leadership, although exhausted by the living conditions due to outside harassments and the embargo imposed on the Camp; were not aware of any weapons in the Camp and were extremely reluctant to return to Iran, despite having no other plans or options. In the case of one individual suffering from advanced cancer, I offered to facilitate his return to Iran to be treated at the cost of the Iranian Government, but he declined. The two couples I interviewed requested they be reunited with their family members but outside Iran. To convince the cancer patient to take my offer to help retuning him to Tehran, I told him that he might wait for years for the refugee status while cancer will not wait for that long. It needs to be treated urgently. His reply, as translated by Mr Khodabandeh, he prefers to die of cancer rather than returning to Iran.

During the spring of 2009, the pressure on Camp Ashraf mounted. This pressure had been pre-planned. The Council of Ministers' decision of 17 June 2008 prohibited any Iraqi or non-Iraqi organisation, party, institution or individual in Iraq from cooperating with MEK members in Ashraf and considered any contravention of this ban as a breach of the anti-terrorism law; requested the MNF-I to hand over all matters related to the MEK, including Camp Ashraf itself and the surrounding checkpoints to the competent Iraqi authorities; and to implement arrest warrants against members of the MEK for alleged crimes committed against the Iraqi people. This decision was however opposed by al-Iraqiya (a coalition of political parties of secular orientation, Sunni confession lead by Ayad Allawi a Shiite), the coalition with the largest number of seats in the Council of Representatives (parliament). Meanwhile, few days prior to the said decision, religious and tribe leaders declared the support of 3 million Iraqi Shiites to the PMOI and the residents of Ashraf.

The purported CoM decision on Ashraf, has not been officially promulgated. I asked the MoHR to provide UNAMI with a copy but was told it is not available. I wonder what legal value one would attribute to a governmental act that remains unpublished, in other words kept secret. Also, when I came to work with the so called "Ashraf Committee", I asked a number of authorities dealing with Ashraf matters to provide me with the constitutive act of the "Ashraf Committee", together with its membership and its functions. I was told its establishment was upon a verbal order from the Prime Minister. The "Ashraf Committee" remained a phantom body managed by the Prime Minister's Office. Its membership, functions and prerogatives are decided on *ad hoc* basis by the National Security Adviser in post. This is how the 'State of Law' Coalition of the Prime Minister al-Maleki governs the country.

Ashraf used to be full of activity, with manufacturing works, agriculture, health and education, even at university level. Before the handover to the GoI, because of their protected person status, the MNF-I allowed Ashrafis to undertake income generating activities in compliance with the Fourth Geneva Convention. At a time when Iraq was falling into chaos and suffering from shortages of basic necessities, there were over a 1,000 Iraqi workers earning their livelihood from Ashraf. Since the handover from the US, the Iraqi armed forces had set up a check point at the Lions' Gate, the main entrance into Camp Ashraf, and started to monitor vehicles and people coming in and going out. Iraqi workers were prevented from entering the camp. The residents were facing restrictions on supplies and had difficulties reaching the Iraqi market and the population. In early July 2009, the USF-I confirmed that the Iraqi armed forces had prevented several trucks loaded with food and other utilities from entering the camp and harassed vendors who delivered services to the residents. Since the establishment of the military check point at the Lions' Gate, access to the Camp became a challenge even for diplomats and international dignitaries. Human rights NGOs, ICRC, UNHCR stopped visiting Ashraf. During the first six months of 2009, only UNAMI visited the Camp twice.

Nonetheless, UNAMI, under the leadership of both former SRSG Steffan de Mistoura and SRSG Ad Melkert, kept advocating that MEK members at Ashraf must be protected from forcible deportation, expulsion or repatriation in violation of the *non-refoulement* principle and must not be displaced inside Iraq in violation of international humanitarian law and that only solutions acceptable to both the Iraqis and the Ashrafis could be supported by the United Nations. In this context, the Secretary-General reported to the Security Council on 14 May 2010 that "UNAMI ... has continued to advocate for the residents' unhindered access to goods and services of a humanitarian nature, as well as for their right to be protected from arbitrary mass displacement or forced repatriation against their will in violation of the universally accepted principle of *non-refoulement*"[5]. On 31 March 2011, the Secretary General reported that "UNAMI reiterates its call for ... respect for the universally accepted humanitarian standards and applicable international human rights law, in particular the International Covenant on Civil and Political Rights to which Iraq is a party"[6]. And on 7 July 2011, the Secretary General called upon Member States "to support and facilitate the implementation of any arrangement that is acceptable to the Government of Iraq and the

---

[5] Report of the UN Secretary General S/2010/240 of 14 May 2010, paragraph 54

[6] Report of the UN Secretary General S/2011/213 of 31 March 2011, paragraph 52

camp residents"[7]. However, on the arrival of SRSG Martin Kobler in Baghdad, he made a U turn and initiated a plan to displace Ashraf residents. To the surprise of everyone involved, his position was supported by New York. Previous public pronouncements and the SG's reports to the Security Council on this issue were ignored, at the cost of serious damage to the credibility and integrity of the United Nations.

---

[7] Report of the UN Secretary General  S/2011/435 of 7 July 2011, paragraph 66

# Iraqi Army Attack on Camp Ashraf, July 2009

In July 2009 the Iraqi armed forces were instructed to establish a police station inside the Camp to exert better control over the Ashrafis. The residents challenged the purpose of bringing a large number of armed security forces inside the Camp particularly after repeated hostile statements from Government authorities. On 28 July, Colonel Saadi, the commanding officer of the security forces around Ashraf went with a number of army and police officers into the Camp to discuss with the Ashrafi representatives the opening of a police station by the water pumping plant. Around 2:00pm, Colonel Saadi walked away from the negotiating table. Two hours later, around 3:30-4:00pm, hundreds of Iraqi soldiers and police officers gathered at the three gates leading into Camp Ashraf (East, North and Lions' Gates) and staged an assault on the camp. They used HUMVEEs and bulldozers to destroy fences and walls around the camp, recklessly moving in all directions at high speeds and targeting crowds of residents. The ISF, on foot, armed with batons, some with nails, metal rods, cricket bats, chains, sickles, axes, teargas, sound grenades and water cannons, broke into the camp and attacked hundreds of unarmed residents who had formed a human chain. At some point, the Iraqi armed forces opened fire on the residents. According to USF-I eyewitness accounts, the attack was extremely violent and lasted for hours, ceasing some time after nightfall. The following morning, July 29, the Iraqi armed forces returned to the camp at around 10:15am and gathered at Tulip Square, near the Camp's water plant. They again attacked the residents in the same manner and with the same weaponry used the day before. At FOB Grizzly, the USF-I, Task Force 134, silently watched events.

In addition to the Iraqi armed forces permanently based around Camp Ashraf, the other participants in the attack were army units from Baghdad, police units from Diyala province and Iraqi army Special Forces from the notorious 56th Brigade under the command of the Prime Minister. Students from a police academy, located two miles from Ashraf, also participated in the attack. The USF-I claimed they could not clearly identify the origin of all the forces involved but confirmed that 800 to 1,000 troops participated in the assault.

Some Ashrafis, when interviewed, reported that some of the attackers spoke perfect Farsi, indicating that these men might have spent time in Iran and might have been former members of the Badr Brigade, now incorporated into the Iraqi security forces. These Farsi speakers could even have been members of the Iranian Security Forces assisting the Iraqi army.

USF-I Task Force 134 (which I called 'Big Brother' because of its remote electronic surveillance systems), reported that the Iraqi armed forces prevented Iraqi doctors and USF-I medical officers from entering the scene to evacuate the wounded. Iraqi forces also prevented some attempts by the press to approach the area. The Camp Ashraf ambulance was shot at several times during the attack as MEK doctors tried to take the wounded to the Ashraf hospital. During the fact finding mission, UNAMI examined the ambulance riddled with bullets holes.

Once the Ashrafis had been overwhelmed, the Iraqi armed forces went on a looting spree, taking goods belonging to the residents such as generators, air conditioners, fans, tables, chairs and anything and everything of use for their poorly furnished base outside Ashraf. In addition, 39 vehicles were seized. All the looting was witnessed by Big Brother. In January 2012, when UNAMI-GoI representatives met at the Iraqi Army base during the talks for the relocation of Ashrafis to Camp "Liberty", Behzad pointed at the tables we were sitting around and told me these were looted in the attack of July 2009. By way of teasing, I asked an Iraqi army officer from where they obtained the tables. His response was a piercing stare and a fake half smile.

In Baghdad, at the time of the 28-29 July attack on Ashraf, we received only partial and sketchy information – some reports of skirmishes taking place, perhaps a massacre. The diplomatic community looks towards UNAMI for information. In turn, UNAMI looks towards the US Embassy and the Department of State. I decided to dispatch a fact-finding mission. It took eleven days for the GoI to agree to such a mission. We were told that a cooling-off period was necessary for the safety and security of the UN staff. This was an inadvertent admission that something drastic had happened.

On 10 August, the UNAMI Human Rights Office and the UN Office for the Coordination of Humanitarian Affairs (OCHA) were finally granted access to the Camp. The mission visited Camp Ashraf hospital, met the Camp's representatives, USF-I and senior Iraqi army officers, interviewed victims, medical staff and a number of residents as well as collecting photographs, documents, medical reports and video footage of the attack. At the end of the mission the delegation met with USF-I officials to examine the evidence collected. They confirmed what the evidence indicated.

Col. Saadi, and his deputy, Lt Col. Abdel Latif, were the senior Iraqi officers in charge at Camp Ashraf. When Col. Saadi was asked about his version of events, he answered in a low voice, as if he was trying to pass unheard. He said that, on the morning of 28 July, he received orders from the Prime Minister's Office to enter Camp Ashraf. He then added that he had been ordered to enter the camp without weapons. Col. Saadi went to the camp with 50 unarmed soldiers and six regular army vehicles (armoured personnel carriers). At the gate, he and his men faced fierce resistance, he said, with Ashrafis attacking them with knives, batons and stones. Col. Saadi explained that his men did not expect such resistance and were rapidly outnumbered. They had to call for reinforcement from the police at Diyala, and from the Iraqi Special Forces and army units from Baghdad. The mission did not receive any evidence supporting this version of events. Nor did the USF-I corroborate the use of any weapons by Ashrafis. USF-I confirmed however that hundreds of troops stormed the camp on 28 July around 4:00pm in what seemed to have been a very well planned operation.

On 12 August, UNHCR met in Baghdad with Ali al-Yasseri, Director of the Department of Operations at the Iraqi Prime Minister's Office and Chair of the "Ashraf Committee". Al-Yasseri told UNHCR that the Iraqi authorities had discovered heavy weapons, including rockets and rocket launchers, inside Ashraf. UNHCR kept this "valuable information" as an internal secret. It would later be used to support UNHCR's stand vis-à-vis the Ashrafis and to justify its refusal to deal with them unless they "defect". Paradoxically, in contrast to its position on the MEK, UNHCR had registered members of the Kurdistan Workers' Party (PKK) and its sympathizers assembled in Camp Makhmour in the north of Iraq as refugees in spite of the designation of the PKK as a 'terrorist organisation' by the US, the EU and the United Nations. Clearly, the determining factor here is political not humanitarian. UNHCR had acted exactly as the Iraqi political authorities wanted it to do. The PKK members in the north of Iraq enjoy the sympathy of the Kurdish Regional Government (KRG). Due to the existing sensitivities between the Arabs and the Kurds, the Federal Government in Baghdad cannot oppose the wishes of the KRG in this matter. This is not the case for the MEK which is combated by both the Iranian regime and al-Maleki's government. And this is what explains the UNHCR double standard justified by its doctrine of working hand in hand with governments.

Al-Yasseri, in making the claim about the supposed discovery of heavy weapons, had forgotten that the Iraqi Ministry of the Interior, the Governorate of Diyala province and the MNF-I had repeatedly searched the Camp and found no weapons. A document of 20 April 2009 from the Iraqi Ministry of Interior, issued following a search with police dogs on 18 April 2009, confirmed the absence of weapons in the Camp. Successive events in the coming months would prove that al-Yasseri's allegations were devoid of any credibility. The man was either misled by the forces on the ground or he intentionally made baseless claims. Despite of that, the UNHCR remained deeply convinced that there are weapons hidden in the Camp which is a proof of terrorist intents of the MEK, enough to disqualify the Ashrafis from UNHCR's protection.

When Col. Saadi was asked about the fire arms used, he confirmed having heard gun shots but said he had *"no idea where they came from"*. He then added that *"some mistakes may have been made but certainly unintentionally"* and, then, suddenly, he became vague and evasive on the matter, saying that many residents threw themselves under the advancing vehicles of the Iraqi army. In the days following the attack, some officials within the Prime Minister's Office claimed that MEK snipers had killed or wounded Camp Ashraf residents. In a conversation I had had with al-Yasseri on 4 August, he had also claimed that Camp Ashraf residents were shot by the MEK and not by Iraqi forces. The dead were dissidents within the group, he asserted. Al-Yasseri also claimed that there were 100 injured police officers and 13 injured soldiers on the Iraqi side. However, UNAMI had not been presented with any evidence to substantiate such an allegation. Evidence and testimonies presented to the fact-finding mission clearly established responsibility as belonging solely to the Iraqi security forces (army, police and security agents) for the shooting, the reckless and dangerous driving and the looting.

At the time of the attack, USF-I soldiers were located at three different sites: East Gate, North Gate and Lions' Gate. They also monitored the situation directly from FOB Grizzly. USF-I watched and filmed events as they were unfolding. UNAMI requested a copy of the footage. USF-I promised to do so provided that the material had not been classified. Subsequently, however, UNAMI did not follow up on its request and USF-I did not volunteer the video footage, as no party was willing to be seen by the Prime Minister's Office as stirring up a forgotten matter.

At the end of the fact-finding mission, the UNAMI delegation mixed informally with several USF-I soldiers who had witnessed the events on the ground. They confirmed what happened, the identity and the numbers of forces involved, and the numbers of killed and wounded. Senior USF-I and US Department of State officials in Baghdad admitted to UNAMI on 6 August before the dispatch of the fact-finding mission, that the Iraqi armed forces had lost control of their troops during the attack. In the same meeting at the US embassy, a USF-I Deputy-Commander explained that the role of the USF-I was to observe and report and not to intervene on either side. The SOFA agreement prevented them from such intervention. He added that this had been made clear to the MEK leadership, Camp Ashraf residents and the GoI. Later, a USF-I officer told the mission 'off the record' that they did not intervene or try to prevent the Iraqi armed forces from attacking the camp because they had received an order from General Odierno[8], the General Commander of the USF-I not to do so.

---

[8] General Raymond T. Odierno served as the Commanding General, Multi-National Force - Iraq and subsequently United States Forces - Iraq, from September 2008 until September 2010.

Eleven residents of Camp Ashraf were killed during the attacks; six on 28 July, two on 29 July, two on 30 July and one who succumbed to his injuries on 14 August. The USF-I confirmed the number of the dead. Ashraf residents' representatives produced the list of the dead and 443 names of residents who had been wounded, including 42 seriously injured. USF-I confirmed having seen at least 200 injured residents. A UNAMI physician who checked photographs and medical records of the deceased wrote: *"Some of the victims were killed by a single, deadly gunshot to either the chest or the head. I conclude that these shots have been targeted and intended to kill. A random shooting would likely cause a different injury pattern"*. According to medical documents given to UNAMI by the residents' representatives, 138 residents presented head trauma, 56 had fractured bones and 25 were wounded after being run over or hit by a military vehicle.

Both UNAMI and the High Commissioner for Human Rights expressed concern over the excessive use of force and called for an independent inquiry. I explained to the Iraqi authorities on a number of occasions that it was in the interest of Iraq to investigate the incident and to hold those responsible to account. The Directorate of Operations at the Prime Minister's Office naively or irresponsibly put together a file as a conclusion of their supposed inquiry. It consisted of the statements of some Iraqi members of the ISF together with few pictures of hand grenades, pistols and some night vision devices displayed on a table. When they showed me the file and claimed this was the evidence that the MEK was armed and responsible for the killing in Ashraf, I advised them not to circulate it as it was clearly a laughable, amateurish manipulation that no one would take seriously. As far as the UN was concerned, this was now history. The call for an independent investigation would never be invoked again.

After the July 2009 attack, the Iraqi forces had opened a police station inside Camp Ashraf and renamed the Camp as "Camp New Iraq". In practice, only UNAMI persistently kept using this name for fear of being perceived antagonizing the Iraqi authorities while the Iraqis themselves used the name Ashraf and even called the committee in charge of the MEK file as Ashraf Committee. In his speech at the Security Council, the Iraqi Ambassador had never hesitated to refer to Camp Ashraf. However, as the coming months and years would prove, the real objective of the police presence inside the Camp had nothing to do with the maintenance of law and order.

### Ashraf Detainees after July Attack

During the attack of 28-29 July 2009, 36 residents were arrested and charged according to article 230 of the Iraqi Penal Code related to assaulting officials on duty. The 36 were detained in al-Khalis Police Station. On 24 August, Judge Thamer H. Khalil, investigative judge, ordered their release for lack of evidence. The public prosecutor immediately appealed against the release order. The appeal was scheduled for consideration by the Court of Cassation in the week beginning 13 September. In addition to the appeal against the release order, the public prosecutor brought new charges against the 36 detainees consisting of illegal entrance into the country and entries without duly established identification papers.

*Name and Protected Person ID Number of the Detainees*

| | |
|---|---|
| 1. Mohammadzadeh Gholamreza 2E5ED94F | 20. Ahmadi Djehon Abadi Seyyed Hossein 0417F34B |
| 2. Mohammadi Abbas 9A3C49E6 | 21. Tolammy Moghaddam Ali A9524BAB |
| 3. Hoshmand Mohammad Reza 8AA0A21E | 22. Farsy Hossein 585525A8 |
| 4. Haydari Rahman 5DD5C075 | 23. Sarveazad Hossein 29F3C8E4 |
| 5. Ghorab Habib C8BBE695 | 24. Abdorrahimi Mehdi FCC69AC8 |
| 6. Sanaie Mostafa 255D12BA | 25. Zare Mehdi 6A2B6A9D |
| 7. Latifi Ezat 9A3792CE | 26. Ashtari Hamid 39220E97 |
| 8. Besharati Hassan D66A31A1 | 27. Balaee Mehrban 0E0130B2 |
| 9. Majidi Manouchehr BF7C5855 | 28. Gougerdi Javad D4843A17 |
| 10. Ghadermazi Omid 154A655A | 29. Komarizadeh Ebrahim |
| 11. Shojaee Mohsen | |

| | |
|---|---|
| A1CF99BD | D3D7A424 |
| 12. Khorrami Gholam-Reza 493520FB | 30. Kargarfar Jamshid BB49F880 |
| 13. Malaipol Ebrahim F14E80DE, | 31. Ahmadi Jihonabadi Iraj 9BBEF582 |
| 14. Forghany Jalil F8B49815 | 32. Ghasemzadeh Mohammad Reza F63E014D |
| 15. Tajgardan Ahmad 9B77F119 | 33. Tatai Mohammad Ali D74E9A1F |
| 16. Kongi Moshfegh 6DD86679 | 34. Dayhim Homaun 7F9346D4 |
| 17. Shahbazi Asad 0364B037 | 35. Gholamizadeh Azizollah 2281AC81 |
| 18. Ghorayshy Danaloo Mir Rahim 2E69CFB9 | 36. Gholamzadeh Golmarzi Jalil 6B368E7D |
| 19. Mohammadi Karim 723674C2 | |

In protest, the 36 detainees started a hunger strike from the day of their arrest. The ICRC visited them on 12 August and I received information that they would not be allowed to return to the Camp. I was worried that they might just disappear. All it takes is to keep them incommunicado, move them around the country and all trace of them would be wiped out.

There were rumours about moving the Ashrafis to Camp Echo, near Nasireyah in the south or to Nigret al-Salman in the desert of Samawa in al-Mouthana province near the Saudi border, a former prison for political detainees. The nearest water source to Nigret al-Salman is several days walk. I expressed concern to the ICRC and we agreed to keep a close watch on the case.

By the end of the first week of August 2009, a group of 136 Camp Ashraf residents, joined by other groups in Europe and America, were on their tenth day of a hunger strike in solidarity with the detainees. My immediate concern was that the 36 detainees were about to enter into a dry hunger strike. With temperatures reaching 50° Celsius in August, I was concerned that they would soon die of dehydration or cause themselves irreparable damage. The Camp's leadership were worried too. They asked me to intervene to convince the 36 to give up their fast.

Behzad called me in September 2009 to say that the 36 were now on dry hunger strike and asked if I could do something to stop it. I decided to go to al-Khalis to see them, look them at the eyes and urge them to stop.

I spent days trying to secure clearance for the mission. I explained to al-Yasseri, Chair of the "Ashraf Committee" in the Prime Minister's Office, that it was in the interest of Iraq to be transparent on the issue; obstructing the UNAMI monitoring mission would aggravate concerns. We finally got the go ahead. On 8 September, Lt. Col. James Blackwell, UNAMI military advisor, arranged with the USF-I for transport on two Black Hawk Helicopters and by 11.30 we were at FOB Grizzly.

Four USF-I HUMVEEs and two Mine Resistant Ambush Protected vehicles (MRAP) escorted us to al-Khalis. The Iraqi Provincial Police authority received the delegation at al-Khalis Police Station. They served some refreshments and briefed us on the conditions of detention. They showed us a sample of meals served to the detainees. It consisted of a plate of rice with a chicken leg together with a can of Pepsi Cola. It looked freshly delivered from a takeaway restaurant. I expressed my appreciation to the officer in charge but said to myself that this demonstration was not necessary since the detainees were not eating anyway. The 36 were divided into three groups, each group of 12 housed in a room of 5 x 6 m, equipped with air conditioners. The three rooms were in a row sharing a corridor about 15m long and 1,5m wide. The hunger strike had weakened them. They were mostly confined to their beds.

At my request, two lawyers of the detainees were allowed to join me at the detention facility. They explained to me the conditions of the arrest and the way the detainees had been treated. They showed me those who were assaulted during the arrest. One had a broken arm; others had injuries to the face and the limbs. They complained that their clients were kept in detention despite the order of the investigative judge to release them. The public prosecution, as mentioned above, had appealed against the release order and added to the primary charge of assault a new charge of illegal entry to the country. The two lawyers explained to me how the presence of these individuals in Iraq was perfectly lawful and that they had not broken any laws or regulations. On these grounds, an al-Khalis court had dismissed the case and ordered the release of the 36 on 24 August 2009.

At the time of my visit, 8 September 2009, the 36 detainees had been on hunger strike for 41 days. I went to each room, shook hands with each and every one of the detainees, looked them at the eyes and urged them to stop the hunger strike. They were determined to continue until their deaths or their release and return to Camp Ashraf.

Diyala province, particularly al-Khalis, is a highly dangerous area. The road between Ba'qubah and Ashraf had the highest record of attacks by insurgents. After an hour, my PSDs were telling me that it was time to move. The American soldiers of the escort squadron were also getting nervous. We had to leave. In any case, I still had to get to Ashraf to visit the 136 on hunger strike in solidarity with the 36 detainees. As soon as we came out of the built up area, the HUMVEEs left the main road and plunged into the desert at high speed, raising large clouds of dust giving an extra layer of protection to the convoy. We turned into limestone statues as the dust settled on our sweaty skin but we were safer than on the main road.

On arrival at Camp Ashraf, we went to Tuloo Building where meetings took place. There, the

Camp's leadership explained the circumstances of the July attack with supporting documents and demanded both an independent investigation into the raid by Iraqi armed forces and a UNAMI permanent presence in Ashraf for the residents' protection. We then went to see the hunger strikers at the Camp. They were in the City hall in two vast conference rooms. The first hosted 75 men and the second 61 women. They were stretched out on hospital beds. The place was very clean. The Camp doctor was there monitoring the health of each hunger striker. Some of them were being fed intravenously. The doctor complained that he was not receiving adequate medical supplies. I made a tour of the beds together with the doctor. I told the hunger strikers that their cause had been heard by the international community and urged them to call the strike off. As in al-Khalis, the determination of the strikers was unshakeable. Their demands were: the unconditional release of the 36 detainees they considered held as "hostages"; the establishment of an independent commission of inquiry; that the GoI renounce the plan to relocate Ashraf; that the GoI guarantee the implementation of the principle of *non-refoulement*; that the GoI pay compensation for looted or destroyed property during the 28/29 July attack; and that UNAMI establishes some UN presence in the Camp.

Before I left Ashraf to return to Baghdad, the Camp's leadership handed over to me a number of documents related to their protected status including a letter signed by Major General Geoffrey D. Miller, dated July 21, 2004, which I reproduce verbatim:

> *I am writing to congratulate each individual living in Camp Ashraf on their recognition as protected persons under the Fourth Geneva Convention. This determination will assist in expediting the efforts of international organizations in your disposition as individuals in accordance with applicable international law.*
>
> *You have signed an agreement rejecting violence and terrorism. This sends a strong signal and is a powerful first step on the road to your final individual disposition.*
>
> *In our effort to reach a peaceful future for the people of Camp Ashraf, we will continue to seek the best disposition for each individual and commend you all for your patience and cooperation during this lengthy process.*
>
> *Very respectfully,*
>
> *Geoffrey D Miller, Major General, US Army, Deputy Commanding General*

An earlier letter from the same source dated 25 June 2004 reads:

> *Prime Minister Allawi of the Interim Iraqi Government (IIG) has given Ambassador Bremer, of the Coalition Provisional Authority, his assurances that the provision*

*of essential services to the individuals living at Camp Ashraf will continue after sovereignty is transferred on 30 June, 2004. These services will be commensurate with the level of service at the quantities and prices as those received by Iraqi citizens living in Diyala Province and will remain in effect until the final disposition of the individuals living at Camp Ashraf is determined. Prime Minister Allawi said that the IIG would agree to allow the MEK to purchase commodities and services (including oil/fuel, electricity, commerce, agriculture, and health) thus enabling them to remain self-sustaining at Camp Ashraf.*

*After the transfer of sovereignty, Multi-National Forces Iraq will facilitate transportation of those who need to discuss individual issues with the relevant IIG entities.*

*Very respectfully,*

*Geoffrey D Miller, Major General, US Army, Deputy Commanding General*

Another letter I was given was from General Gardner, deputy commanding General of the MNF-I, dated 16 January 2006, to the General Secretary of the MEK in Ashraf. It reads in part:

*"I would like to assure you that the coalition remains deeply committed to the security and rights of the protected people of Ashraf and*

> *the principle of non -refoulement. We will*
> *continue to work with the residents of Camp*
> *Ashraf, Iraqi authorities, and appropriate*
> *international organizations to resolve the*
> *disposition of the Ashraf residents consistent*
> *with applicable international law."*

Back in Baghdad, I reported the demands of the Ashrafis and warned that the situation remained extremely volatile and that it was likely that some use of force by the Iraqis would take place again after Eid al Fitr or any time within the next 60 days if no lasting solution was worked out. I recommended that some robust intervention with the GoI was the only way to prevent further violence. I reported that the issue was a political one. It could only be solved through high level political dialogue, a dialogue that could be facilitated by the UN, with the active participation of the Americans.

In the late summer and autumn of 2009, UNAMI was submerged in letters of protest and calls for action to resolve the situation from all over the world. In the last few weeks both the High Commissioner for Human Rights (HCHR) and the Special Representative of the Secretary General (SRSG) in Iraq received a large number of letters calling for the protection of Ashrafis, among these letters from: members of the British House of Lords on 2 September; a group of German MPs on 3 September; the Vice- President of the European Parliament on 5 September; and the Vice-Chair of the Sub-committee

on Human Rights of the European Parliament on 3
September. In addition, the US Congress had
conducted a hearing with the American Ambassador
in Iraq.

The standard UNAMI reply to the many letters on
this issue read in part:

> *"We appreciate very much the points you
> raised for the protection of the individuals
> concerned both in Ashraf Camp and at al-
> Khalis police station in Diyala Province.
> Please be reassured that UNAMI has been
> closely monitoring the situation in Camp
> Ashraf since 2004 and we are actively
> searching for a protective solution to its
> residents"*. It went on: *"The physical and
> psychological wellbeing of the thirty-six
> Camp Ashraf residents arrested during the
> events of the 28-29 July is of great concern to
> UNAMI. The fundamental rights of these
> detainees, including their right to a timely
> access to justice, the international standards
> for a fair trial and the due process of law
> must be observed. UNAMI is calling upon the
> GoI to uphold the rule of law in this respect"*.

In reality no one in UNAMI would face Prime
Minister al-Maleki with a request of this kind. He
had been too intimidating. Whenever the situation of
Ashraf was mentioned to him, he would blow up in
rage and would end the meeting. Those diplomats
who dared raise the issue with him, received the

response, "Why don't you take them to your country?". When legislators from the US Congress and the European Parliament came to Baghdad to look into the humanitarian situation of the Ashrafis, they were treated as *persona non grata*.

### *Release of Ashraf Detainees, October 2009*
On 7 October 2009, the 36 detainees were released from al-Muthanna detention centre at Baghdad International Airport where they had been held after a brief stay in the Green Zone. On that day I arrived at Camp Ashraf earlier than usual for the purpose of monitoring the handover of the detainees. Both the ICRC representative and I, together with the USF-I team lead by Brigadier-General David Quantock, commander of the USF-I Task Force 134 , sat at the Iraqi Army HQ in Ashraf waiting for the two buses to arrive from BIAP. Present on the GoI side were Sadiq for the "Ashraf Committee", Hayder for the MoHR and Col. Saadi for the Iraqi Security Forces. The buses entered Ashraf at about 11am but the ordeal of the 36 was not over yet.

The representative of the PM's Office insisted on the residents' representatives signing a document to the effect that when requested by the judiciary, the 36 must immediately present themselves to the police. It was a form of extra-judicial house arrest, not congruent with the court's release order. A long and exasperating argument went on while the 36 sat on the two buses at the Lions' Gate. The 72 days of hunger strike had weakened them to the extent that no one could independently stand up. At noon, the sun was 90° vertically above us at a lead melting temperature. To save the hunger strikers from further suffering, the residents' representative signed the handover document. Now the Government representative wanted the document to be signed by both representatives of the UN and the ICRC, not simply as witnesses of the handover, but as guarantors that the 36 would voluntarily submit to the police when requested. The ICRC refused to sign. I urged Sadiq to redraft the document to the effect that the UN and the ICRC were simply witnesses to the handover. This was done and I signed. Now we needed to go to the buses and do the head count. The scene was truly dramatic.

When Col. Saadi ordered the driver to open the bus door, a smell of dead bodies hit me in the face. I saw carcases hardly alive. I was told by the medical staff that a long fast makes the body consume its own cells, causing organ failure. It was the process of dying I could smell. The ICRC told me it was nothing to worry about - mere dehydration. The detainees will recover with some food and water. Some of them would need to be hydrated intravenously.

The Ashrafis were now allowed to go to the buses. They brought stretchers and carried their men away. That was the end of that chapter in Camp Ashraf's history. No independent inquiry was held; there was no pursuit of the extra-judicial killings. No one would even dare to mention the eleven dead to the Iraqi authorities, much less seek some accountability. As the SRSG told the diplomatic community on 29 September, "UNAMI has a huge agenda with the GoI and does not want to have one issue jeopardize all".

On 9 October 2009, the spokesperson of the Office of the High Commissioner for Human Rights (OHCHR), Rupert Colville, made the following statement: "*United Nations human rights officials today welcomed the Iraqi Government's decision to release 36 members of an Iranian dissident group who had been detained since July when security personnel used force to take control of the camp where they had been staying*"…The spokesperson of OHCHR, told journalists in Geneva that "*the world body was grateful that the Government had responded to a request from High Commissioner Navi Pillay to release the detainees*". As nobody thought al-Maleki would agree to return the 36 detainees to Ashraf, the world body in charge of the promotion and protection of human rights acted as if the release of the detainees was the result of its efforts. On one hand it unduly claimed for itself the outcome of the Ashrafis steadfastness and sacrifices. On the other hand it had given a barely disguised stamp of approval to the GoI for its good conduct. Extra judicial killings and arbitrary arrests were to be put aside so as not to upset al-Maleki's government.

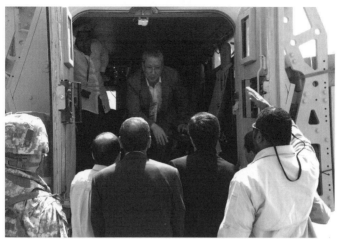

Arriving in Camp Ashraf

Among Ashraf residents

Visiting Ashraf accompanied by delegation from UN High Commissioner for Human Rights

In Street 100 in Ashraf with representatives of the residents

Coming out of Tuloo building in Ashraf after meeting Camp Leadership

Assiyeh Rakhshani, who was killed in April 8 attack by Iraqi forces, explaining about some of her work

In a briefing session in Ashraf attended by US military

Meeting in Ashraf accompanied by UNHCR representatives and US military officers

# UNHCR and Camp Ashraf

UNHCR offices in Baghdad, located a few yards from the Human Rights Office, do not share information with UNAMI. In joint meetings, information from their side was so scarce even though we were operating as part of an integrated mission. We were supposed to represent one UN, one policy, one vision. Conversely, the information withheld from UNAMI was liberally shared with the GoI and some embassies. The same information often comes to me through the Iraqi authorities, the diplomats or 'Uniform Charlie' Plaza.

UNHCR policy on Ashraf was to keep low profile and to abstain from visiting the Camp or providing assistance to its residents. They would only provide protection and assistance to "defectors" who had left the camp, and who were under Iraqi government surveillance in either the al-Muhajeer or al-Zohoor hotels in Baghdad, two facilities used by the GoI to temporarily accommodate those Ashrafis who leave the Camp. These two facilities are also visited by the Iranian Embassy staff. This policy was, and is, meaningless as the "defectors" do not need UN protection. They have no difficulty, at least in theory, in going back to Iran if they wanted to. Those who are in real need of protection are those in Ashraf who genuinely fear persecution and torture if they are returned to Iran. It is worth mentioning that all residents who leave Ashraf are picked up by the Iraqi army and kept in undisclosed locations for up to three months. Only at the end of a debriefing period is their location revealed to the UN and the ICRC.

In September 2005, at the request of the Americans, UNHCR had conducted interviews in order to establish refugee status for those assembled at the American-run Temporary Internment and Protection Facility (TIPF)[9], established outside Ashraf. At the same time, UNHCR kept their distance from those who remained inside Ashraf. Between 20 February and 31 March 2006, 187 people were interviewed via video teleconference (VTC) between Geneva and Ashraf. On 5 May 2006, the interview results were handed over in Geneva to Lt Col. Julie Norman of the MNF-I: 164 persons were granted refugee status; 21 were denied refugee status (and had appealed, of which 17 were accepted and four denied). During June and July 2007, UNHCR sent a team of two to interview newcomers as well as the four whose appeals were turned down. On 16 October 2007, all 204 interviewed were recognized as refugees.

---

[9] After the invasion of Iraq and the consolidation of the mujahedin in Camp Ashraf, the MEK/PMOI declared that those who wish to separate from the movement were free to do so and should be allowed to leave the Country. The TIPF was then established by the MNF-I in the proximity of Ashraf in 2003 to accommodate those who had chosen to separate from the movement and the UNHCR was called in to determine their refugee status in order to facilitate their resettlement outside Iraq.

The reality of the TIPF residents remains untold. Many of those in the TIPF were Iranian troops captured by Saddam's army during the Iran-Iraq war, who had joined the PMOI after their release under supervision of the ICRC in 1990. In 1992 ICRC had done the last call and they stayed in Ashraf, but after the invasion of Iraq they were not able to endure the hardship of being in the resistance. As former POWs, they were of concern to the ICRC. Because some of them had refused to return to Iran, the US Government called in UNHCR to sort out their status so as to enable them to settle elsewhere other than Iran. When UNHCR failed to find countries for them, some decided to return to Iran supervised by the ICRC. UNHCR only became involved in their case at the request of the US Government, not because it was within its remit but simply because the US wanted UNHCR to do so. By the same political logic, on 13 September 2011, UNHCR adopted a new stance towards the Ashrafis and declared that "there is no formal requirement for individuals to disassociate themselves from the PMOI/MEK in order to apply for refugee status". This radical change in UNHCR policy towards Ashraf residents was the results of the steadfastness of the residents and the pressure exerted by the USG and the UN HQ.

On 7 August 2009, the Rapporteur of the Working Group on Arbitrary Detention, the Special Rapporteur on the Promotion and Protection of the

Right to Freedom of Opinion and Expression, the Special Rapporteur on the Right of Everyone to the Enjoyment of the Highest Attainable Standard of Physical and Mental Health, and the Special Rapporteur on Torture and other Cruel, Inhuman or Degrading Treatment or Punishment sent an urgent appeal to the Government of Iraq through its Chargée d'affaires in Geneva regarding the situation at Camp Ashraf. That had an important effect on how the GoI subsequently addressed the situation of the 36 detainees and paved the way for UNAMI and ICRC visits and the detainees' eventual return to Ashraf.

# UNAMI in Search for a Peaceful Solution for Ashraf, Fall 2009

From the time of its inception, UNAMI was caught in a paradoxical situation; between the imperatives of human rights and humanitarian principles, on the one hand, and the dictates of a sectarian, pro-Iranian regime GOI, on the other. As a political mission, UNAMI had been mandated by Security Council Resolution 1770 (2007) and subsequent resolutions to assist the GoI on the latter's request. Given the power-politics and how it is played in Iraq, this limitation of the UNAMI mandate to act on the government request turned the UN organization into a tool in the hands of PM al Maleki's Office, not the Government of Iraq as such. This explains why the successive Special Representatives of the UN Secretary General had been compromising to different degrees particularly on human rights issues. The question that remained to be answered was should UNAMI assist the GoI when it acts unlawfully and violates the principles of international law and the United Nations Charter as it did in Ashraf?

Under pressure from a number of European parliamentary groups, US Congressmen and international dignitaries, on 27 September 2009, SRSG Ad Melkert called a brainstorming meeting to identify feasible and practical steps the UN could take to facilitate a lasting solution to the problem of

Camp Ashraf. The meeting recommended the following:

The first task was to identify an Iraqi interlocutor/s with the capacity to commit the GoI. Thus far, UNAMI had been frustrated in its communications with three people representing the so-called "Ashraf Committee", Ali al-Yasseri, Haqqi Karim and Sadiq Mohammad Kazim. They were not the decision-makers; they always referred matters elsewhere and never came back with answers. Once an interlocutor at the policy making level was identified, UNAMI could then address with him/her the following issues:

- That Iraqi sovereignty over Camp Ashraf was unquestionable and that with sovereignty comes the responsibility to protect and to uphold the rule of law and human rights.
- That the UN stands ready to facilitate a dialogue in order to reach a solution based on respect for Iraq's sovereignty and on the need to guarantee the residents' safety, security and dignity.
- That a peaceful solution to the situation is in the best interests of Iraq and that the international community expects a peaceful solution that preserves the residents' fundamental human rights.

Second, the UN needed clarity as to American expectations and the kind of assistance they would provide. Third, the UN needed to discuss with EU member states and other interested parties grounds for engaging the residents either as nationals or as former residents in those countries, or as candidates for refugee status. Fourth, there should be some form of consultation with the Iranian Embassy in Baghdad to assess the extent and credibility of the Iranian offer of amnesty to the residents.

Once information had been gathered according to the four steps above, the UN could then approach the Camp's leadership with some concrete proposals for discussion. The aim of this exercise was to prevent further violence. Time was of essence.

SRSG Melkert met the Prime Minister's Chief of Staff, Dr Tarik Abdullah, on 29 September 2009 to discuss a number of issues including the coming general elections and relations with Kuwait. Ashraf, however, was the main topic but was deliberately left, as usual, as the last item on the agenda. The SRSG did not want the Iraqis to think he was giving Ashraf priority over other challenges and concerns. It was the first opportunity to share the conclusions of the brainstorming we had had in search of an exit for the residents of Camp Ashraf, and to explore the possibility of establishing a UN temporary monitoring presence in the Camp. It was paramount for the UN to know the plans of the GoI, as well as the views of the diplomatic community, on the way forward.

Dr Tarik Abdullah made it clear that the GoI did not want special treatment be given to the residents of

Ashraf as: they had no legal status in Iraq; were considered a terrorist organization by the governments of Iraq, the United States and other members of the international community; had committed crimes against Iraqis; and posed a problem with a neighbouring country. He added that, despite all that, the GoI was prepared to put aside the political aspects of the issue and focus on a humanitarian solution without forcing residents to go back to Iran. Dr Abdullah made it clear that Ashraf was a highly sensitive issue for the Prime Minister and that Iraq would exercise its sovereign right to temporarily relocate the residents. He welcomed the idea of a UNAMI monitoring presence in Ashraf provided that it remained a neutral player. 'Neutrality' here is understood in the context of "whoever is not with us is against us". It was a general pattern of conduct of the political actors in Iraq and indeed all those who decided to undertake the war in Iraq. Dr. Abdullah agreed that dialogue should be promoted with the EU and North American governments to secure their contribution towards resettling the Ashrafis. We listened attentively to Dr Abdullah. He raised a number of political arguments. None of them could stand before a court of law. However, he did not say that the presence of the Ashrafis in Iraq was unlawful and he did not claim that Ashraf Camp was established on privately owned land in order to justify their eviction as others had previously asserted.

A meeting was urgently convened with representatives of the diplomatic community for 3 October 2009. It was chaired by the SRSG and present around the table were: Ambassador Nicola Trouve (Sweden, chairing the EU); Ambassador Baron Paul von Maltzahn (Germany); Ambassador Mikael Hemniti Winther (Denmark); Ambassador Gary A. Grappo (Minister-Counsellor for Political Affairs, US Embassy), Julie Martin and Kyle Richardson (Political Affairs, US Embassy); Lyn Waring and John Wilks (UK Embassy); Luc Briard (French Embassy); Deane Turnbull (Australian Embassy); Nicola Bazzani (Italian Embassy); Akira Endo (Japanese Embassy); Achin Ladwig, the European Commission (EC) representative; and Martin Thalmanh and Olivier Martin (ICRC). Absent was the UNHCR representative.

The SRSG began the meeting by stating that the Prime Minister's Office considered the issue of the MEK/PMOI to be a matter of urgency. The GoI wanted to move the MEK/PMOI from Camp Ashraf and the SRSG sensed that they wanted this done before the elections scheduled for April 2010. There was a need for all actors to move quickly.

The SRSG then gave the floor to me to provide a brief update on the situation on the ground. I informed the meeting that the hunger strike was now in its 67th day. The 36 residents detained in al-Khalis had now been transferred to the Green Zone, despite the three court orders for their release. They were now detained in some disused premises of the Higher Council for Education, a few yards away from the UNAMI residential compound, 'Uniform Charlie', between the Vice-President's residence and the SRSG's villa (few days later they were transferred to al-Muthanna prison in BIAP). I informed the meeting that the investigative judge had circulated a letter to all police stations instructing the release of the 36 detainees wherever they were held. However, since they were in the custody of the Office of the Prime Minister's security apparatus, the Investigative Judge instructions could not be implemented. I also underlined the international community's concern as expressed in a mountain of letters coming from individuals, Nobel Peace Prize winners, NGOs, churches, tribal leaders, Mayors, parliamentary groups and political parties.

Ambassador Gary A. Grappo told the meeting that the Prime Minister was in favour of UN involvement but that he did not want to return the 36 detainees to Camp Ashraf. Such extra-judicial detention created an obvious political problem for the US.

The SRSG replied that there was a general understanding that the current Ashraf situation could not be sustained and that it was positive that the Prime Minister accepted the support of the UN. UNAMI had been asked by many sides to take a monitoring role, and that naturally, the UN would consider this with the Office of the High Commissioner for Human Rights (OHCHR).

However, there was a need for caution as the UN should not be drawn into monitoring a position that might not change for decades. The UN should only accept a monitoring role if it was part of an overall solution. There were conditions that should be met, namely:

(a) The GoI should provide details on how they were going to conduct the re-location. They should make available good facilities, treat the residents well and make relocation a more attractive option than remaining at Ashraf.

(b) The PMOI leadership should be asked to cooperate with the re-location and allow individual residents to state their preferences to remain or re-locate to another area. There should be no forcible displacement.

(c) Third countries, willing to favourably consider asylum requests from residents and the return of nationals on an individual basis, should be identified. UNHCR would assist as long as its role was clearly defined.

The SRSG added that it would prove difficult to move the residents if there were no prospects of a durable solution. Some might return to Iran and the UN stood ready to assist them. In summary, it was important to have a commitment by third countries to assist the GoI in resolving this issue in order to make the role of the UN meaningful. The SRSG was counting on the UNHCR to play a leading role but the agency had not seen fit to even attend the meeting.

The European Commission representative supported the UN pre-conditions as outlined by the SRSG, and warned that the UN must guard against continuous relocations without eventual resolution of the core issues.

The Italian Embassy representative stated that it was possible that there were 95 persons in the camp that might have been granted refugee status by Italy but this had not been followed up. The Italian government was ready to consider any evidence supporting the claims of these 95 persons. While the Italian government had not visited the Camp, they had been informed that none of those with connections to Italy wanted to leave.

The UK Embassy representative stated that they had a list of 80-85 residents from 2005 that had either past links to the UK or lapsed refugee status. They had visited the Camp in April, June and most recently in September. They had interviewed one-third of those on the list. None of them wanted to leave the Camp and they could not produce any documents showing a connection to the UK. If individuals were granted refugee status by UNHCR then they would be considered like any other applicants.

The representative of the Japanese Embassy appreciated the efforts of the UN but stressed the need for caution; the key issue was that people did not really want to leave the Camp.

The representative of the Australian Embassy stated that there were three people with connections to Australia but one denied that he had citizenship. None of them wanted to return. With respect to re-settling any residents in Australia, the initial assessment was that the residents would be unlikely to meet Australian immigration requirements. The representative also asked if UNHCR would conduct individual refugee status determinations.

The Danish Embassy representative reported that fifteen people in the camp claimed to have a connection with Denmark. Only one wished to return but the Embassy had since lost contact with her. If UNHCR processed the residents they would be considered for resettlement like all other refugees.

Ambassador Grappo asserted that Camp Ashraf had been a problem since 2003 when the US disarmed the PMOI and gave them protected person status. The legal obligation of the US to protect them had ended in June 2004, but, as a matter of policy it had continued protecting them until 1 January 2009. The PMOI rejected the US position and argued that protected person status cannot be terminated before final dispositions are achieved (article 45 of the Fourth Geneva Convention). The US had received written assurances from the GoI that the residents would not be deported to Iran and, notwithstanding the events of July, they would be treated humanely. From FOB Grizzly, a small contingent of USF-I military police monitored the Camp and assisted in resolving problems regarding supplies. Since July2009, the US government had been urging patience and this might have had an effect. Additionally, the US had also pleaded for the involvement of international organizations. The US felt the involvement of international organisations would serve to reassure the PMOI that any transfer was not an Iranian scheme and would also serve to protect the GoI by ensuring legality and the appearance of legality. The US Embassy had been reducing meetings with the PMOI so as not to give the impression that there was a direct link with the PMOI/MEK, and the US military was prepared to completely cut off the existing contacts. There were between five and ten US citizens in the Camp, some with charges against them for providing material support to the PMOI/MEK which is listed by the Department of State as foreign terrorist organization. The status of the MEK/PMOI as a terrorist organization complicated any attempt to settle residents in the United States but, although he could not make a decision, he was willing to raise the question of granting refugee status to a limited number with Washington.

The German Ambassador reported that there were no German citizens in the camp. Nine had refugee status that had since lapsed. He did not think, in view of the current [conservative] government political attitudes to immigration in Germany, that his country would be able to take any of the residents.

The representative of the French Embassy stated that France had appealed against the judgment of the European Court of First Instance of 4 December 2008 (in Case T-284/08 *People's Mojahedin Organization of Iran* v *Council*) delisting the PMOI. He added there were French charges pending against 24 members of the PMOI [these charges were dismissed on 11 May 2011 by the Investigative Judge of Paris]. He added that the French Embassy had been in contact with the MoHR regarding whether any residents had links to France but had not received any information at that point. France was ready to consider individual cases. [It is to be noted that despite my repeated invitations, the French Embassy did not participate in any of the UNAMI-arranged consular visits to Ashraf].

The Swedish Ambassador reported that there was currently no common EU position on Camp Ashraf, (Sweden had the EU presidency at this time). With respect to the Swedish position, he sounded the same note of caution as had others about an endless UN commitment. The Swedish did not want to see the legitimization of the PMOI, which could happen if the UN role was not directed at finding a solution. There were four Swedish citizens in the Camp and twelve others who had valid travel documents. There might have been others who had invalid documents. Sweden would take those who wanted to go, but so far all had said they wanted to stay. The Swedish immigration authorities are independent, and even if UNHCR requested asylum on behalf of some residents it was unlikely that it would be granted due to the background of the PMOI. Finally, the Swedish government had read the reports of both the UN and ICRC on the issue and did not view the humanitarian situation as alarming.

The ICRC head of delegation stated that they would visit the 36 detainees the following day and that they had previously visited them in al-Khalis with a medical doctor and that the ICRC was not alarmed about their safety. It was the right of the GoI he said to enter the camp as it was a legitimate right of the GoI to enforce law and order on its own territory. In the ICRC head of delegation's view, the main problem was that the issue of the PMOI was so politicized. It left no room for humanitarian action he said.

The SRSG then summarized the meeting in the following terms: <u>UNAMI had a huge agenda with the GoI and did not want one issue jeopardize all other issues.</u> The GoI could react badly, but the PMOI could also cause problems. All we could do was to monitor and to refer to the GoI with expressions of concern. It remained in formal terms the domain of the GoI to deal with this issue one way or another. The UN would continue urging third countries to commit their support to facilitating the role of the UN and to finding solutions.

In the following days, I went with the SRSG to meet the Iranian Ambassador, to hear from him about whether there was an amnesty and if so what arrangements if any were in place to effectively implement the amnesty. The SRSG was hoping that the Government of Iran would issue a written document that could be used before a court of law to protect Ashrafis if persecuted for their past activities. However, we were aware that such a document would be meaningful only if the Iranian judiciary was effectively independent and that the Iranian Government acted in good faith. The Ambassador's reply was uncommitted to any written assurances or guarantees.

# The First Attempt at a Relocation Plan, Fall 2009

On 19 October 2009, I made my fourth visit to Camp Ashraf since the Iraqi Army attack of 28/29 July. As soon as I arrived in Ashraf, an Iraqi Officer advised that Ali Al-Yasseri was expected to arrive to announce the closure of the Camp and to propose an alternative location for the residents. I was invited to attend and observe. I had with me Martin Bohnstedt (HRO), Kristen Elsby (OCHA) , Stuart Shepherd, UNAMI Department of Humanitarian Services, Lt. Col. Jim Blackwell (UNAMI Military Advisor) and the MNF-I commander, Brigadier-General David Quantock, as well as US Embassy Political Section Representatives, Moustafa Popal and Philip Trayne. From the GoI side, Ali al-Yasseri, Haqqi Karim, Sadeq Mohammad Kazim and the Ministry for Human Rights representative, Haider Hussein Abdulhasan Al Douairi, were present. Mahdi Baraei led the delegation representing the residents.

The meeting took place outside Ashraf in a trailer at the Iraqi Army base. The atmosphere was highly charged and I had to intervene from time to time to calm the situation. Al-Yasseri announced that Camp Ashraf would be closed; the residents would have to be relocated by 15 December 2009 to al-Muthanna province. The residents' representative retorted that remaining in Iraq or returning to Iran were not options for Ashraf residents as they were persecuted by both governments. They were prepared, however, to move to third countries as soon as this became possible. They asked for time to explore perspectives in third countries. Al-Yasseri did not mention what practical arrangements the Iraqis had planned for the operation. I could not tell from that meeting whether the Iraqi side meant what they said or was just bluffing, nor could my American counterparts.

This visit allowed me to further discuss with USF-I the necessary logistics for deploying a team of human rights officers to FOB Grizzly starting from 25 October. The idea of a UNAMI monitoring presence was well received by the Camp's representatives, the USF-I and, seemingly, the GoI representative. The residents' representatives went as far as to offer some premises they held at FOB Grizzly to UNAMI. I made it clear to the Camp's representatives that part of the HRO monitoring role would include face-to-face meetings with non-accompanied individual residents. Such a guarantee of non-interference by the Camp's leadership was essential if UNHCR was to become involved in assessing cases for possible relocation to third countries. This was unreservedly accepted.

Although the residents had now announced their willingness to leave Iraq for good, the shift had received no acknowledgement from al-Yasseri. By imposing a deadline and emphasising the GoI's sovereign right to forcibly transfer residents, al-Yasseri left no room for any further discussion. The meeting ended on rather confrontational terms with no indication of when the parties would meet again and with no indication that these critical issues could be resolved.

On 21 October the SRSG, Melkert, called for a second meeting with the diplomatic community. The following embassies were represented: the United States, Germany, Denmark, the EU, Switzerland, Italy, the Netherlands, the Vatican, Sweden, the United Kingdom, France and Australia. In addition, the UNHCR and the ICRC attended.

I reported what happened during my visit to Ashraf on 19 October and that the likelihood of further violence could not be ruled out and indeed could be anticipated if the GoI maintained its present position. The MNF-I was no longer in a position to act as an interposition force. If further attacks took place, casualties would be considerable and would not have access to suitable medical services. In the absence of any political breakthrough, the UN, the US and the diplomatic community should continue consultations and urge the GoI to allow more flexibility.

SRSG Melkert pointed out that it was urgent that states make clear their positions as to whether they were ready and willing to accept residents. Such clarity would help define our strategy vis-à-vis the Government of Iraq, the PMOI, and any potential UN monitoring role. He then opened the floor for individual states to comment.

The German Ambassador spoke first. He said he now believed that there were 300 persons in Camp Ashraf with links to Germany. He could not say that Germany would take any of them and that the time limit set by the GoI would not make it possible to assess these cases. The Danish Ambassador stated that determining who had claims to residence in Denmark was very difficult; ten or twelve might have had a resident permit but these had since expired. Denmark was currently returning failed asylum seekers, so the environment for acceptance of asylum seekers from Ashraf was not favourable. However, Denmark would assist its nationals, if any in Ashraf, in the context of normal consular support.

The normal consular support was offered by all delegations but no concrete action was suggested for those who had no third country nationality. The UNCHR Chief of Mission's intervention did not help diplomats to move forward as he spoke about the presence of a large number of people who had been tricked into the Camp and should be treated as victims. This allegation was pushed a bit further by the US representative who said most of population was not there by choice and, although they might not agree with the leadership, would stay there and die. The German Ambassador added there would only be a change of mind if the Government of Iraq sticks to its timetable because it would allow residents to make up their minds.

As the person who was permanently in contact with the Ashrafis, I was outraged with this kind of statements as I knew it was not true. I learnt from my extended interactions with the individuals and with the leadership in Ashraf that they were all determined to stand shoulder to should in defence of their convictions. I personally had deployed tremendous discrete efforts to convince some individuals who have compelling reasons to leave. My advice had always been turn down. Time will later on prove that the UNHCR representative, the US and German Ambassadors were just repeating falls allegations against the Ashrafis as no change of mind happened and no one had departed from the group when relocation began in February 2012.

The SRSG, trying to direct the meeting more positively, commented that the date set by the GoI for closure of the Camp had given the UN a sense of urgency and we had to look at the situation from a humanitarian point of view. If there was violence, we would be asked why we did not act and we will have to give an account of ourselves. He asked the assembled representatives if he could speak on their behalf to the Government of Iraq. He requested that the states put in place a facility near the Camp where individuals could go and receive help. The Danish Ambassador asked whether consular officials could go. The German Ambassador replied that he would prefer that the facility be established first. After the close of the meeting, discussion continued in the corridor and, as usual, there was wild speculation about what was happening inside the Camp, fuelled by rumours from those who claimed to have contacts with defectors.

UNAMI meetings with the diplomatic community were now set to take place on a fortnightly basis, coupled with a fortnightly briefing of the human rights officers of the embassies of the EU member states and a weekly meeting at the PM's Office with members of the "Ashraf Committee". Ad hoc meetings between the SRSG and Ambassadors, the Prime Minister and other Iraqi dignitaries would continue. The essence of the matter was not as complex as it has been portrayed by diplomats and politicians. The GoI wanted to put an end to the presence of the MEK in Iraq. The Ashrafis, persecuted by both the government of Iran their home land, and the current GoI led by PM al-Maleki, their host country, wished to leave Iraq but they were not prepared to trade their dignity. In addition they had nowhere to go. The solution and the primary responsibility over the fate of the MEK members in Iraq is that of the coalition governments who waged a war to introduce change in Iraq. The war has reversed the status of the MEK members in Iraq from being honourable gests of Iraq to that of unwanted foreign terrorists. The duty to protect in international law is not a licence for states to wage war against those who failed their citizens as was perceived during the April 2003 invasion of Iraq. It is rather the opportunity to extend protection to those who are left without a protective government.

## *UNAMI-OHCHR Presence at Ashraf, Fall 2009*

Following the consultative meetings with the diplomatic community on 3 and 21 October, the SRSG and the HCHR in two separate telephone discussions, agreed on the establishment of a joint monitoring office under the direct supervision and the overall guidance of the SRSG, with the following purposes:

- Monitoring human rights and the humanitarian situation in Camp Ashraf;
- Liaising with American and Iraqi counterparts as well as Camp Ashraf representatives;
- Regularly reporting on the situation to the SRSG and OHCHR Geneva HQ and recommending possible action;
- Assessing the possibilities and the presence of enabling conditions provided by the GoI for possible deployment of UNHCR staff;
- Performing other tasks as required.

The Mission drew its mandate from a request by the Government of Iraq and from the Camp's representatives. On 19 October, the Camp's leadership gave UNAMI a verbal guarantee of unhindered access to Camp Ashraf and all its residents. Three UNAMI Officers, together with their security support, were to be present at Ashraf at all times.

The team was to be accommodated at US Army FOB Grizzly, located on the north part of Camp Ashraf. It was expected that the mission members would have daily access to Camp Ashraf, and that movement, logistics and security would be provided by the USF-I. The staff were accommodated in pre-fabricated units of a similar standard to normal USF-I FOBs. A large, one-room office container was made available, with furniture, IT equipment and Internet connectivity. All meals were provided at the FOB's central dining facility; and essential services such as emergency medical care, laundry and some recreational facilities were accessible within the FOB. US helicopter flights linked FOB Grizzly and Baghdad's International Zone, where UNAMI headquarters were located.

In place by the 25 October 2009, the UNAMI monitoring team at FOB Grizzly faced major challenges from the outset. While we had planned for three substantive officers to form the team, we could not find enough staff to volunteer for this mission. It was often manned by only one person. Most officers were afraid to go to Ashraf because of the perception that Ashrafis were dangerous terrorists. These 'terrorists' could turn against them if things went wrong. Those who found enough courage to go, do so for personal reasons, predisposed towards proving that Ashrafis act in bad faith. The distance of two km between the FOB and Ashraf, and the security regulations to be observed, also proved to be off putting for staff. Most team members stayed locked up at FOB Grizzly and were rarely present on the ground when and where they needed to be. As they were required to send daily reports, they end up collecting rumours heard from the soldiers at FOB Grizzly. Once, Big Brother reported having spotted a group of Ashrafis practising indoor martial arts. By the time the story reached me in Baghdad, it was dramatised into a report that the residents were training under cover in martial arts possibly for an attack against the Iraqi army. This was simply paranoia. Ashrafis are a community of highly educated people who lived in different parts of Europe and America. Sports were part of their daily life.

The UNAMI presence in Ashraf is supposed to be staffed on a weekly rotation. As there was no political, cultural or institutional homogeneity among the staff, there were noticeable discrepancies in the reports in terms of objectivity. As advisor to the SRSG on Ashraf related matters, all reports should have been distributed through my office in Baghdad. Some zealous officers, contrary to reporting procedures, circulated reports directly to a large list of non-concerned recipients. This uncontrolled reporting fuels rumour and speculation and causes periodic panics among the diplomatic community. This is the nature of the UN multi-agency works with its multi-polar allegiances and interests.

The UNAMI monitoring mission was to observe the situation on the ground and verify any allegation about violations of human rights. The golden rule was supposed to be impartiality. The reality in practice was otherwise. For fear of being accused of sympathising with a terrorist group, monitors were often too cautious in their reports. They tended to close their eyes to certain Iraqi officers' conduct and extensively used words such as "allegedly", and "reportedly", a method of disseminating the unverified information while disclaiming responsibility. There should be no need for such hedging by direct observers. A fact-finding mission is supposed to verify, confirm or refute any allegations on the ground. The Mujahedin- and Camp Ashraf-related stories often began as rumours and then turned into allegations. Because they went unverified, they often mutated in certain minds as hard facts. These, 'hard facts' are then transmitted to the new comers among diplomats and UN staff as absolute truths. 'Uniform Charlie' Plaza and the UNAMI undercover bar play an important role in perpetuating rumours that eventually find their way into the UNAMI reports and become a source of information. This had severe consequences for the Camp's residents.

However, from the perspective of the duty to protect, and separate from UNAMI's mandate and reporting, the mere presence of a UN team on the ground is perceived as a deterrent against violence. All parties tend to show the best of their public image. So was the case at the Camp; all acts of violence against

Ashraf residents took place in the absence of the UN monitors.

As the 15 December deadline, announced by al-Yasseri on 19 October, arrived, the GoI invited a number of media representatives to observe the relocation operation. The Prime Minister's Office sent buses to Ashraf and the Army went roaming up and down the residential areas of the Camp using loudspeakers and distributing leaflets calling upon the residents to board the buses. The residents just ignored the whole scenario. Some of them spoke to the media to say they were not going to move. A few hours later, the buses left empty.

# Humanitarian Crises at Ashraf, Winter 2009-10

The December failure to relocate Ashraf residents created frustration and bitterness among the "Ashraf Committee" members. As a consequence, they decided to further tighten the embargo on the Camp in the hope of softening the residents' resolve and determination. A scheme of collective punishment and deprivation was now at work.

By January 2010, the residents faced fuel shortages which had a direct impact on a number of utilities. The Camp's representatives sent a letter on this issue to the SRSG on 17 January and pointed to the fact that no fuel supplies, with the exception of 5,000 litres for the Ashraf Hospital, had entered the camp since 5 October 2009. When two fuel tankers attempted to bring in kerosene supplies on 4 November, the tankers were confiscated by the Iraqi Army and the drivers were arrested and held in al-Khalis police station for 20 days before a judge ordered their release.

Between 2003 and 2006 fuel for Camp Ashraf had been purchased directly from the Iraqi Oil Ministry according to the assurances given to the residents by the Interim Iraqi Government (IIG) as stated by Major General Geoffrey D. Miller in his letter to Mr Baraei of 25 June 2004, reproduced above. However this arrangement had ceased from late 2006 under

Ibrahim al-Jaafari Premiership due to the pro-Iranian Daawa Party position towards the MEK and to Iranian pressure. The residents had since purchased most of their needs from Kuwait, with smaller amounts from local vendors, at costs considerably above the unit market price. Since the events of 28/29 July 2009, the GoI made it increasingly difficult for fuel to enter the camp. The fuel shortage had a direct impact on the generators used to power the water purification plant, cold chain facilities, personal heaters, refrigerators and all other electricity powered facilities. This puts the health of residents at risk particularly during the extremely hot summers and the freezing cold winters.

In a meeting with the residents' representatives on 21 January 2010, UNAMI monitors were warned that current fuel reserves would be unlikely to last more than two weeks on the basis of current demand. Rationing was already in place. The monitoring mission observed that vehicles were now rarely seen on the streets of Ashraf. Hot water in the residential areas was only available for less than two hours a day. Still, the UN, as usual, was cautious about the Ashrafis' claims. The monitors went to check the reservoirs and found that the residents' claims were justified.

Col. Saadi had been transferred to Basra by this time and Lt. Col. Latif was now the officer in charge of Camp Ashraf. There was mutual respect between the two of us. He did not usually turn down my requests.

I urged him to do his best to maintain the fuel at the level supplied during the American control of the Camp. He whispered near my ear "I am a soldier. I only implement the orders I receive from above". Later, in an informal discussion with Iraqi officers in Ashraf, I was told 72,000 litres of fuel had entered the camp before the tightening of restrictions in early October. On a separate occasion, I asked the USF-I if there were any available records detailing the quantities of fuel entering on a monthly basis prior to the restrictions. Major Julian did not have such data, having only been in command at FOB Grizzly for the last four months. However, to refute some Iraqi allegations, he said there was no indication that supplies were being smuggled into the Camp from surrounding villages as such activity would have been picked up by USF-I.

Following a monitoring visit in January 2010 to three utilities in Ashraf, namely the electricity distribution centre, the water purification plant and the power generating plant, the Mayor of Ashraf, Ms Mandana, explained that most of the equipment dated back to the 1980s. Maintenance of such equipment becomes increasingly difficult as the years passed and the ban on spare parts was exacerbating the maintenance problem. Residents were increasingly unable to use the generators assigned to each of the individual collective housing units and were now relying on candles and lanterns in the evenings. All residents relied on electrical stoves to cook meals in the evenings. This was now increasingly disrupted. Ms Mandana complained that no spare parts for the electricity distribution centre had been received in the last ten months in spite of repeated requests to the Diyala authorities. Even requests for light bulbs and halogen strip lights were being denied. This was in evidence at the distribution centre where nearly half the lights were not functioning.

Three years ago, the residents built their own power plant at the cost of over \$3 million to reduce the level of reliance on the national grid. When fully operational the plant had a capacity of $5 - 5.2$ MW which met most of the Camp's needs. In the last three months of 2009, the plant was out of use due to the lack of fuel. Each of the six generating units consumed 250 litres of diesel per hour and this fuel had not been available due to the imposed restrictions.

The water plant consumed three tons of chlorine per month and a similar amount of aluminium sulphate. The stocks were rapidly being depleted and the residents were encountering problems getting chlorine into the water supply at the required level. The machine that injected chlorine into the water had technical problems in the absence of spare filters, and the residents were re-using existing filters at the risk of degrading the water quality. This was independently confirmed by Iraqi technicians at the water plant during a visit by UNAMI on 11 August 2010. Furthermore, due to a lack of the required technology, the residents were forced to test the water quality by unconventional methods. They used two sample buckets containing tadpole-like amoeba. If the amoeba died from the water entering the buckets then it was judged not fit for human consumption. This was an ingenious way of bypassing the embargo.

The residents also complained about the difficulties they encountered in accessing the water source. They relied on two water pumping installations, one at Zarganieh, 30 km to the west of Ashraf and a smaller unit at Marfou, six km to the east. The residents had spent over $3 million on the two stations over the years in terms of the cost of the buildings and restoration, purchase and installation of equipment, generators, wages, fuel and maintenance. The Zarganieh station relied on four pumps and two generators to draw and process water from the Tigris. These pumps needed continuous servicing and maintenance. To make things more complicated, the Iraqi water authority opportunistically connected extra pipes to the Zarganieh main pipe and diverted the water to the nearby villages. This considerably reduced the pressure and disrupted the distribution of water in Ashraf.

I reported to the "Ashraf Committee" that the lack of regular fuel supplies, compounded by a ban on spare parts and equipment, was impacting on the ability to run essential public services. I urged the Committee to restore the supplies to the existing levels at the time the MNF-I handed over Ashraf to the Iraqi authorities. They replied that allowing the Ashrafis to make life too comfortable for themselves would mean that they would never leave.

### *Medical Services*

Ashraf had a 23-bed hospital outside the Camp's perimeter on the southern side of the Lions' Gate. It opened in May 2009 as an out-patients day care centre and at a later stage expanded its capacity to provide a more substantive service including surgical interventions. It was run by the Diyala health authority and staffed by three physicians, twelve nurses, one dentist, four lab technicians, two pharmacologists and administrators. All the staff were Iraqi nationals. The cost of the equipment, the drugs, the canteen, the water and the power are met by the Ashrafis. A separate 97-bed hospital inside Ashraf, owned by the residents, had recently been converted to a convalescence home. USF-I told me the hospital was converted at short notice due to fears that it would be seized by the GoI.

During my visits to Ashraf, I usually paid a visit to Dr. Umar Khalid, the acting director of the hospital, to inquire about the state of the services and supplies since there were always problems with the delivery of essential equipment and drugs. The visit on 19 January 2010 coincided with the arrival earlier in the day of a consignment of medicines and surgical equipment that had been ordered by the residents and had been pending for a number of weeks. Some two weeks previously, on 1 January, I received a letter from the Camp's representatives complaining that two previous attempts to bring in these supplies had been turned back on the orders of the "Ashraf Committee". In a follow up visit to the hospital on 21 January, Dr. Khalid confirmed that the receipt of these essential medicines and equipment meant that he would be able to perform small surgical operations.

Operations requiring advanced expertise were performed by visiting consultants. They too faced challenges as access to the hospital was tightly controlled. A laissez-passer had to be issued from Baghdad. On a number of occasions, consultants arrived at Ashraf to undertake operations and were turned back for trivial bureaucratic reasons. Dr. Khalid acknowledged that the Iraqi Ministry of Health barely provided one third of all drugs required (approximately 70 out of 210). The remainder were ordered by the residents from the private sector at a much higher cost than from the national health authority. In terms of the Ashrafis' ability to access local hospitals and doctors for specialist treatment, Dr. Khalid acknowledged that some Ashrafi patients who were sent to Ba'qubah hospital had not been treated after waiting for several hours. This was not necessarily malpractice or discrimination he explained. It was rather due to the inherent difficulties in the Iraqi health service. However, he also pointed out that there was reluctance on the part of some specialists to visit the Camp because of the highly charged and sometime intimidating political atmosphere.

Soon Ashraf hospital would reveal its limits in providing the necessary care to residents. Iraqi medical personnel did not want to be seen to be providing more care than the absolute minimum required for fear of raising suspicions of collusion with the Mujahedin. Lt. Haider Zab Mashi, the military intelligence officer in Ashraf, was always watching. The "intimidating political atmosphere" and interference by the "Ashraf Committee" made it impossible for the doctors at Ashraf hospital to perform according to professional standards.

In addition, most Ashrafis of a certain age had experienced torture in Iranian prisons. Torture scars the person for life. As age catches up with them, the person becomes more fragile and vulnerable. In addition, Dr. Umar Khalid told me that at least 200 residents needed surgery for cancer and heart disease. There were also those needing care for the injuries sustained during the July attack, most of whom needed urgent surgical interventions in specialized hospitals.

Until June 2011, I was able to obtain "concessions" from the "Ashraf Committee" allowing the transfer of Ashrafi patients to Irbil in Kurdistan for advanced surgical interventions. By July, twelve cancer and heart disease patients needed to be transferred urgently to Irbil hospital. Unlike in previous transfers, the "Ashraf Committee" requested a UNAMI letter to guarantee the return of the patients to Ashraf after treatment. I immediately drafted a letter of guarantee even though the UN cannot guarantee anything in the conditions of Iraq. Anything could happen on the way from Ashraf to Irbil. Arrests, kidnappings, and insurgent attacks are common in the area. However, this was a humanitarian necessity that needed to be addressed proactively. I sent the letter to Sadiq and followed it with a telephone call. He said that we needed a letter from the Kurdistan Regional Government (KRG) to authorise such a transfer. Working in the field of human rights, I was used to these marathons. I called my colleagues at the UNAMI Office in Irbil and asked them to follow up as a matter of urgency with the KRG Ministry of Interior. Unfortunately, the Minster turned out to be out of the country until August. On his return, a UNAMI officer met him and explained to him the humanitarian situation of the twelve patients. He signed the letter which was immediately forwarded to me. I passed it to the "Ashraf Committee". By now al-Yasseri was no longer in charge. The new National Security Adviser, Faleh al-Fayadh, had the Ashraf portfolio. Haqqi and Sadiq referred the matter to him. He banned all transfers to Kurdistan on the ground that there were sufficient services in Baghdad. Since the July 2009 attack, ten patients from Ashraf had died due to similar bureaucratic obstruction.

### Seized Vehicles

A total of 39 vehicles belonging to the Ashrafis, worth $1.177 million, including fuel and water tankers and minibuses for public transport, were seized by Iraqi Forces on 28 and 29 July during the attack against Ashraf. These vehicles were clearly visible, decaying in the conditions of heat and dust, in a holding area controlled by the Iraq Police. Some were cannibalised by the Iraqi police for spare parts. When I raised the issue with the "Ashraf Committee", I was told the matter was before the court. The vehicles were in police custody and the "Ashraf Committee" had no jurisdiction. In the coming months and years, the UNAMI monitoring team was never able to establish whether or not this matter was actually put to the court.

### *Food*

The issue of inadequate food supplies, including delays in deliveries and mishandling during cargo checks, was always a matter of contention between the Camp residents and the Iraqi authorities. Supplies had to be contracted in Kuwait and transported from there to Ashraf along the MNF-I convoys, an unnecessary and costly journey. Local contractors refused to supply Ashraf for fear of falling under the anti-terrorist law. Those who did were harassed and sometimes arrested. Needless to say, had there not been an embargo imposed on Ashraf, arrangements with local merchants would have speeded up the sourcing and delivery process and would have provided fresher and cheaper food. Such arrangements would also have benefited the local economy of the Diyala Province.

Under pressure from the diplomatic community, eager to know the reality of access to food, I visited on 4 August 2010 the warehouses where the residents stock their food supplies. The visit to the warehouses was not pre-arranged. I went through all the stocks. From the reports I received earlier, I was expecting to find mountains of food. In reality I was shocked to see in the cooling rooms small quantities of dried fruits and vegetables and a quantity of frozen poultry and red meat. Although the warehouseman told me there were enough supplies for a week, from what I saw, I thought this was an overestimate. In another surprise visit on 11 August 2010 to both the water plant and the food warehouse, in the absence of High-level PMOI representatives, the UNAMI team reported that food deliveries still came from Kuwait due to harassment of local Iraqi vendors and that delayed cargo inspections by the Iraqi Army resulted in an average loss of 40 to 60% in the refrigerated food supply.

From the warehouse, I went back to the Tuloo Building near the Lions' Gate to meet the Camp's representatives. There, our delegation was served a rather copious meal. Ashrafis are proud to show Persian hospitality. Being of the same cultural background myself, I knew they were making a sacrifice. In the regional tradition, passers-by would never leave a house before a goat or a chicken is killed for them, even if it is the only asset the household possesses. Guests get the best, and God will provide if nothing is left for the next day. When we returned to Baghdad, colleagues reported, in different directions, that the alleged embargo against Ashraf was an illusion. We were served food in Ashraf in better quantity and quality than what we get at the UNAMI dining facility, they said. One of the military advisors went to the extent of observing, from the other side of the meeting room, what kind of nail polish and what brand of headscarves the women were wearing. Such remarks are not as innocent as one might think. They are damaging when put in the context of whether the Camp was effectively subjected to an embargo. They contribute to the building of false perceptions and undermine the credibility of the Ashrafis.

# Psychological Pressure:

# Iranian 'Visiting Families' and the Loudspeakers

The sequence of events in Ashraf since February 2010 indicated that the Iraqi authorities were set to carry out a plan announced in 2009 by the former National Security Advisor, Muwaffaq al Rubaie. It consisted of a series of measures to make life in Camp Ashraf "unbearable" with the aim of breaking the bonds between the residents and their leadership. The imposed restrictions on goods and services were aimed at destroying the infrastructure of the Camp. It was hoped that continuous hardship and violence would undermine the residents' endurance, solidarity and discipline. At that point, the Prime Minister's Office believed, the residents would willingly give up and go back to Iran.

The Prime Minister Office in cooperation with the Iranian Embassy in Baghdad arranged the so-called "family visits" of some Iranian government-operated NGO (or GONGO in the jargon of human rights activists) to destabilize Ashraf. Assisted by the Iraqi army, they set up camp at the Lions' Gate and fixed nine loudspeakers to the Gate's metal frame to broadcast aggressive messages to the residents. Over a period of two years, the loudspeakers multiplied to reach 300 units blaring threats and insults day and night at the residents.

The residents naturally saw this as a provocation orchestrated by the Iranian Ministry of Interior and Security (MOIS). As a counter measure, they in turn installed their own loudspeakers on the top of a vehicle to broadcast music shielding the residents from the aggressive and sometime obscene messages coming from the other side of the fence.

Powerful loudspeakers on perimeters of Ashraf broadcasting deafening noise as part of psychological torture of the residents after US handed over of the camp to Iraqis

On 15 April, the USF-I informed the UN monitoring team that approximately 100 soldiers in anti-riot gear and 5 HUMVEEs had arrived in Lions' Gate at 15.23 and began to threaten the residents if they did not switch off their audio system. At about 16.00, the USF-I outpost informed us that more vehicles had arrived at Lions' Gate and began to push the residents away from the area using batons. The anti-riot force was dispatched to remove the residents' loudspeakers as they rendered those of the Iranians ineffective. As a result of this confrontation, five residents were hospitalised. On 18 April, I received the following update from the USF-I:

*[- Reportedly, the injuries were to lower extremities only.*

*- ISF claims that upon entering the compound they laid razor wire between themselves and the MEK protestors.*

*- MP Battle Captain believes that this could account for lower extremity "injuries" if the MEK cadre tried to cross the wire (do not know if they did...this is mere supposition).]*

When I contacted Haqqi of the "Ashraf Committee" on 16 April, he denied that there were any disturbances and claimed that the situation in Ashraf was calm and that the Iranian visiting families were still camped at the Lions' Gate waiting to see their relatives. Our officer in FOB Grizzly confirmed that since the incident of 15 April the situation had calmed down but the Iranian visiting families were still entrenched in their position at the Lions' Gate.

On 16 April 2010, I briefed the SRSG and DSRSG on the current situation on the ground and suggested a way forward as follows:

- *Engage the Iraqi authorities in the context of capacity building*
  1. Advise the Iraqi authorities to manage the Camp by civilian specialists with expertise in crisis management from the MoHR/MoFA.
  2. Advise on how to manage the Camp consistently with international humanitarian standards.
- *Engage the diplomatic community and exploit the dynamics that led to the removal of the MEK/PMOI from the European Terrorist List*
  1. The EU removed the PMOI from its terrorist list following a decision of the European Court of Justice. UNAMI should address the diplomatic community to exploit these judicial dynamics to galvanise the immigration and refugee services of the EU Member States.
  2. Member States of the Coalition Forces that invaded Iraq should be persuaded to share responsibility for Ashraf residents, separately from the political issue of the PMOI.
- *Engage the PMOI*
  1. There was a perception that UNAMI could protect. A dialogue should outline the limits of the protection that UNAMI could provide and bring the PMOI to a more realistic understanding of their reality.

2. The PMOI should be engaged at the HQ level.

On the same day as my briefing, the SRSG had two meetings, one with the PM al-Maleki and the other with the Iranian Ambassador, Hassan Kazemi-Qomi. He discussed with them the way forward. Al-Maleki repeated the usual message that Iraq would assume its responsibility, and, in doing so, would comply with international humanitarian standards. The Iranian Ambassador complained about the biased and partial conduct of the UNAMI monitoring team. He said the UNAMI monitoring team interacted only with the MEK leadership in Ashraf and had not met with the families asking to see their loved ones detained in Ashraf. He asked that UNAMI receives a delegation representing the visiting families.

The SRSG was aware that if there was any bias at UNAMI, it was against the MEK, but, for diplomatic reasons, he accepted that a meeting with the Iranian visiting families be convened as soon as possible.

On 19 April 2010, a meeting was arranged at UNAMI HQ at 11:00am for a delegation consisted of Ms Thuraya Abdullah, Ms Mah Veer Jalali, Mr Ridha Ramadhani and Mr Falah Alshaybani, a Farsi-Arabic interpreter.

It was not the kind of meeting the SRSG would attend in person, nor would the DSRSG. He delegated the matter to his Director of Political

Affairs, Mr Madhu Acharya. Present with him was Ms Birgetta Holst Alani, political advisor to the SRSG, and myself, as Chief of the Human Rights Office. As the meeting was improvised at short notice, we did not have a professional Arabic-English interpreter. I ended up playing that role and so did not effectively participate in the discussion.

Madhu, new in the mission, had not yet gained a full understanding of the situation. He welcomed the visitors and expressed his apologies for the difficulty the visitors faced while entering the Green Zone. He then gave the floor to Ms Thuraya Abdullah.

Ms Abdullah, nicknamed 'Captain Thuraya' because of her alleged authority over the Iraqi army officers, introduced herself as the spokesperson of the Iranian families picketing the Lions' Gate. The families wanted to see their loved ones detained inside Camp Ashraf. She apologized for her voice as 75 days of shouting and crying had taken their toll. Ms Abdullah recited a long repertoire of grievances against the Rajavis (leaders of the MEK) and the MEK 'cult', quoting the confessions of some defectors such as Ms Batool Sultani and Iman Yagani. In summary, she rehearsed all the allegations of the Sahar Family Foundation and Iran-Interlink web sites. She said that all attempts to see their 'children' (all adults) had failed. Ms Abdullah claimed that Naheet (a female resident) and Basheer (a male resident) had attacked her in the presence of the Iraqi army while the latter did nothing to protect her. She said she intended to press charges against the two attackers and against the Iraqi army for failing to protect. Ms Abdullah said that they were here to seek help from UNAMI to reunite the families with their loved ones.

Birgetta Holst Alani, political advisor to the SRSG, asked how the families had spent the past 75 days. Falah (the Iraqi interpreter) intervened to answer the question himself. He said the families were enjoying the hospitality of the Iraqi government. Ramadhani expressed the families' gratitude to the government of Iraq for providing them with all means of comfort, including accommodation and medical services. He added that the current government and army were entirely different from those of Saddam's regime. The Iraqi Army in Ashraf had been so generous as to provide an Iranian cook so that the picketing families felt at home.

Ms Mah Veer Jalali said her son had been kidnapped 13 years ago in Kermanshah while travelling in search of work. He had been taken to Europe and from there to Ashraf, she said. Ms Abdullah handed some compact discs and documents to Madhu Acharya, the Director of Political Affairs, to corroborate their stories.

Madhu concluded by saying that UNAMI would do everything possible within its mandate to resolve the issue while the primary responsibility for finding a lasting solution remained that of the GoI. He thanked the delegation for attendance and closed the meeting.

While the meeting was in progress, Ms Abdullah had placed what we thought was her mobile telephone on the table in front of her. In fact, she had recorded the entire meeting. Within 24 hours, the tape was transcribed, edited to attribute to Madhu more than he intended to say, and then posted on Iran-Interlink with the UNAMI Logo pasted in to give it more authenticity.

On 20 April at about 11.00am, the UNAMI Public Information Office (PIO) picked up the information and circulated it among the UNAMI leadership. Everyone was dismayed with the way the mission had been used for propaganda purposes. We needed to act. Given that the meeting was requested by the Iranian Ambassador, I immediately called the Iranian Embassy to protest at the breach of confidence and the illegal use of the UNAMI logo. I was told it had nothing to do with the Embassy and I should address the NGO with whom we met. The Chief of the UNAMI PIO then contacted the website administrator and requested the immediate withdrawal of the text and the misused UNAMI logo. It was done without delay.

The Deputy Special Representative of the Secretary General (DSRSG) for political affairs, Jerzy Skuratowicz, arrived at the mission in February 2010. In addition to his solid academic background, he was also very experienced UN diplomat. The DSRSG requested a meeting with the "Ashraf Committee" to hear the GoI's planning for the closure of FOB Grizzly and the USF-I pull back to FOB Warhorse outside Ba'qubah on 1 July 2010. I went with him to that meeting on 18 May. After the usual courtesies, the DSRSG informed al-Yasseri that UNAMI would no longer be able to retain a monitoring presence in Ashraf in the wake of the US withdrawal. He asked al-Yasseri for his views on how the Camp is currently managed in terms of supply and control and what his vision was of the relationship between the PMOI/MEK and GoI in the coming months.

Al-Yasseri replied that USF-I would hand over FOB Grizzly to the Iraqi Army Unit responsible for Camp Ashraf led by Lt. Col. Latif. The police force there, under the leadership of Major Agad, would take over the Iraqi Army location at the Lions' Gate. Al-Yasseri was concerned at the decision to withdraw the UNAMI monitoring team from the Camp following the withdrawal of US forces. He noted that the Iraqi Security Forces were fully trained and equipped to protect the UN, as had been demonstrated throughout Iraq since the drawdown of the USF-I.

The DSRSG explained that the decision by UNAMI stemmed from the mandatory security procedures of the UN.

In order to guide the discussion towards the necessity of closing Camp Ashraf and relocating the residents, al-Yasseri expressed concern that when the US withdrew from the area there was the possibility that Iran will strike Camp. Al-Yasseri complained that countries in the region were trying to interfere in Iraq's affairs. The threat from Iran was of particular concern. Iran had not so far attacked Camp Ashraf [in fact Iran did launch a number of attacks on the Camp with Skud missiles before and after the 2003 invasion of Iraq] because of the presence of the USF-I and the UN. The "Ashraf Committee", he said, had tried to meet regularly with the PMOI but had had little success. The "Ashraf Committee" dealt with the residents as individuals through 'representatives' rather than with the PMOI leadership. The Committee had tried to find common ground with the PMOI but had not been successful. If the group would like to live in peace they could go and resettle elsewhere but, without legal status in Iraq, the group could not 'run free throughout Iraq'. The GoI would not allow the PMOI to meet with Iraqi citizens or foreign nationals living in Iraq because of the organization's possible linkages to terrorist groups.

Al-Yasseri raised another issue, that of the alleged MEK interference in the Iraqi elections. As evidence of such interference, he showed printouts of digital photographs of al-Iraqiya campaigning posters hanging in a conference room at Camp Ashraf. The DSRSG asked with disbelief for the links between the posters and any possible interference in the elections, since the residents were locked up in Ashraf and forbidden from contact with Iraqi citizens.

Al-Yasseri insisted that, despite the PMOI's unacceptable conduct, and the fact that UNHCR did not recognize them as refugees, the "Ashraf Committee" had always allowed in all supplies they ordered such as food, medicine, and clothing, "with the exception of military fatigues and items of possible military use".

To conclude, al-Yasseri requested an official letter from the United Nations testifying to the *"GoI's good conduct in controlling the camp. This will be an encouragement to the military who have demonstrated considerable restraint toward the PMOI, even when they were attacked with stones when the GoI attempted to open a police station"*. The security forces had been instructed not to use force, and to remain calm, even if provoked, he said. Al-Yasseri was trying to clear the Iraqi Army of any wrongdoing particularly in the events of 28/29 July 2009 by obtaining a letter of good conduct from UNAMI.

The DSRSG insisted that the GoI must develop a clear strategy on how to move forward on Ashraf within the framework of Iraqi domestic law and its international legal commitments. The UN did not want to witness another incident in which people were hurt. The GoI needed to demonstrate to the international community that it had a cohesive and well-defined approach to the issue.

I provided a short briefing on the meeting with the 'Iranian families' and the hijacking of that meeting for pure propaganda purposes. Regarding the loudspeakers, I informed the meeting that the residents had removed their loudspeakers but the other side had not; in fact, more speakers had been added. The DSRSG emphasized that the use of loudspeakers was a form of collective punishment and was counter-productive. He reiterated that it was not serving any purpose and needed to cease. A more responsible approach was needed. We agreed to continue meeting as a joint working group.

The UNAMI-Ashraf Committee working group met regularly every Sunday at 10am at the PM's Office, acting as a channel of communication between the Ashrafis and the GoI. Subsequently, I encouraged my counterparts from the American Embassy to join the meeting. Their presence had always been of great help. UNAMI was to take the lead with US support.

## Ashraf Committee-Iraqi Army Operations in Ashraf as of 2010

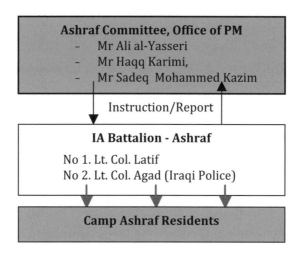

On 7 June 2010, I received a letter from the American Embassy notifying UNAMI of the USF-I pull out of FOB Grizzly on 1 July. Ambassador Grappo asked me to verbally convey the content of the letter to the Camp's representatives. They did not want to be seen writing directly to the Camp's leadership since the American policy was now to minimize contact with the Ashrafis.

That same day, I had a telephone conference with Mehdi Baraei and Behzad Saffari. Having informed them of the US withdrawal from FOB Grizzly, I then conveyed the message that, "*the US no longer has any legal obligation or authority to provide for the protection of the residents of Ashraf*", and that "*the US government's policy of continuing to treat Ashraf residents as protected persons ended when the UN mandate for the Multi-National Forces expired at the end of 2008...*" I also relayed the message that the US "*will continue to monitor the situation closely to ensure that the GoI abides by its assurances and obligations*".

Mr Baraei argued at length that the residents were protected persons. The protected persons' status was granted by individual agreements signed between top military US commanders and each and every resident. Each resident was given a "protected person ID card". In an official letter, dated 7 October 2005, Major General William H. Brandenburg reiterated the right of the residents, as protected persons, as follows:

i. *"The residents of Camp Ashraf have the right to protection from danger, violence, coercion, and intimidation and to special protection for the dignity and rights of women;*

ii. *They have the right to help in contacting their families outside Camp Ashraf and their families have the right to help in contacting them;*

iii. *They have the right to seek assistance from the International Committee of the Red Cross, the UNHCR and from other international humanitarian organizations;*

iv.    *They have the right to freedom of thought, religion, expression, intra-community association, and political opinion; they have the right to freedom from persecution and forced unpaid labour;*

v.    *They have the right to food, health care, and a quality of living which meets the standards of local residents of the territory in which they are protected;*

vi.    *They have the right to fair treatment under the law, in accordance with Iraqi domestic law and international standards;*

vii.    *They have the right to pursue employment opportunities and profit-making activities which are constant with local laws and can be taken without compromising their overriding rights to personal safety;*

viii.    *They have the right to speak with representatives of the Coalition, the protecting power, privately and with confidence in the Coalition's humanitarian interest in their situation;*

ix.    *They have the right to refuse to return to their country of nationality, regardless of their legal status in the country in which they are protected;*

x.    *They have the right to depart the territory of conflict at any time for their country of nationality or for any other country for which they possess valid travel documents.*

*All these rights are essential for the protection of the residents of Camp Ashraf, and under the terms of the Fourth Geneva Convention, and they cannot be renounced, either by the residents of Camp Ashraf or by the Coalition*".

Mr Baraei argued further that the rights of protected persons were fundamental rights and could not be renounced by either the MNF-I (now USF-I) or the residents. Handing over the residents to the exclusive authority of the GoI knowing that the latter was not willing to respect these rights was a violation of article 45 of the Fourth Geneva Convention. Mr Baraei argued that USF-I should at least keep a small unit to ensure that the guaranteed rights of the residents were duly respected until the departure of the USF-I from Iraq at the end of 2011. He asked whether UNAMI would keep a monitoring mission in Ashraf. The pull out of the USF-I from FOB Grizzly, leaving the residents defenceless against daily threats, amounted to sending them to their deaths, he said.

I replied that the UNAMI presence in Camp Ashraf was entirely dependent on the USF-I in terms of logistics and security. Once the USF-I pulled out, the UNAMI presence in FOB Grizzly would be unsustainable. The decision was not UNAMI's. It was dictated by the UNHQ security policy. However, UNAMI would continue to monitor the situation with weekly field visits, and to engage the

Iraqi authorities and the diplomatic community, as it had done before the events of July 2009.

On 29 June 2010, I met with Ambassador Gary A. Grappo and Brigadier General Joseph Anderson at the US embassy to discuss the needs and the format of the new monitoring mission. Both men were very keen to provide support in accordance with the USG policy set in January 2009 to avoid direct involvement but to support the UN in handling Ashraf issues. I put it to them that UNAMI needed to monitor and to be seen doing so. This would require frequent visits to Ashraf and USF-I assistance in terms of security and air transport would be essential. I requested that the first flight to Ashraf be within a month at the latest. This was agreed. It was also agreed that representatives of the diplomatic community and other UN agencies would occasionally join UNAMI on these flights. Col. Bryndol Sones, the USF-I/UNAMI coordinator and Col. Nelson and Lt Col John Hagen, UNAMI military advisors, would coordinate the missions. Later that day, I sent an open invitation to all relevant embassies to join UNAMI visits for consular or monitoring purposes. I also informed both the "Ashraf Committee" and the Camp's leadership about the new monitoring arrangements.

On 18 July 2010, I went to the PM's office to coordinate the first visit to Ashraf after the departure of the USF-I from FOB Grizzly, planned for 20 July. The UNAMI delegation was to be accompanied by consular officers from the US and UK embassies who would meet with their nationals in the Camp. Haqqi told me his government had no objection to consular visits as long as their aim was the resettlement of the Camp's residents; diplomatic visits for monitoring purposes would not be permitted. Sadeq was to be at Ashraf on 20 July to receive the UNAMI delegation. I guessed that Sadeq's presence was to ensure that the delegation comprised no diplomats other than consular officers.

As a start for the new monitoring mission, I requested clarifications regarding the arrest warrants against Camp residents and the loudspeakers.

Haqqi replied that the GoI intended to implement the arrest warrants issued against some camp residents (the initial list was 37, but by January 2012 it had reached 121). This would happen after the return of the Committee's Chair, Ali al-Yasseri from his trip abroad. Al-Yasseri would obtain approval from PM al-Maleki and then the warrants would be served at Camp Ashraf by the ISF. Haqqi did not disclose the nature of the alleged offences for which the arrest warrants were issued. He said the GoI had information confirming that the persons concerned were presently in the Camp. I had the list of the 37 warrantees and I knew some of them were based in Paris, not in the Camp. I raised my concern about the interference of the executive in judicial affairs, and I urged the Committee to adhere to the rule of law and to respect human rights. Haqqi assured me that the ISF would observe human rights in enforcing the warrants; those detained would be screened, and those deemed innocent would be released, he said.

On the issue of the loudspeakers, I reminded Haqqi of the pledge he made during our last meeting. He replied that the Camp residents had failed to comply with agreements on removing their loudspeakers and that PMOI leaders had concealed weapons in the camp and refused to remove portraits of the Rajavis, despite several requests by the GoI. As a matter of fact, UNAMI had documented the removal of the residents' loudspeakers from the time we had made the request.

The UNAMI leadership was anxious to have uninterrupted visits to Ashraf to compensate for the withdrawal of the monitoring team. Everything was done to send a message to the international community that UNAMI and the USG were not abandoning the Ashrafis. On 24 July 2010, I lead a delegation comprising British and US consular officers into Camp Ashraf. This was done with the agreement of the Iraqi authorities.

The visit coincided with the first anniversary of the Iraqi Army attack on Ashraf of 28 July 2009 and with the publication of the 15th Human Rights Report covering the period 1 January-30 June 2009. Paragraph 52 read: "*In March, UNAMI interviewed former residents of Camp Ashraf who had escaped from the Camp. They confirmed some of the previous findings that some residents may have been brought into the Camp on false pretences, while trying to leave Iran for western Europe or the United States of America, and once there, were denied the right to leave. UNAMI was told, on this and on previous occasions, of the alleged psychological pressure, intimidation, and physical abuses that the PMOI rank and file might be subjected to.*"

The residents' representatives strongly criticized the report, arguing that it reflected one-sided and biased information. The report had only recorded allegations coming from proxies of the Iranian regime – a regime currently torturing residents through continuous broadcasting of threats on loudspeakers at the Camp. People who had left Ashraf in the 90s could not be reliable sources of information. The report had omitted the fact that the Camp representatives had repeatedly invited UNAMI monitors to talk to the residents privately, individually and collectively, but that invitation had always been turned down. They further complained that the report had neglected the human rights violations against the residents; it did not mention the embargo imposed on Ashraf and the difficulties residents encounter in accessing food, fuel, utilities, equipment, medical services, and lawyers. It did not report on the restrictions on Ashrafis' freedom of movement. It did not report that the real families of the Camp's residents were denied entry visas to Iraq. The representatives expressed their alarm that UNAMI had reported events with bias and without verification and had summarised in one paragraph events extending over six months. The report had given the Iranian regime carte blanche to treat Ashraf residents as they please. They warned that the Iranian regime, with the support of al-Maleki would attack Camp Ashraf again and that UNAMI would be held responsible.

I told the meeting that UNAMI strictly observed the UN reporting guidelines. We had produced a number of reports on Iraq and these had always contained a chapter on Camp Ashraf. It was normal that reports did not have the agreement of all parties. We were extremely cautious in reporting and always referred to 'allegations' when we used information from third party sources.

Looking back now at paragraph 52 of the said report, I realize how scandalous it was. I have since traced the source of the information provided by the HRO to the RAND Report referred to above, page 63, paragraphs 2 and 3, and to the Human Rights Watch (HRW) report of 2005, page 14 onwards. The HRO report was nothing more than plagiarism. It was not the outcome of duly organized interviews of former residents of Ashraf.

As the Head of the HRO, I had arrived in March 2009 when the report was already in preparation. I had not been able to have a meaningful contribution to it or to question the work already done by my colleagues. Later, when I had gathered first hand information, I understood why my predecessor had been pushed out of office. At the UN, there are those who work to do their jobs and those who work to keep their jobs. The latter are those who know well the UN establishment. They know that certain realities are not well-received in Geneva and New York. Forget about integrity, professionalism, accountability and all the values the UN advocates but does not uphold. The reality is that UNAMI is in Iraq to serve the Iraqi Government. The checks and balances that exist are there to keep that government happy. Raising human rights issues, particularly when it concerns Camp Ashraf residents, upsets the decision makers in Iraq. Consequently, human rights reports are first drafted in Baghdad, moulded and shaped in Geneva and New York and then presented to the Government concerned for comment before they are released. Even though I felt duped and betrayed by those who had drafted the report, I comforted myself with the thought that even Secretary of State, Colin Powell, had been misled by his own staff when he presented on 5 February 2003 the Security Council with false evidence of Iraq's failure to disarm.

After a few months in the mission, I had developed good relations with the Council of Representatives, the Government officials as well as a large number of tribal leaders, NGOs and independent personalities. Unlike other UN staff, I had the privilege of sharing language, culture, history and religion with the Iraqis. I came to understand that as long as the Ashrafis are in Iraq, they will be denigrated and hated by some, honoured and protected by others. They are an important element in the sectarian equation of Iraq. Moreover, the Iranian influence over al-Maleki's government will make their presence in Iraq as an opposition group impossible. Tarnishing the MEK as a terrorist organisation and as a cult has been an effective way of marginalising them in Western thinking about the Middle East. Tehran has been successful in horse trading them with the West and in stigmatising them with allegations which distort their aspirations for democracy and human rights. Thus, the pressures kept mounting on Ashraf: the loudspeakers multiplied; supplies were scarce; and access to medical services became a serious challenge. Complaints from the residents to UNAMI and the US Embassy became overwhelming.

On 13 October 2010, after having duly notified the "Ashraf Committee", I went on a scheduled visit to Camp Ashraf, accompanied by a representative of the US Embassy. Our delegation was met this time at ex-FOB Grizzly by the Commanding Officer of the Iraqi Army at Ashraf, Lt Col Latif. He told me apologetically that the "Ashraf Committee" had given instructions to the army not to meet UNAMI. The delegation, escorted by three USF-I Strykers, then moved into Camp Ashraf to meet with the residents' leadership at the Tuloo Building. After a two hour meeting with the Camp's leadership, the Commander of the USF-I Strykers platoon came to inform me that he had credible information that the

Iraqi Army would attack following the departure of UNAMI and that he intended to keep his force in Ashraf to monitor developments.

The UNAMI Delegation terminated the meeting with the residents' representatives at noon and returned to ex-FOB Grizzly to meet with the Iraqi Commanding Officer in order to probe the likelihood of violence. The Iraqi Commanding Officer informed me that he had firm instructions to remove the residents' road block by force if necessary and that he had no choice but to do it. He admitted that it would be an ugly scene but as a soldier he would obey his orders.

On the same day, after returning to Baghdad, I contacted the "Ashraf Committee" to urge them to calm the situation and to do everything to avoid violence. The Committee replied that responsibility for events lay not with them but with the Mujahedin-e Khalq. I contacted the residents' leadership and urged them to immediately remove their road blocks. They responded that they were ready to move their road blocks if the Iraqi Army simultaneously did the same. Continuous contacts were maintained with both sides till 8pm when Sadiq from the "Ashraf Committee" called to inform me that the USF-I were maintaining three Strykers at ex-FOB Grizzly and had located an additional ten Strykers outside Camp Ashraf. He expressed serious concern saying that this act violated the sovereignty of Iraq and was a breach of the SOFA. I was told that, since I had brought them in, I was to get them out. Sadiq wanted me to ask the USF-I platoon commander to withdraw his forces immediately.

Given the dangerous security situation in the Diayla region, and the corresponding risk involved in moving forces at night, I suggested to the "Ashraf Committee" that the Iraqi Army treats the USF-I platoon as guests for the night on condition the platoon leaves the next day with the understanding that the Iraqi Army would refrain from taking any violent action against the residents. The Committee agreed. By 5pm on 14 October, the USF-I left Camp Ashraf to return to FOB Warhorse in Ba'qubah. When the news reached Prime Minister al-Maleki, he called Ambassador Jeffrey and protested at the breach of the SOFA and asked him to ensure such an incident did not happen again. The Americans considered court-martialling the commanding officer who took the decision to stay overnight at Ashraf. I had to affirm that the officer had in fact saved lives by his action and that he should be commended, not court-martialled.

On Sunday, 17 October 2010, I called my counterpart at the US embassy (for the obvious reason I will not give a name) and explained that I needed the embassy's support in my meeting with the "Ashraf Committee". We discussed the situation and agreed to meet at the PM's Office at 10.00am. The meeting was attended, on the Iraqi side, by Haqqi and Sadiq. Al-Yasseri, the "Ashraf Committee" chair, has been distancing himself or more likely distanced from Ashraf meetings. In sombre mood, Haqqi requested an explanation for the presence of USF-I at Ashraf on 13 October following the departure of the UNAMI delegation. Below, part of the note to the file:

*(American Embassy Rep): I would like to convey to you on behalf of Ambassador Jeffrey the following: The US and Iraq are friends. Friends should be able to speak to each other openly and frankly; after having been here two months, it became clear to me that there is a pattern of conduct of the Iraqi Armed Forces confronting and harassing Camp Ashraf residents... To avoid further provocations and escalations, we recommend that you:*

- *Allow shipments of food items and other items to maintain the standards set by the USF-I when they were in control;*
- *Remove additional army checkpoints located inside Camp Ashraf;*
- *Remove loudspeakers;*
- *Stop inhibiting Iraqi judges and lawyers from visiting Camp Ashraf and speaking to its residents.*
- *Stop threatening to expel the residents from Ashraf by force.*

[When urged to not forcibly move Camp Ashraf residents, the Committee representatives cautioned that Iraq had only committed not to forcibly repatriate them. There was no commitment not to relocate them within Iraq using any means necessary].

*TB (UNAMI): UNAMI did not know that the USF-I platoon had actually stayed behind in Ashraf at the end of the monitoring mission until Sadiq called at 8pm demanding that they leave immediately. As soon as I was informed, I contacted UNAMI military advisors (MILAD) and USF-I to convey that information. In order to save face for all, I suggested that the Iraqi Army would accommodate the USF-I platoon as guests for the night to spare them a dangerous journey at night back to FOB Warhorse in Ba'qubah. This was agreed with Sadiq.*

*Haqqi (AC): The USF-I platoon did not leave in the morning as agreed; they stayed until 5pm.*

*(American Embassy Rep): Frankly, I was in Ashraf on Sunday (13th October) and from what I saw on the ground it was clear that there would be an attack and that the USF-I platoon's delayed departure saved lives. The Commander on the ground was trying to prevent what he saw as an imminent loss of life.*

*Haqqi (AC): What made you believe that there would be an attack?*

*(American Embassy Rep): My observations from the last two months. The Iraqi Army has been behaving in a provocative way. We have documented the unacceptable behaviour of Army officers beating up harmless and defenceless residents. There is no reason for additional army check points inside the camp apart from harassing the residents. There is no*

*reason for restricting or delaying foodstuffs to the residents. On behalf of Ambassador Jeffrey, I would like to urge you to stop these provocations and remove these loudspeakers the Iraqi Army is installing everywhere. The whole scene is unacceptable and is not dignifying to the Iraqi army's image.*

*TB (UNAMI): UNAMI has been monitoring the situation for a long time and I would like to draw your attention to the fact that UNAMI has never received a complaint against American officers. On the other hand, complaints about the behaviour of Iraqi Army officers are reaching us on a daily basis. We recommend that the Iraqi authorities uphold human rights and the humanitarian standards set by the American Army. Doing otherwise will not serve the image of the country. I would also draw attention to the fact that the loudspeakers are creating a hostile environment and they are undermining our trust-building efforts. UNAMI has repeatedly brought to your (the "Ashraf Committee") attention the conduct of certain officers, namely Lt. Haider, Capt. Ahmad and Lt. Col. Nazzar. These named officers were in charge last year during the 28-29 July events. It was under their command that eleven residents were killed. As long as these officers are still in charge, there is no way of trust-building. I sincerely think these officers should be deployed elsewhere if a dialogue is to be restored between the Camp and the Iraqi authority.*

*Haqqi (AC): You raised this issue before and we requested their removal in writing. We have not received any reply from the leadership. But on the standards, apart from the banned items, all shipments of food were allowed and we supplied UNAMI with documentation to that effect.*

*(American Embassy Rep): I want to leave this room confident that the "Ashraf Committee" has taken measures for trust-building and I would like to report to the Ambassador that you have taken measures to remove the loudspeakers.*

*Haqqi (AC): No, we will not remove the loudspeakers. There are families camping there waiting to see their relatives. If the Munafiqin (a derogatory term meaning 'hypocrites' used by the Iranian authorities to refer to members of the PMOI) let the families meet with their relatives, then the loudspeakers will be removed. I cannot make a decision on my own; that is a decision for the Committee.*

*TB (UNAMI): The residents claim that these 'families' are either Iranian agents or sent by the Iranian intelligence services?*

*Haqqi (AC): Not the residents; the leadership claim that.*

*TB (UNAMI): The next visit to Camp Ashraf will be on Wednesday 20 October. Are we going to have the privilege of meeting the commanding army officers to brief us?*

*Haqqi (AC): Sadiq will be there to meet you and brief you. The Army officers have no authority to brief you. End of meeting.*

On 21 November 2010, I returned from rest and recuperation leave. The Ashrafis were bitterly complaining about Dr Khalid and the treatment they get at Ashraf Hospital. On 24 November, I went to Ashraf together with Ambassador Gerard Sambrana, Political Advisor to the SRSG, Col. Bryndol Sones, USF-I/UNAMI coordinator and Col. Ronald Laden, UNAMI military advisor. We went directly to the hospital to get first hand information from the authorities there on the recent claims that the residents had been prevented from accessing medical services. The general atmosphere at the hospital was tense and highly emotional. I could feel a mutual lack of trust between the medical staff and the patients. The deputy director of the hospital explained that medical access is guaranteed to all residents. Each individual patient is treated on a case-by-case basis and treatment is always delivered according to professional norms. "The challenges surrounding the issue of medical care are mostly due to the fact that the residents don't observe the profession's rules and regulations and the realities of the general medical services of Iraq", he said.

While the meeting was in progress, some patients (males and females) forced their way into the room to report their grievances against the Deputy Director, accusing him of obstructing their efforts to access medical services. To avoid any escalation of this challenging situation, I terminated the meeting and left the hospital to go to the Tuloo Building to meet with the residents' representatives. On the way out, a small group of very excited and emotional residents tried to approach me. Lt. Col. Laden and Col. Bryndol intervened, holding me between the two of them and rushing me out of the crowd, leaving Ambassador Sambrana and my personal security detail running to catch up. Our USF-I escort was on full alert, fingers on triggers moving towards the Lions' Gate. It was a false alert I kept telling Lt. Col. Laden. It was simply a case of desperate people trying to communicate their plight to the representative of the UN.

At about noon, the delegation met the residents' representatives lead by Ms Mojgan Parsaei, Vice President of the Iranian Resistance. I first reported that the visit to the hospital had to be cut short because of the disorderly manner in which some individuals had interrupted the meeting with the Deputy Director. Ms Parsaei, jokingly, replied that it was because they were missing Mr Boumedra who had been away for some time. She then went on to update the delegation on the specific issues related to medical care, supplies, security, the Iraqi Army's harassment of the residents, and the issue of the arrest warrants. As advice, I recommended that a procedure for solving the existing challenges by keeping a logbook for each patient by the designated representatives of the residents so that disputes and allegations could be documented and addressed in a transparent manner. This filing system has been adopted in the management of logistics supplies and has successfully introduced transparency in monitoring goods and services that are allowed or denied. Ms Parsaei welcomed the idea and promised to act accordingly.

When we returned to Baghdad, the news – or rather a distorted version of the day's events - had, as usual, circulated speedily through 'Uniform Charlie' Plaza. Apparently, there had been an attempt by Ashraf residents to kidnap the UNAMI delegation!

On 8 December 2010, on arrival at Ashraf, I conferred with Lt. Col. Latif on the possibility of visiting the east wing of the camp to check the newly installed loudspeakers as well to meet with Dr. Khalid to discuss the cases of the seven patients who needed emergency treatment. Lt. Col. Latif made a call to the "Ashraf Committee" in Baghdad and the request was authorized.

Accompanied by Col. Bryndol Sones and Lt. Col. Ronald Laden from USF-I, we set off with a platoon of three Strykers to the east wing of the camp. I inquired about the newly erected stand of twenty loudspeakers placed high-up and close to residential quarters. The Camp's representatives told me they had information that the number of speakers would be increased to sixty and expressed the fear that the use of the loudspeakers might incite violence. At my next visit the number of loudspeakers had indeed expanded massively.

At the hospital, I presented to Dr. Khalid the details of the patients who needed urgent medical care and referrals to Baghdad, Ba'qubah and Erbil hospitals. Dr. Khalid brought out the medical files of all the patients and recited the dates they were transferred to various hospitals, the nature of each illness and the treatment each received. He stated that the hospital never denied patients medical care. Lt. Col. Latif supported Dr. Khalid's assertions. I suggested that both parties should keep records and document all referral cases in a logbook to avoid falling into a repetitive situation of claims and counter claims.

Back in the Tuloo Building, the residents' representatives complained that in a meeting between Prime Minister Nuri Al-Maleki and the Commander of Diyala Police, the Prime Minister issued instructions to arrest whoever entertained any ties with the MEK and to charge them under the anti-terrorism act. Following these instructions, a physician, Dr. Rashid, who had delivered some flowers to one of the MEK patients in Baghdad, was detained. The residents also expressed concern over the statement made by Judge Kazim al-Aboudi, the Head of the Iraqi Higher Criminal Court, on state TV affirming that the MEK was a listed terrorist organization that had committed crimes in Iraq. The Camp's leadership deemed such a statement as laying the ground work for a full-scale attack on the residents.

As with all allegations, I followed up on this one. Back in Baghdad, I called the office of Judge al-Aboudi and asked for an appointment to discuss his reported and very public condemnation of MEK members without any legal proceedings. Presenting myself at the agreed time on 8 December 2010, I was kept waiting for some time. Also waiting were a number of parliamentarians, including Sheikh Khalid Attiyah, Chair of the Human Rights Committee and Deputy Speaker of the Council of Representatives. I knew that the state of Iraqi prisons was high on the agenda of the CoR's Human Rights Committee; however, we are not in a position to ask each other about our reasons for seeing the Judge; issues such as prisons, the Mujahedin and human rights in general are minefields. We just exchanged few polite words and remained suspiciously and embarrassingly silent.

When I was called in, I found seven judges chatting to my host. Among them was a judge who, together with a UNAMI colleague, had tried to initiate a project for the de-Ba'thification of Iraq, based on the East German experience of uprooting the communist party. We went into the usual endless greetings then I broke from the courtesies and came straight to the point. I told Judge al-Aboudi that I had come to see him regarding his televised statement about the MEK and that I wished the meeting to be confidential, a way of hinting to the other judges to leave the room.

He ignored my hints and said loudly, 'Oh you are here to defend those criminals'. I reminded him that I was a UN human rights officer. The presumption of innocence until proven guilty was a paramount principle of justice. His response was that he had tangible evidence that the MEK were terrorists and had committed crimes against the Iraqi people. The Judge then asked his secretary to bring a pile of dossiers and had him exclaim some of the testimonies of the alleged witnesses. As the secretary read aloud, the seven judges listened attentively while people came in and out of the office. The scene was more like a 'souk' than a judicial arena.

I listened carefully to the secretary's reading. The 'testimonies' were mere hearsay at second and even third hand; there was nothing of substance. A judge of his calibre should have known better, especially in a post-conflict situation where there is a rush to settle scores and curry favour with the new regime.

I did not go to see Judge al-Aboudi to give him a moral lesson or tell him how to do his job. I went there to hear from him the actual allegations against the people he had condemned on television before any charge had been brought. I left his office convinced that justice would not be done in the prevailing circumstances of Iraq. The judiciary had been so politicized and "sectarianized"; it had become a mechanism for settling historic religious and political scores.

On 11 December, three days after my meeting with the Judge, the Ashrafis were attacked by demonstrators ferried to Ashraf by the "Ashraf Committee" and a number of them were injured. Some video footage of the attack was circulated on YouTube. I wrote to the diplomatic missions in Baghdad inviting them to attend a meeting with the "Ashraf Committee" on 12 December 2010. The following missions were represented at the meeting: Mr Russell J. Hanks, Deputy Political Counsellor, American Embassy; Mr Ville Varjola, EU delegation; Ms Sharon Diaz and Mr Neale Jagoe, British Embassy; Mr Renato Diporcia, Deputy Commissioner, Italian Embassy; Ms Tanya Spisbah, Acting Deputy High Commissioner, Australian Embassy; Ms Elisabet Hellsen, Chargée d'Affaires, Swedish Embassy; Mr Lars Tummers, Embassy of the Netherlands; and Robert Zimmerman, ICRC.

I first provided a brief update on the key issues raised by the residents' representatives during the monitoring visit to Camp Ashraf on 8 December. I brought to the attention of the "Ashraf Committee" the proposed high level meeting of the Security Council on Iraq scheduled for 15 December 2010, emphasizing that media reports of the ill-treatment of camp residents might impact negatively on the GoI. I urged the "Ashraf Committee" to pro-actively manage tensions at the Camp as the Security Council discussions would focus on political progress in Iraq. In particular, there would be an examination of the completion of the negotiations on the formation of the government and that might entail a focus on the termination of some of the sanctions under Chapter VII the UN Charter imposed on Iraq. The negative reports on Ashraf would not be helpful to Iraq in those Security Council discussions. In that context, I requested that the "Ashraf Committee" provide an update on the challenges faced in running the Camp, focusing on how the humanitarian needs of the residents were being met, as well as the status of the presence of the Iranian groups outside the Camp.

Haqqi stressed that Camp Ashraf should be a concern not only of Iraq but of the international community. He reiterated that the problem had been inherited from the previous regime and requested the diplomatic community's assistance in re-settling the Camp's residents in their respective countries. Haqqi went on to explain how the GoI, despite its own internal challenges, was doing the best it could to ensure that the residents receive the best treatment. He informed us that patients requiring critical care were transferred to hospitals in Ba'qubah, Baghdad and Erbil under the supervision of UNAMI, underlining that Iraqi nationals had to wait several months for specialist care while Ashraf residents were given priority.

I intervened to highlight the need to build trust between the residents and GoI officials and, to illustrate my point, raised the case of a cancer patient, Mr Mehdi Fathi, who had recently died when he could have been saved had he been admitted to

Erbil hospital for specialized treatment in time. I elaborated the wholly avoidable difficulties and delays entailed in transferring patients. Since the residents were prepared to pay for these medical services, such difficulties were inexcusable.

Haqqi and Sadiq alleged that those residents who acted as escorts for patients attending hospitals outside the Camp were engaged in distributing propaganda materials against the GoI. Haqqi denied that the Committee would in any way deny a patient's access to healthcare as it was a basic humanitarian issue.

On the issue of the supplies to the Camp, the Australian Deputy High Commissioner said he understood the decision to ban dual-use items but wondered why such things as whiteboards, paper, microphones and dictionaries were not permitted. In response, the Committee members explained that publishing materials were used to interfere in Iraqi elections. Of course, all the diplomats around the table knew that Ashraf is under full control of the Iraqi Army, they have no freedom of movement or contact with the local population. The contention that Ashrafis interfere in the elections was simply absurd.

I raised the issue of security around the Camp, including the nature of the visiting Iranian 'families'. Haqqi denied the allegations that the Iraqi authorities were facilitating harassment of the residents by agents of the Iranian Ministry of

Intelligence and Security (MOIS), reiterating that they were in fact relatives of some of the residents and because they were prevented by the Camp's leadership from meeting their relatives, they were forced to picket the Camp until their demands were met.

On the issue of the arrest warrants, the Committee stated that there were 38 warrants issued against the MEK's leaders and six warrants against the rank and file. In addition, there were 55 international arrest warrants issued by Iran, all under anti-terrorism laws. When asked how soon the warrants would be executed, Sadiq responded that they were just awaiting the approval of the Prime Minister. I cautioned that the recent televised statement by the Head of the High Criminal Court, Judge Kazim al-Aboudi, condemning the warrantees as terrorists undermined the principle of the presumption of innocence and raised questions about the independence of the Iraqi judiciary.

The EU delegation representative requested the timeframe for the relocation of the Camp's residents. The Committee representatives said that, although there would be no relocations in the immediate future, the plan to relocate the Ashrafis within Iraq was still live. UNAMI would be informed of timings in due course.

Coming out of the meeting, I was told Ali al-Yasseri was no longer the Chair of Ashraf Committee. Al-

Maleki has appointed Faleh al-Fayadh, a member of the CoR from the National Reform Trend, as National Security Advisor (NSA) and chair of the "Ashraf Committee". This was confirmed on 11 January by the National Iraqi News Agency. The post of NSA was first held by Muwaffaq al-Rubaie (until April 2009) and then by Safa' al-Sheikh, who, like al-Fayadh, was also from the National Reform Trend. This is a pivotal post as the holder plays a decisive role in appointing security ministers and other senior security officials.

The NSA post-holder is usually a close ally of PM al-Maleki. The National Reform Movement or National Reform (*Islah*) Trend is Ibrahim al-Jaafari's wing of the *Daawa* Party *(Hizb Al-Daawa Al-Islāmiyya)*. Al-Jaafari was the Prime Minister of Iraq in the Iraqi Transitional Government from 2005 to 2006. Al-Fayadh had been a member of the *Daawa* Party since 1973 and had close relations with the Iranian Government and its religious leaders. During the Iran-Iraq War, *Daawa* fought on the side of Iran against the Ba'athist regime. In the 1980s, Daawa was widely viewed as a terrorist organization. It was thought responsible for a number of assassination attempts in Iraq against the then President and Prime Minister, as well as attacks against Western and Sunni targets. *Daawa* moved its headquarters to Tehran in 1979 and supported Khomeini's Islamic Revolution. In turn, *Daawa* received support from the Iranian government. It was believed that the followers of *Daawa* were behind the judicial murders and torture carried out in Iraq during the two mandates of al-Maleki's premiership. The appointment of al-Fayadh did not bode well for Ashraf.

My weekly shuttle between Camp Ashraf and the Ashraf Committee in the Prime Minister's Office went on uninterrupted from December 2010. By March 2011, the Ashrafis were still complaining about the restrictions on access to fuel, electricity and medical services but their main concern was the loudspeakers and the unwanted visits and demonstrations organized by the Iraqi army. During the last three months, demonstrations had taken place every Friday. Crowds were ferried in on buses from as far afield as Basra and these demonstrations had become more confrontational, with attempts to tear down the protective fence and breaks into the Camp are no longer denied by the authorities as they used to be. It was clear something violent was on the horizon.

The diplomatic community, receiving the same complaints from the residents as UNAMI, also sensed that there was to be a planned escalation of pressure on the Camp. They frequently called my office to verify the information they were receiving and to express concern that the new NSA, Faleh al-Fayadh, was not available as an interlocutor. On 15 March 2011, I wrote a briefing note to the diplomatic missions in Baghdad in reply to their queries:

*"1. 'Ashraf Committee' is the Inter-Ministerial Committee for the closure of Camp Ashraf (in Arabic they use the word 'liquidation'). In theory, it is composed of the following: MoHR, MoJ, MoFA, MoD, MoI, Ministry of Immigration and IDPs and the PM Office. In reality only representatives of the Prime Minister's Office conduct the business and report directly to the Prime Minister. Previously, it was Ali al-Yasseri, Haqqi Karim and Sadiq Mohammad Kazim. Now the file is in the hands of Faleh al-Fayadh who reports to the PM. Haqqi and Sadiq are continuing as the executive officers. The main task of the Ashraf Committee is to implement the GoI policy for closing down the Camp and expelling MEK members from Iraq…*

*2. The loudspeakers, according to the GoI's public statements, are used to allow the visiting families to communicate with their loved ones living inside the Camp. The real purpose, as I have repeatedly been told by those in charge of the "Ashraf Committee", is to soften the resolve of the Camp's residents in order to dissociate them from their leadership and facilitate their departure from the Camp. The policy set by Muwaffaq al-Rubaie, the former security advisor to the Prime Minister, aims at making life in the Camp, as he put it, "unbearable" in order to break the residents' will and determination. Both the Iraqi authorities and the Iranian Embassy officials are firm in keeping the loudspeakers going. The Iranian Embassy officials told me they are prepared to switch off the loudspeakers only during UNAMI visits. I have however explained that the loudspeakers are not helping in anyway. They constitute a collective punishment of the residents and collective punishments are contrary to international law and international humanitarian law. Furthermore, according to the statistics provided by the "Ashraf Committee", 30 residents left the Camp in 2009 (before the installation of the loudspeakers). These have decreased in 2010 to 20 (after the installation of the loudspeakers). This figure is even lower in 2010 according the residents' account. Based on these statistics, it is clear that the loudspeakers policy is counterproductive and self-defeating besides being a violation of international law.*

*3. I met officials from the Iranian Embassy. They reiterated their determination to get rid of the "Munafiqin" from Iraq. The Iranian presence around the Camp is getting more visible and more assertive".*

# Iraqi Army's Second Attack on Camp Ashraf, 8 April 2011

The Ashrafis informed me on 3 April that they were told the Iraqi $3^{rd}$ Battalion of the $21^{st}$ Brigade of the $9^{th}$ Division is going to be replaced by a battalion from Iraq's $5^{th}$ Division. On 4 April, I was told by the Ashrafis that forces of the Iraqi $5^{th}$ Division had entered Ashraf with 30 BMP1, armoured personnel carriers and HUMVEEs and taken up positions around Ashraf. Instead of replacing the $9^{th}$ Division, it seemed the new force was in fact reinforcing the existing battalion which remained in place. The Ashrafis feared a bloodbath awaits them.

On the afternoon of 7 April, convoys of Iraqi forces arrived at Ashraf including a number of engineering vehicles. In the evening, I received information that the USF-I contingent based in FOB Warhorse, which would move every day to the proximity of ex-FOB Grizzly on monitoring missions, had left. The residents raised the alarm about unusual movement of the Iraq Army around the Camp and a number of senior Iraqi officers, including Lt. General Ali Gheidan, the Commander of the Iraqi Infantry Army; Lft. General Tariq al-Azzawi, commander of Operations of the Diyala province and an officer known as General Zia, Commander of the 5th Division had gathered at Ashraf.

By now, I was receiving calls from Ashraf nearly every half an hour updating me on the movement of the Iraqi army. When it became clear that an attack was imminent, I picked up the phone to raise the alarm. It was Thursday, the beginning of the Iraqi weekend. The US Embassy and the USF-I/UNAMI coordinator were not reachable. At the British Embassy, which accommodates the EU Delegation and a number of EU member states' Embassies, there was a party going on. I called my counterpart at the EU delegation to raise the alarm. I was told that a high ranking Iraqi military officer was at the party and was reassuring party goers that nothing untoward would happen. I called Haqqi and Sadiq. Their phones were turned off. I knew MILAD had access to the USF-I through secured lines, so I called the UNAMI military advisor, Lt Col Ronald Laden, and asked him to contact the USF-I to verify the information I was receiving from Ashraf. Even on the secure line, there was no reply. At 11pm I decided to rest briefly when Behzad called to say the Iraqi army was removing the fence on the north side of the Camp. In the absence of any authority I could contact in Baghdad, and in order to alert the international community, I called an MEP in Brussels to let him know that the fence around Ashraf had been removed and an attack was imminent. I also called a few numbers in Geneva, New York and Washington. Unfortunately, by now, most people on the American east coast had already left work.

At 4:45 am on Friday, 8 April, Behzad was on the line again. This time he told me the attack has begun. The Iraqi Army was moving in, using mechanized infantry, engineering, rapid deployment and anti-riot forces. A few minutes later, the phone rang with the news that two residents had been killed. By 5am the number of casualties had reached 12 dead and numerous injured. The 7am update reported 16 dead.

With SRSG Melkert out of Iraq, I called DSRSG Skuratowicz as the designated officer (DO). In order to end the violence, we agreed to take the extraordinary step of going to the home of Faleh al-Fayadh, the NSA. Contacting Iraqi government officials on ordinary days was a challenge let alone on a Friday morning. By the time we arrived at his house it was 9am and the number of the dead had reached 22. We asked him to stop the attack immediately if he wanted to save life and save the image of the Iraqi army and, indeed, that of the country. An attack on unarmed protected persons by three battalions of the Iraqi security forces was unacceptable. Al-Fayadh's response was to tell us that we had merely been alarmed by false rumours. I pulled out my mobile phone and asked him to speak to people on the ground to hear for himself what was happening. Instead, he made his own call. I guessed that he called his lieutenants, Haqqi and Sadiq. Al-Fayadh then reiterated that nothing had happened

Victims of April 8 attack on Ashraf by Iraqi forces

save a minor incident in which three residents had thrown themselves on some vehicles. The three were being cared for at Ba'qubah hospital. I requested authorization to visit Ashraf that day. NSA al-Fayadh turned down the request on the pretext that my weekly visit took place on a Wednesday, and that another visit in the same week was not necessary. The DSRSG insisted that it was important that UNAMI was seen on the ground. It would be an assurance to the international community that nothing had in fact happened. NSA al-Fayadh said he would consult and let us know.

By the end of the day, Friday, 8 April, the cumulative reports I had received from the residents indicated that General Ali Gheidan was personally present at the scene supervising the operation. In its move into Ashraf, the Iraqi army used sound and smoke grenades and teargas. When the residents gathered to create a human barricade in the face of the advancing forces, the army opened fire at them. Snipers were used to hunt camerawomen who were filming the attack and HUMVEEs were driven at high speed into crowds of residents.

The attack stopped on the Friday evening. The Iraqi Army had taken the north side of 100th Street running across Ashraf from west to east. The residents had been pushed south of 100th Street. Almost one third of the Camp was now occupied by the Iraqi Army. Most buildings in the occupied area had been flattened and their content vandalized or looted. There were 28 dead.

The US Embassy outlined the US government 'dilemma' in the event of an Iraqi attack on Ashraf in a cable: "*In order to break up the cult-like nature of the organization, the GOI is threatening to separate the leaders of the organization from the rank and file. Unless done over time and according to careful preparation and planning, this act (or the decision to seek to arrest the leaders) will cause a humanitarian crisis. If the GOI acts harshly against the MEK and provokes a reaction (or the MEK provokes the Iraqi Security Forces), the USG faces a challenging dilemma: we either protect members of a Foreign Terrorist Organization (FTO) against actions of the ISF and risk violating the US-Iraq Security Agreement, or we decline to protect the MEK in the face of a humanitarian crisis, thus leading to international condemnation of both the USG and the GOI.*"[10]

It was in the face of this dilemma that the order was given to the USF-I force unofficially stationed outside Ashraf to leave the scene on 7 April to avoid them witnessing people being killed without being

---

[10] See "*US government outlines 'dilemma' in event of Iraqi crackdown on Iranian dissidents*", US embassy cables published by The Guardian, 8 April 2011, http://www.guardian.co.uk/world/2011/apr/08/us-iraq-iranian-dissidents-mek

able to intervene. Once the dust had settled at Ashraf, the USF-I discreetly negotiated the dispatch of a medical team, which entered Ashraf on the 10 April. Thus, a dozen of residents identified with life threatening injuries were transferred to the USF-I military hospital in Balad. UNAMI only found out about the USF-I medical mission three days later during its fact-finding visit.

Although NSA al-Fayadh never did come back to us on the requested authorization to visit Ashraf, Wednesday, 13 April 2011 was the normal UNAMI scheduled weekly visit to Ashraf and the GoI could not prevent it from taking place. I went with a delegation comprising: Daniel Augstenberg, UNAMI Chief of the Department of Humanitarian Services; Dr Bernhard Lennartz, Chief of the UNAMI Medical Section; Despina Saraliotou, Office of Political and Constitutional Affairs; Bikem Ekberzade, UNAMI Photographer, Public Information Office; Col. Bryndol Sones, USF-I/UNAMI Coordinator; Lt. Col. Ronald Laden, MILAD; and the USF-I escort platoon.

We were usually received by the Commander of the battalion, Lt. Col. Latif in person; on this occasion, we were met by junior Iraqi army officers. They verified that all members of the delegation were UNAMI staff. Members of the diplomatic missions were not permitted to enter Ashraf. We were then escorted to the hospital. On the way, we took photographs of the scene. The fence protecting the north and west sides of the camp was completely removed, the land was flattened, buildings demolished and a berm of about six km erected along 100th Street. As had been earlier promised by the Iranian Ambassador, the loudspeakers were silenced for our visit. At the hospital, I asked the Iraqi Doctor, Umar Khalid, face-to-face, to tell the delegation what he had witnessed and the number of casualties he had received. He stated that only three people had been killed, although prior to the events, he said, he had *"anticipated the worse and had prepared his staff and the hospital"* for any eventuality.

As there was not a single patient on the premises, the delegation left the hospital without any information of substance, except the statement of Dr Khalid which inadvertently reinforced the suggestion that the attack was premeditated. We moved into the Camp to speak to the residents and their representatives. We were taken to a location east of the Camp near Tulip Square as the usual meeting centre in Tuloo Building in the west, near the Lions' Gate, was judged unsafe. Five BMPs (Russian tracked infantry fighting vehicles) were placed a few yards behind the building with their cannons directed towards it.

We were first taken to what seemed to be a makeshift clinic, a residential dwelling crammed with hospital beds. I visited every casualty. The Ashrafis' own doctor explained the state of health of each patient using x-ray images to show the bullets and shrapnel

145

in each body. He explained how some of the injured were run over by HUMVEEs. A USF-I medical team, had already done the triage of the casualties on its visit of 10-12 April, and transferred the critical cases to the USF-I Hospital in Balad. Others were transferred by the Iraqis on the day of the attack to Ba'qubah Hospital. My delegation counted 72 injured in the makeshift clinic.

Outside the clinic, relatives of the deceased stood holding photographs of their loved ones, calling on UNAMI to protect the living. Among them was a 14 year-old girl who had lost her sister during the attack. She spoke emotionally and very eloquently about how the residents were left to be slaughtered without any organisation coming to their aid.

The delegation was then split into two teams. The first team, lead by Dr. Bernhard Lennartz (a UNAMI physician), together with Ms Bikem Ekberzade, PIO Photographer, Col. Bryndol Sones (USF-I) and Lt. Col. Ronald Laden, UNAMI/MILAD, went to do the body count and to take pictures. The second team, comprising Daniel Augstburger, Despina Saraliotou and I, went to hear from the Camp's leadership.

Ms Mojgan Parsaei described the sequence of events on 7 and 8 April when the Iraqi Generals came to Ashraf and forces from Diyala joined the battalion on the ground before the attack was launched at 04.45am. Ms Parsaei expressed certainty that among the soldiers were Iranian agents and snipers recruited to execute residents since most of the dead were killed by single bullets to the head or to the heart. She said they were heard speaking in perfect Farsi as they cursed the residents. She informed us that the army has taken the northern part of the camp, demolished some buildings and blocked access to some vital areas such as the fuel storage facility. She confirmed that the attack lasted approximately seven hours. Some 318 were injured and 34 killed. Forty-four wounded had been taken to Ba'qubah hospital while four had been transferred to Baghdad. Of those transferred to Ba'qubah, six had been discharged and had been taken to a detention centre in al-Khalis, (the six were visited by the ICRC on 12 April and were subsequently released and returned to the Camp on 14 April). She deplored the lack of appropriate medical assistance that lead to the deaths of some of the injured in Ba'qubah hospital.

Back in Baghdad, I sat down with the team to assess the events. I noted: the indifference of the diplomatic community, at least on the eve of the attack; NSA Faleh al-Fayadh having denied that anything had happened while refusing to authorise my mission to Ashraf; and the USF-I covert dispatch of a medical team to Ashraf on 10 April. I noted that the Iraqi doctor's assurance to me that there were only three dead while 28 bodies and 72 casualties lay at a short distance from him. All this confirmed previous speculation about Iraqi intentions towards Camp Ashraf. The GoI spokesperson, Ali al-Dabbagh, had declared that the Prime Minister had vowed to close down Camp Ashraf by "all means"; he had indeed begun to do just that. The northern half of the Camp has been taken. Property had been looted, including the Camp's vehicles. Access to the generators providing electricity had been impeded and the provision of food had not been allowed for the past 15 days. These measures were further indicators that the PM's Office was determined to close the Camp by "all means" regardless of the humanitarian consequences.

Prime Minister al-Maleki expected the criticism of the international community, thus, some diplomatic action is not excluded from his agenda. While discussions on finding a solution might be taking place with different international interlocutors, recurrence of events like those on 7-8 April should not be excluded and could be used as an additional wake-up call to the international community to expedite negotiations for immediate removal of the residents. The Iraqis seem to be determined to close the camp within the deadline set by the Prime Minister, i.e. end of the year 2011. Human Rights and humanitarian concerns had become tactically part of the Iraqi government's rhetoric, what happens on the ground was completely different.

On 14 April, I called Dr Hamid K. Ahmed, Chief of Staff of the Prime Minister's Office and requested an urgent meeting with those in charge of the Ashraf file. He responded promptly and positively. We met the same day at the PM's office. Present on his side were: NSA Faleh al-Fayadh; Political Advisor to the

PM, Georges Y. Bakoos; and Haqqi Karim and Sadiq Mohammad Kazim, Security Officers of the PM's Office. I was accompanied by Despina Saraliotou from UNAMI's Office of Political and Constitutional Affairs as well as Ambassador Lawrence Butler, Foreign Policy Adviser to the Commander, USF-I. The meeting was chaired by the Chief of Staff, Dr Hamid Ahmed.

Dr Hamed began by praising the existing cooperation between UNAMI and the GoI, reiterating the GoI commitment to uphold human rights and humanitarian standards at Camp Ashraf. NSA al-Fayadh spoke about the urgent necessity of finding a durable solution within the timeframe set by the Prime Minister. None on the Iraqi side mentioned the 8 April attack. I told the meeting about my fact-finding mission the previous day. My team had done the body count and recorded 28 dead and 72 injured at the Camp. Other casualties were to be found at hospitals elsewhere. Dr Hamid Ahmad and Georges Bakoos were visibly shocked. The others kept silent looking down at their notebooks, avoiding eye contact with me. NSA al-Fayadh persisted in denying the attack had taken place at all. I had to offer them my pen drive with the pictures of the dead. Of course they declined to look, knowing what had happened better than I did. On behalf of the UN, I requested an independent commission of inquiry to investigate the case and to hold those responsible to account. Ambassador Butler supported my request. Al-Fayadh, his irritation obvious, replied nervously that the inquiry was a matter for Iraq; "No one will dictate to us how to do an inquiry".

### *United Nations' Response to the Second Attack*

What happened in Ashraf on 7-8 April 2011, in my assessment, was premeditated extra-judicial killing. That it was planned could be evidenced by the following facts: the GoI's rhetoric before the attack; the movement of different forces of Iraqi Army the preceding week; the presence on the ground of three generals and the same officers responsible for the 28/29 July 2009 attack; the presence of snipers as evidenced in video clips provided by the residents; the large number of victims shot with a single bullet to the chest or to the head; the use of hollow point ammunition; and the lack of credible reporting of any Iraqi casualties. Having despatched a fact-finding mission, which had confirmed the attack and the casualties, the UN should have unreservedly condemned the attack. However, UNAMI was not prepared to put its very existence in Iraq in jeopardy. It is worth recalling at this point the SRSG's statement at the meeting held with the diplomatic community on 3 October 2009; "*UNAMI has a huge agenda with the GoI and does not want to have one issue jeopardize all*". Thus, UNAMI's statement on the issue, dated 16 April 2011, merely noted "*the initiative of the GoI to establish a commission of inquiry*" and UNAMI's expectation that such a commission "*be independent*" and to start its work "*without delay*".

Knowing that UNAMI was not going to condemn the attack on Ashraf, I decided to share the report of the fact-finding mission with the Office of the High Commissioner for Human Rights outside of the regular reporting procedure. With the report and pictures of the dead in Geneva, the UN High Commissioner for Human Rights, Navi Pillay, had to "*condemn the lethal Iraqi military operation*". She said "*The Iraqi military were well aware of the risks attached to launching an operation like this in Ashraf... There is no possible excuse for this number of casualties. There must be a full, independent and transparent inquiry, and any person found responsible for use of excessive force should be prosecuted*".

As usual, the UN did not follow up on this call for an independent investigation. The reality was that UN decision-makers had other priorities in Iraq. In the case of the Mujahedin e-Khalq, the UN, at different levels of management was misinformed, misled or, as events will reveal, was intentionally keeping quiet for a mixture of personal interests and political expediency. In terms of political expediency, it should be underlined that the United Nations is not taking into account that UN agencies and programmes had an agenda in Iraq that will outlive the presence of UNAMI. At the same time al-Maleki's government was not necessarily going to outlive UNAMI, and this reality was not factored into the UN's throwing its weight behind him.

Outside of the UN system, the individual governments of the coalition expressed indignation but kept silent on the issue of investigation. They too had their own agendas and interests. They had an eye on the Iraqi post-conflict reconstruction cake. Al-Maleki's Office has the upper hand in awarding projects and no government was prepared, for the sake of a "bunch of presumed terrorists", to lose its place in a very promising market. There was however universal condemnation of the attack from parliamentarians and civil society.

## *Stevenson Initiative*

The European Parliament had adopted four resolutions on Camp Ashraf. On 12 July 2007; 4 September 2008; 24 April 2009 and 25 November 2010. By these resolutions, the EU Parliament recognized the rights of Ashraf residents in accordance with the applicable international law and the relevant international conventions including the Fourth Geneva Convention. The 4 resolutions were duly communicated to the GoI. After the second attack on Ashraf and in the follow up, a delegation of the European Parliament led by MEP Struan Stevenson visited Iraq from 26 to 29 April 2011 with the issue of Ashraf on its agenda in search for a lasting solution. Before the arrival of the delegation, the EU diplomatic mission in Baghdad, embarrassed by such a visit, tried to push the protocol arrangements to UNAMI. In that respect, the SRSG refused that UNAMI plays the role of the EU mission in hosting the delegation but arranged for a meeting on 26 April in the SRSG villa for consultation and exchange of views. UNAMI too was somehow embarrassed by that visit as the GoI had already warned that the delegation was not welcome in Iraq. Although the UN helicopters were put on standby to fly the MEPs to Ashraf, it was not a surprise to anyone when the Iraqi government refused permission for such a visit. A ban on NGOs, diplomats and parliamentarians visits had been in force since early 2009.

In a statement made public on 29 April 2011, the delegation offered to work on the resettlement of the residents to third countries such as the US, Canada, EU member states, Switzerland, Norway, and Australia, as the long term solution for all Ashraf residents without exception. The issue of ownership and properties of Ashraf residents and the People's Mojahedin Organization of Iran inside Iraq will be negotiated for compensation payable to residents of Ashraf. During the negotiations for a comprehensive solution and until the transfer of all the residents to third countries, the Iraqi authorities commit to end all judicial harassment and restrictions on Ashraf, and to respect the rights of the residents in accordance with international humanitarian law. The UN and the USG would guarantee the protection of the residents. The GoI openly rejected the MEPs' initiative while the UN and EU member states discretely distanced itself from it and the USG stated that as a matter of policy it only supports UN initiatives.

Had this initiative found enough support, it would have provided comprehensive, peaceful and durable solutions as it involves all Ashraf residents without exclusion. Any solution envisaged under the condition of obtaining the UNHCR refugee status risks politicizing the process and would exclude a category of residents particularly those in the MEK leadership which is in itself a dangerous obstacle to a peaceful solution. It is the policy of the UNHCR to work with the government in place. The government in place in Iraq under pressure from the Government of Iran wants the arrest of Camp Ashraf leadership. This explains why the GoI had rejected the EU parliamentarians' comprehensive plan for a durable solution.

# UNAMI's Search for a Peaceful Solution for Ashraf, Spring 2011

UNAMI had understood since the July 2009 attack that further action against Ashraf was in prospect; it was only a matter of when. As SRSG Melkert put it to the diplomatic community, UNAMI had to be seen to be taking steps to prevent further violence. "We will be blamed for what would happen if we remain indifferent", he said. On the other hand, he did not wish to be seen to be too much concerned with the protection of a group of MEK members. Al-Maleki would not appreciate it. In order for UNAMI to reconcile these competing demands, it was decided that a third party had to be called in, preferably an NGO. Before the events of April 2011, an approach had been made to the Centre for Humanitarian Dialogue (the HD Centre). The HD Centre was known as an independent organization dedicated to facilitating dialogue between parties in conflict, and providing support to the broader mediation and peace-building community.

Upon invitation from UNAMI, Angelo Gnaedinger, the then Acting Director of the HD Centre, visited Baghdad in January 2011 to assess the Centre's involvement in an initiative to find a viable solution for the future of the 3,400 Ashrafis. Over the course of a week, Mr Gnaedinger was able to meet several interlocutors on the issue in Baghdad including representatives of the USG, the EU, the UK, France,

Italy, Australia, the ICRC and UNHCR as well as representatives of the GoI. All welcomed the proposed initiative. I spent long hours briefing him and explaining the complexities and sensitivities of the issue. However, for reasons that remained unexplained, UNAMI pulled out of the project and started looking for a direct interlocutor within the GoI while the USG designated Ambassador Lawrence E. Butler, the Foreign Policy Adviser to the Commander of the USF-I Gen. Lloyd J. Austin III, to find a solution before the end of August 2011.

### UNAMI meets Ashraf Representatives, May 2011

Since the April attack, the residents' representatives had been persistently requesting that SRSG Melkert visit Camp Ashraf. The UNAMI leadership were worried that a visit to the Camp might give al-Maleki the impression that UNAMI was protecting those whom the GoI wished to expel from Iraq. At the same time, UNAMI did not wish to be criticized for its inaction and indifference. It wanted to be seen working towards a solution without alienating the concerns of the GoI. It was in this context that UNAMI suggested that Ashraf representatives visit the SRSG at UNAMI instead him going to them at Ashraf. I managed to convince the Ashrafis that it was worthwhile making the trip to Baghdad. I assured them that their transport and security would be guaranteed by UNAMI and that I would ensure there was a written statement from the GoI authorizing such a move. On 22 April I drafted a text in Arabic, discussed it with Haqqi and Sadeq, and sent it to NSA al-Fayadh and the DSRSG for signature. Here is its unofficial translation:

*In the Name of God, the Most Merciful, the Most Compassionate*

*Date 22 April 2011*

*Subject: UNAMI meeting with Camp New Iraq Representatives in Baghdad*

*Within the framework of the existing cooperation between the Government of Iraq (GoI) and the United Nations Assistance Mission for Iraq (UNAMI),*

*taking into consideration the decision of the Council of Ministers concerning the future of the residents of Camp New Iraq, and*

*within the framework of the ongoing consultations to find solutions for the residents of the Camp on humanitarian grounds,*

*the GoI agrees to and facilitates all necessary arrangements for representatives of the Camp's residents and UNAMI to meet in Baghdad at the request of the latter.*

*UNAMI shall make arrangements for transporting the Camp's representatives from the Camp to Baghdad and back to the Camp in the context of its weekly visits subject to the same security arrangements.*

*For and on behalf of the GoI*

*For and on behalf of UNAMI*

*NSA Faleh Fayadh*

*DSRSG Jerzy Skuratowicz*

Having secured the GoI's cooperation, the UNAMI Department of Safety and Security expressed the absurd reservation that the Camp's representatives might refuse to return to Ashraf. I gave a personal guarantee that this would not happen and consent was given.

On the morning of 3 May 2011, I went to Ashraf and accompanied Ms Mojgan Parsaei, Ms Zohreh Akhiani, Mr Mehdi Baraei and Mr Behzad Saffari back to Baghdad on two UN helicopters. I had the letter signed by both NSA and DSRSG in my pocket. The first disappointment for the Ashrafis was the absence of the SRSG. He was away on other commitments. It was DSRSG Skuratowicz who received the delegation and chaired the meeting. It was not an easy meeting and the discussions on both sides of the table were very candid. Ambassador Butler, Political Advisor to General Lloyd Austin, General Commander of the USF-I, had already coordinated how to manage the meeting with the DSRSG and had asked to be introduced at the meeting as a member of UNAMI staff. He quietly observed and took notes. The following is the verbatim transcript of the discussion:

DSRSG: We are happy to welcome you to UNAMI. We appreciate that you agreed to visit us here and I hope that we can exchange views and come to some kind of a way forward to address the issues of Camp Ashraf. As you are aware, UNAMI has a mandate limited to monitoring the humanitarian and human rights situation in Camp Ashraf. In fact, what we are doing is stretching our mandate as we realize what has happened on 8 April has dramatically changed the situation. It is important to note that the GoI has clearly announced that the residents of Camp Ashraf should be out of Ashraf by the end of the year; all indications show that the GoI is serious about this. We have also to look at the situation in the context of the withdrawal of US troops from Iraq by the end of the year. Until last year, when USF-I was in FOB Grizzly, UNAMI could station monitors permanently there; but since the departure of the USF-I, our presence became unsustainable. So far we have an agreement with the GoI to visit Camp Ashraf once a week, Wednesday or Thursday. As you know, we have been informed by USF-I that, by the end of June, they will not be able to support us. The security situation is complicated and we are reviewing the continuation of our monitoring mission which will be more complicated after June and, in fact, by the end of the year, when USF-I will have withdrawn, monitoring in Camp Ashraf will be extremely difficult. This is why it is so important today to meet and discuss and explore together the options for a lasting solution for the residents of Camp Ashraf; to see what UNAMI can do within its mandate. I must mention that our mandate is based on the fact that whatever we do in Iraq, it must be with the approval of the GoI. Considering this new difficult situation, I believe that we must consider a humanitarian option which gives certain guarantees; we need to find a lasting solution. I understand that we will not come to final decisions today but we are in touch with you through Tahar (Boumedra). I appreciate that our contact is based on trust and in the spirit of discussing all the different solutions which will ensure the life, dignity and wellbeing of Ashraf residents. This is my introduction. Welcome.

Ms Parsaei: I will also make an introduction before entering into a discussion on the issue. First my name is Mojgan. The residents in Ashraf are waiting to see Mr Melkert there, particularly after what happened on 8 April. We were encouraged to come here by Madam Maryam Rajavi in Paris and we have not informed the residents yet. We will inform them later, but they are waiting to see a delegation in Ashraf. We are aware of the mandate of UNAMI and the limitations you have and difficulties and challenges in Iraq. I do not go into the details of 8 April. I am confident that you are aware of the whole event but I want to make a few points to reiterate that this was not just an ordinary attack. It was a raid with a huge army commanded by General Ali Gheidan; 2600 troops were involved in an attack against defenceless people. So far 36 have been killed and 345 injured, 225 injured by direct gunshots. If we had free access to medical care, and if the US had helped, the number of dead would not have been so high. We are under medical siege; we are not allowed to bring in the medicines that we bought ourselves. Some of the Quds Force[11]

---

[11] The Quds Force is a component of the Islamic Revolutionary Guards Corps (IRGC), formed during the Iran-Iraq war, and responsible for planning and conducting

elements were involved in this attack. They spoke Farsi to each other. Most of the casualties took place around the residential areas.

DSRSG: We are aware from our mission on 13 April and we have a clear account. We receive information through Tahar, and I am aware of the statement regarding the involvement of Iranian elements in the 8 April attack, made by the Chair of the Foreign Affairs Committee of the NCRI, Mr Mohammad Mohaddessin, and of Madam Rajavi's letter on the same subject.

Ms Parsaei: I want to emphasize what the real issue is on the table. We cannot bury the 36 dead; we must address this issue and find a solution. The next attack is already looming. After 28/29 July 2009, international pressure prevented another attack on the residents. One preventive measure was to open a UNAMI office in Ashraf. Unfortunately that office was closed. On 15 December 2009 the GoI planned another attack but because of the UNAMI presence it was averted and that is why we have invited Mr Melkert to visit Camp Ashraf. We need a stronger condemnation by UNAMI and by the Secretary-General of the 8 April massacre. We have not seen any pressure by the UN to form a commission of enquiry. The existence of such a commission and report would be a preventive measure. This could be initiated by the UN. The scale of the problem is now

---

foreign operations, intelligence gathering and terrorist activities.

much larger than in 2009. We are still dealing with injured people. The crimes of 8 April, if left un-investigated, will aggravate our worries. We cannot wait for more and more people to be killed before taking such measures. The Iranian regime has joined in to annihilate Camp Ashraf. The residents have written to the SG a letter requesting his personal intervention to prevent another massacre by the GoI. It is most appropriate that UNAMI take this up with the SG's office. We need a monitoring team stationed in Camp Ashraf and a Security Council representative to investigate the events of 8 April. I am sure that Maleki's government is under pressure from the Iranian side to mount another attack. The Iranian regime is bombarding the world with a misinformation campaign to show that there is a solution but Ashraf residents are not willing to accept it. The blame is put on our side, as if we are not ready to negotiate. The raid of 8 April took place under the pretext of claiming back agricultural land in Ashraf when, just 48 hours before hand, we made proposals to UNAMI and the US, which were welcomed. In 2009 we had Iraqi inspectors everywhere; for three days they inspected and they fingerprinted everyone. We fully cooperated. They interviewed every resident privately and asked if they wanted to stay in Ashraf or leave. We signed a joint letter with GoI in 2009 when they came to inspect for weapons. (*She hands a copy of the letter to the DSRSG*).

DSRSG: May we keep a copy of the letter?

Ms Parsaei: Yes. There is an accusation that we still have weapons in Ashraf. In all aspects, we cooperated. In 2003 we had an agreement with the US that everyone who wants to leave can do so. This is to show you that it is not a question of us not wanting to negotiate or not cooperating or keeping people by force or any other allegation, which are simply the pretext for the use of force. They want us to kneel down to the Iranian regime and the mullahs, to force us to surrender. Another example of misleading information was that, in 2002/03, the Iranian regime spread propaganda of WMDs in Iraq hidden in Ashraf.

DSRSG: I do not want to talk about past history: we need to look to the future.

Ms Parsaei: Experience from the past can guide us in the future.

DSRSG: Let us talk openly and frankly. Let us first agree and understand what happened in 2009 and this year. The GoI is today a sovereign authority. No state in the world would concur with the view that a foreign community living in a camp like Camp Ashraf would have extra-territorial rights, immunities and privileges. Until 2008, the USF-I controlled the Camp. The gradual handing over of authority to the GoI will formally end in December 2011. The important point is that the UN, the US, or any other country, cannot tell the GoI to treat Camp Ashraf residents as a diplomatic mission. I do not want to enter into historical detail but UNAMI/UN does not have an official stand; as far as your organization is concerned, we have no official position. We are only concerned by the humanitarian and human rights situation of the residents. We can work with the GoI to develop their capacities and understanding of their international obligations, but we have no power to force them to comply. If the GoI tells us today that we are not allowed to go to Camp Ashraf next week, we shall not be able to go. I am aware that you have a lot of friends in the world, in the European Parliament and in the US Congress, many former politicians, but I have not seen any government authority speaking on your behalf. In terms of your situation, and this is important, it is not parliamentarians that take decisions but governments. All the proposals and concepts you mentioned are decisions to be taken in the Security Council by governments, not parliaments. I do not want to conclude on a negative note but when you said that your only option is to go on your knees, I do not think so, there are a couple of options of different scales which can be good, better or worse. We need to come to a humanitarian solution that would maintain the dignity of Ashraf residents. Let me put something on the table for your views. I must underscore that I am not talking about politics; I do not wish to make an assessment of the governments of Iran or Iraq. We want to search for the best solution to save lives and ensure the wellbeing and dignity of the residents and the approval of all. We have to take the decision of the GoI seriously. After the 8 April events we saw some governments express concern and the UN appealed for an independent investigation. But after two to three days, the indignation stopped and the attack became an event of the past. I am afraid that if there is a next time, more will be killed and more will be wounded, and once more there will be international indignation for one week or so and that's it. This is why we must consider a solution; we have seven months until the end of the year. So I would say that option 1 is a return of those willing to do so to Iran; option 2 is relocation within Iraq; option 3 is relocation/resettlement in a third country. I would say that options 1 and 3 would require a fundamental decision from you that basically every resident of Camp Ashraf be treated as an individual. Option 2 could be considered as a community move within Iraq. As far as UNAMI is concerned we are aware that a formal amnesty, guarantees, conditions would be needed for a return to Iran. As for resettlement in a third country, UNAMI would try to facilitate. Realistically, no country will accept Camp Ashraf as a community. However, individual applications for refugee status would give you some international protection. I believe that the alternative to the said options is continued harassment and a gradual extinction. The international community could only look on and express concern. I understand that this is an important decision for you, and I understand the implications, but the UN cannot help you without you leading in this approach.

Ms Parsaei: The options you have mentioned are not new ones; they have been on the table in the past. Option 3 we have discussed with the US since 2003; option 2 was suggested in 2009 and we replied to it and we made our views and conditions public. However, the issue now is the massacre. We have not been able to bury the dead. You do not want to discuss politics but we are facing criminals. How can you talk of dignity, humanitarianism and human rights with criminals? You ask us to talk about the future, but what about the close past, the commission of inquiry? You told us that there would be another massacre...

DSRSG: You told us this.

Ms Parsaei: There are preventive measures to avoid another one.

DSRSG: I agree.

Ms Parsaei: The issue is that the GoI is determined to close Camp Ashraf by the end of 2011 and the practical message of this is the massacre of the residents. When you say that the situation is serious, what does that mean? Is UNAMI waiting to see people killed? The GoI has issued an ultimatum; at least an EU parliamentary delegation should come to Camp Ashraf to discuss the situation. The ultimatums should stop. These ultimatums and threats are the obstacle to any practical solution. After the 2009 attack, we provided three lists to the UN of people who wished to go abroad or who needed medical treatment abroad. No one on those lists was taken care of. When Iraqis say that they are serious about closing the camp, it means they are serious about killing. The Iranian regime is on the verge of collapse.

DSRSG: I cannot react to this; we agreed no politics.

Ms Parsaei: We do not need an amnesty from that type of regime. An amnesty is for criminals; this is not acceptable. They have killed hundreds of people and executed our families.

Tahar (myself): Madam, we have been discussing the issue for a long time and you know my views well. As Jerzy explained, you seem to be addressing the wrong interlocutors. UNAMI has a specific mandate within the UN. It is true that many parties expect a lot from UNAMI, but UNAMI cannot act without the approval of the GoI. We discussed the issue of the Security Council and you took the right steps; this is not an easy issue because the Security Council agenda needs to be sponsored by member states - it is not UNAMI who will put this matter on the agenda of the Security Council; this will remain your work. UNAMI cannot advise you on this; it is up to you to decide where to take this matter and which specialized UN agency you approach. We also discussed at length the fact that you are a group of foreigners on Iraqi territory and we discussed the legal status you could enjoy in Iraq. Whether the Fourth Geneva Convention is still applicable? The ICRC is the mandated agency and is the custodian of the four conventions. So, it is not within UNAMI's competence to determine your status; determining the status of refugees under the 1951 Geneva Convention falls under the UNHCR mandate. UNAMI monitors the general humanitarian and human rights situation in Camp Ashraf under its own mandate as set in Security Council resolution 1770 and article 2 of the Covenant on Civil and Political Rights. I mention this to show how restricted UNAMI's action is. You noticed that during our visits to Ashraf, we discuss humanitarian and human rights issues and report on the situation as observed on the ground. We came to Camp Ashraf after the 8 April events, not to conduct an enquiry; and you could see that we were not a specialized delegation to investigate, but to monitor and to inform the international community about what we observed on the ground. It is now left to the international community, including the specialized UN agencies, to take responsibility and you must convey your message in that direction. We are observing that the GoI is determined to close the camp. The UN made it clear (UNAMI and OHCHR) that the use of force is unacceptable. Let us think together how can we prevent the use of force, and if it happens, what can the UN do? These are the issues we have to address.

DSRSG: We should come to a logical conclusion of our discussion. You will stay with us a little longer, so let us have a small break. I will not be able to stay for the entire time of your visit, I have other obligations, but Tahar will accompany you the whole time and will further discuss these issues.

After the break, Mr Baraei intervenes: allow me to say that we understand UNAMI's limited mandate but there is an issue to recognize which, if not tackled, will lead to more bloodshed. In all your remarks you pointed to the ultimatum to leave by the end of the year.

DSRSG: This is not an ultimatum this is a decision by a sovereign government.

Mr Baraei: The main issue is that there has been a massacre and it should be investigated and determined who did it; those killed are still not buried. If you do not touch on these issues, other parties will be rewarded for what they have done. First we must tackle this and investigate to prevent another massacre. This issue has been put aside. The decision of the GoI to close Camp Ashraf by the end of 2011 is not realistic. The solution to leave Iraq has been discussed since 2003; and, when they say by the end of the year, they know that this is not practical or possible unless they intend to kill us. We do not expect you to act beyond your mandate but we want to concentrate on the massacre that took place otherwise we will encourage al-Maleki government to attack again.

DSRSG: I was mistaken; I thought that our common interest was to save lives and maintain the dignity of the residents of Camp Ashraf. This is what I wanted to discuss. Tahar has explained that the international community is calling for an investigation but the international community has no means of imposing an investigation on the GoI. You can publish, you can talk but you cannot impose. A sovereign government has the right to expel foreigners from its territory, look at France and Italy (a reference to the expulsion of the Roma people from these countries). As for the 8 April events, I want to prevent further attacks, knowing there is no possibility of forcing the GoI to investigate. The UN has already requested an independent investigation. Today we have to focus on what can we do to save lives. Let us move forward. Suppose the GoI could relocate you to a former US base. We could try to discuss with US partners before the end of June. This could be organized with US assistance and USF-I. You could move to a former military base with normal living conditions as a community. This is a possible option. Of course your agreement is very important. From the UN point of view this must be on a voluntary basis. As for option 3, we could explore different possibilities. This would not be an easy process, but there are chances. The residents would move out of Iraq under international protection and supervision, but the fundamental issue requires the residents to register as individuals. Some would be located in one country, others elsewhere. I believe these two options are possible, at least from my perspective in terms of creating dignifying conditions for all. If you do not take it, there isn't more to offer. I personally do not know what to do. From our perspective, the simple monitoring of

Camp Ashraf is not a solution in any way. We do not wish to be witnesses to dramatic events. We shall review our monitoring role, but if you accept option 2 and 3 we will help create a conducive environment to solve the problem, including getting GoI guarantees and commitments for the whole process. I have nothing more to tell you. I hope that you make the right decision for the interests of all of you.

Ms Parsaei: We have talked of options 1 and 3 in the past. These two options were initiated by the PMOI.

DSRSG: History is for the records and for our children.

Ms Parsaei: We have to be patient in discussing options.

DSRSG: What are the main elements of your proposal?

Ms Parsaei: We have prepared a 10-point set of demands.

DSRSG: Point 1 is for the Security Council; point 2 is a GoI decision; point 3 must be negotiated with the GoI; point 4 is not for us; point 5 we cannot take these decisions; point 6 is for the Security Council, not our business; point 7 is policy of GoI; point 8 we cannot force; point 9 we cannot speak for the US government. These points are not for us.

Ms Parsaei: Then if UNAMI is not accepting any responsibility, what does it accept? The options you speak of were initiated by us and amnesty by the

Iranians is to shame us. Amnesty is for condemned criminals. We are not criminals.

DSRSG: You said yourself, be patient.

Ms Parsaei: You are sitting here to discuss a solution; remove the guns from our heads.

DSRSG: The starting point is the agreement on individual registration. This is not the end but the starting point. Only this will allow other UN agencies to explore other countries. We need to look to the future and to think of Ashraf residents. We must realize that in eight months from today, Camp Ashraf will not be where it is now; we may protest but, if we are committed to save lives and the dignity of every resident, you have to consider with us the different options. You have to think seriously about the people. The situation in 2009 and now is different.

Ms Parsaei: The situation is the same.

DSRSG: Not only is the environment different; the US will not be here, and no one will recognize that you have protected status and nobody will be able to help. If you accept individual registration with UNHCR you will have some protection. If you think about saving lives, you have to consider realistic options. We can talk a little about option 3. This rests on the decision of individual registration. It is your decision and responsibility if you accept or refuse, with all positive and negative consequences.

Ms Parsaei: If Jesus Christ had not stood against the Emperor, he would not have been crucified.

DSRSG: I do not want to talk about crucifixion.

Ms Parsaei: We too do not want crucifixion. Regarding option 2, relocation inside Iraq simply under the pretext of agricultural land is a joke. It is rather a pretext for more killing. The Iranians attacked us with 1000 missiles. On 18 April 2001, there were 77 Iranian missiles, but only one person was killed. The casualties of all the Iranian air attacks were much fewer than the killings in July 2009. The issue of relocation is a pretext for more killing.

DSRSG: If done before the end of June, it would be with support of USF-I and under supervision.

Ms Parsaei: Camp Echo was suggested by the US. It is under bombardment. Why should we accept relocation inside Iraq? Mr Jeffrey Feltman, during a Congressional hearing, stated that relocation would be the beginning of the killings; and forceful relocation is against international law.

DSRSG: Of course we would require your agreement.

Ms Parsaei: As for Option 3, we do not object to UNHCR coming and talking to the residents individually. But why does the UN put all the responsibility on UNHCR? Who is the main party responsible, the US or the UN for the whole process of option 3?

DSRSG: The formal process is with UNHCR as a refugee organization.

Ms Parsaei: There is a history on this issue (a reference to the TIPF residents explained to above).

DSRSG: I know this history.

Ms Parsaei: The ICRC and UNHCR cannot do anything serious. They provide a thick book about communications with UNHCR. Some people left and talked to UNHCR; one person was sent abroad and two drowned in the river at the Turkish borders.

DRSG: Many errors were made. Now there is a fundamental difference; in this different context, UNHCR will lead the process for all the residents, if there is a commitment from your side that every single person can register.

Ms Parsaei: If the practical end is not back to the Iranian regime.

DRSG: The objective is to get you out of Iraq, not back to Iran, unless that is where some want to go.

Ms Parsaei: The families of Camp Ashraf residents are staging a sit-in in front of the UNHCR in Geneva. So UNHCR could talk to our representatives in Europe and sign a memorandum with them.

DSRSG: Your organization is not accredited with the UN and therefore we can only talk informally. If we have an agreement, then we shall discuss the details of the process and UNHCR will make an agreement with individuals.

Ms Parsaei: From the beginning we were protected as individuals.

DSRSG: That status was the decision of USF-I and ended in 2008.

Mr Baraei: We are under siege; we cannot have our lawyers come to Ashraf to discuss our rights. In any negotiation we should have our lawyers. We are under siege, in prison, not able to consult our lawyers.

Tahar: As a practical step we could arrange this; access to a lawyer is a fundamental right. Once we agree on the main principle, UNAMI as a facilitator will request the GoI to allow access.

Mr Baraei: We have no objection. For any decision our lawyers should be here or our representatives go to Europe. Under this siege we do not even have a lawyer.

DSRSG: If we talk like this we will talk forever, how to move forward?

Mr Baraei: There are obstacles.

DSRSG: What are the positive elements?

Ms Parsaei: We are trying to see a light, to move towards a light.

Tahar: To summarize the issue of refugee status, we do not want you to tell us your decision now, but we understand that you do not object to proceed with applying for refugee status. You can inform UNAMI when you are ready to proceed with UNHCR. Once we reach this stage, we will proceed with other practical steps with other stakeholders.

Ms Parsaei: Naturally we do not do anything without consulting our lawyers. In principle, as long as the process is not leading us back to the Iranian regime, as was our previous experience with UNHCR, we do not have objections. Our lawyers should come to discuss.

DSRSG: Can we agree that next Wednesday? Tahar will visit and you will discuss further? Understand the seriousness of the situation; at the end of this year Camp Ashraf will be closed.

Ms Parsaei: We understand. They are insisting on covering up that attack and do not want to be accountable for the massacre.

DSRSG: We are not conveying anyone's message. This is our assessment, understanding, in honesty and with concern for what could happen if nothing is done. This is a courageous step from your side and a lot of preparation from our side. It was not easy to bring you here and to get guarantees that not a hair on your heads would be touched. So, let us go away today with some optimism. END.

At the end of the meeting I felt I was personally used and betrayed as the meeting turned into an exercise to force the hands of Ashraf leadership to accept Butler's relocation plan. The Ashraf delegation came to Baghdad because I convinced them that it is worth making the extra mile to be part of a negotiated solution. But when the discussion deviated from the search for a lasting solution outside Iraq and turned around the proposed relocation in Iraq, I felt I had misled the Ashrafis. The meeting had only deepened the mistrust in the UN efforts in search for a solution acceptable to all. In silence I accompanied the delegation back to Ashraf to ensure their safe return. I felt deep disappointment and embarrassment as they already argued with me for hours and hours that relocation is the beginning of more suffering for them. They insisted that they have information from their sources and they have experience dealing with the Iranian regime and the Iraqi government. They believed that appeasing the Government and not holding it accountable for the killings of July 2009 and April 2011 is an indication of lack of intention to get anything tangible done. They also warned that if the GoI is left unchallenged about the killings and maiming it committed against protected persons in Ashraf it would be more emboldened for further attacks. For me it was a complex situation but based on information I gathered from the Iraqis, I had reasons to believe the Ashrafis concerns. Deep in my heart I had sympathy with the residents' argument and genuinely feared for their safety and security. UNAMI did not have the necessary political will to press the government. Instead it went pushing the residents to accept what all knew it would be a dangerous move.

Following the meeting with the Ashraf representatives, the DSRSG sought a meeting with NSA al-Fayadh to thank him for his personal support for the idea of meeting the Camp's leadership in Baghdad and for guaranteeing their safety and security. The meeting took place on 8 May 2011 in the NSA's office.

The DSRSG informed al-Fayadh of the substance of the discussion that took place and emphasised that, realistically, there were two solutions: the relocation option, being developed by Ambassador Butler; and the resettlement of individual residents in Europe. A decision on which option to follow was not made in the course of the meeting. There was agreement in principle on the approach, but the representatives would need further consultation with the Camp's residents and their leadership. Consultations within the UN system in relation to the resettlement option were also necessary. The DSRSG informed the NSA that the representatives of Camp Ashraf had raised concerns regarding guarantees in connection with all three options and had had a negative reaction to the idea of relocation to a new site in Iraq.

The NSA emphasised that it was important that the residents heard the message about the necessity of relocation "clearly" from UNAMI. It was noted that if such a message was also delivered "by our friends in the international community", it would facilitate a "compromise solution". He felt it was important to give the residents of Camp Ashraf time to rethink their position and stressed the need for UNAMI to continue repeating it. He also said that the GoI had its "own way of conveying its message". Drawing attention to the efforts of Ambassador Butler, the NSA was thankful for his assistance towards "solving problems" and noted that Butler had delivered his own message to the Camp's residents "similar" to that of the UN.

The NSA informed the DSRSG that the GoI was in contact with the Government of Iran which is "prepared to offer guarantees" for an amnesty. He requested that UNAMI continue to engage with Iranian officials in that direction.

The DSRSG reassured the NSA of UNAMI's wish to cooperate with the Government of Iran in finding a solution for the residents.

I raised humanitarian matters related to food, logistics and medical supplies. I also voiced concerns regarding the delayed burial of people killed on 8 April, contrary to Islamic teaching.

The NSA assured us of the GoI's wish to abide by humanitarian principles. He sought clarification as to the number of people who would attend the burial; given the current emotionally charged atmosphere and the risk the residents would make some military display, he had security concerns.

The DSRSG stressed that UNAMI had requested that the Camp residents exercise restraint and avoid any confrontation with security forces.

# US Attempt at a Relocation Plan
# Butler Initiative - Summer 2011

In May 2011, Ambassador Lawrence Butler, political advisor to the General Commander of the USF-I, General Lloyd J. Austin III, engaged in shuttle diplomacy between Baghdad and Camp Ashraf on behalf of the Department of State to try to reach an agreement for relocation within Iraq before the final departure of the USF-I from Iraq. He made 7 trips to Ashraf and I accompanied him on most of these trips. Buttler's initiative aimed at creating the conditions for a mutually agreed relocation of the residents of Camp Ashraf to a transitory facility elsewhere in Iraq that both ensured humanitarian treatment while their refugee status was determined, ahead of an eventual resettlement outside Iraq. The model he built on was the Makhmour refugee camp in the south of Ninewa province where the UNHCR registered 10,240 Turkish Kurds affiliated to the Kurdish Workers' Party (PKK). They received residency documents and work permits. The PKK is listed as a terrorist organization by a number of states and organizations, including the United Nations, NATO, the United States and the European Union. This did not prevent Makhmour from being officially recognized as a refugee camp. Butler's plan considered reproducing this camp at the former USF-I Takkadum Base in al-Anbar. It had a capacity for 10,000 people.

## *Proposed Sites of Ambassador Butler Relocation Plan*

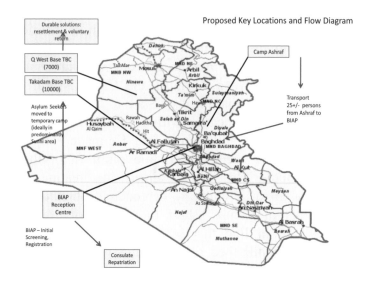

Butler's initiative came with a number of obligations, including the requirement that the Ashraf population agreed to register with UNHCR individually during the process of transferring from Ashraf to the new transitional location (NTL). Other conditions were that UNHCR or another body be associated with the administration of the NTL, and that the GoI was allowed to routinely inspect the facility. Butler's initiative also required that the GoI observe a number of commitments, including: a public announcement of the formal acceptance of the transfer and the new status of the former Ashraf residents; a formal request to the UN/UNHCR to take a role in administering the NTL; a pledge to prevent harassment, including the psychological harassment of the loudspeakers, and attacks against the NTL residents; an agreement to observe a moratorium on serving arrest warrants to permit all NTL residents to resettle peacefully; the establishment of a "protest free" security zone around the NTL; and an agreement on permitting unfettered access to telecommunication and medical services .

Butler's initiative was challenged by the Camp's leadership mainly on two grounds. First, they have accepted the European Parliament plan for settlement outside Iraq, thus questioning the logic of relocation inside Iraq given that the central problem would remain unresolved. In their view, relocation in these circumstances amounted to illegal eviction. They argued that relocation is setting stage for another massacre. Second, they questioned the mechanism suggested for their protection in the proposed NTL. They asked if the USF-I or UN blue helmet were going to enforce protection or would the NTL be left at the mercy and goodwill of the Iraqi Army. They argued, as Ms. Parsaei told the DSRSG in Baghdad that if they are to be attacked and killed in Ashraf, no doubt that they would face more threats in the new location. Thus, they rather stay in Ashraf rather than be relocated, humiliated and then killed.

The main drawback of the Butler plan was the fact that it was conceived with the presumption that the Ashrafis were members of a military terrorist organization that needed first to disband and then individually seek asylum by applying for refugee status with the UNHCR. As a UN human rights officer, taking the lead in the search for a solution to this humanitarian situation, I found Ambassador Jeffery's public comment that PMOI must disband itself damaging and destructive to all confidence building I achieved so far. It undermined the fundamental right to freedom of association recognised in the Universal Declaration of Human Rights and protected by the ICCPR to which both the US and Iraq are party. Such a statement had further fuelled the already existing mistrust. Thus, making the environment ever less conducive for the search of a lasting solution.

The residents had no problem with seeking individual refugee status, although they argued that they have been refugees for years, however, they were aware that the real objective was to disband the organization and this was a red line for the residents. They repeatedly cited the massacre of 30,000 of the PMOI members in 1988 who were executed in a matter of few months simply for refusing to deny their affiliation with the PMOI. The residents argued that any suggestion that they should disband their organization is tantamount to asking them to surrender to the Iranian regime and is thus a clear concession to Iran. Whatever, that may have been in the mind of Ambassador Jeffrey and Butler, considering the existence of an ocean of blood between the resident and the Iranian regime, the residents' position was understandable. Almost one third of the residents had spent several years in prisons in Iran as political prisoners, suffering degrading, inhumane treatment and torture. A large number of them have lost family members. Every single one of them had lost friends in the course of their struggle.

When Ambassador Butler visited Camp Ashraf, he crudely addressed the Ashrafis as terrorists and portrayed himself as their saviour. In doing so, he felled victim to the same contradiction the USG faced when it granted the Ashrafis protected person status in 2004 while maintaining the MEK on the Foreign Terrorist Organisations list. The PATRIOT Act 2001, section 805 as amended by the Intelligence Reform and Terrorism Prevention Act 2004, prohibited "expert advice or assistance" to terrorists. He was thus doomed to failure as he was acting beyond the US legal framework.

Furthermore, Ambassador Butler made a series of mistakes in his interaction with the Ashrafis that cost him credibility. He irreparably undermined the trust-building process between him and the residents' Leadership. First, when he attended a meeting on 3 May 2011, organized by UNAMI with the residents' representatives at UNAMI HQ, he asked to be introduced to Ms Parsaei and her colleagues as a member of UNAMI staff. A few weeks later he visited Ashraf as a senior US Embassy representative. Second, in one of his visits to Ashraf, he took with him a journalist and introduced him as a US embassy officer. The following day, this fake US embassy officer turned out to be Tim Arango of *The New York Times*. On 22 July 2011, Arango quoted Ambassador Butler in his report for *The New York Times*: "*These people slaughtered Americans*"; "*They have blood on their hands*"; "*To the outside world, you look like a paramilitary organization*"; and "*As a group, you are dangerous*". There was sharp reaction from the Camp Leadership, as well as from members of the European Parliament and the United States Congress, to both Butler's conduct and to the article.

As a senior diplomat, Ambassador Butler had failed to observe the most elementary rule of diplomacy: trust-building. Even though, comparatively, Ambassador Butler's plan offered more protection and guarantees to the residents than that of UNAMI, what scuppered Butler's initiative were two things: the precondition of disbanding the PMOI which was the residents' red line and the overtly biased and politically motivated attitude Butler had shown towards the Ashrafis. He went to Ashraf to dictate, not to bridge the gaps between the political realities of Iraq and the residents' demands. The final straw was his involving *The New York Times*.

Butler's initiative collapsed after Butler's negative remarks about the Camp Leadership were reported in *The New York Times* on 22 July 2011. On 1 August 2011, Ambassador Butler came to see me in my office. He acknowledged that his plan had failed and he would no longer pursue his initiative since it had been rejected by both the GoI and the MEK. Nonetheless, the USG would continue supporting UNAMI's efforts in search for a durable solution. In the meantime, the Camp's leadership informed UNAMI that since they have accepted resettlement outside Iraq as proposed in the European Parliament plan, relocation within Iraq or a return to Iran were no longer options.

The MEK responded to the Butler initiative by suggesting at least seven alternative plans, some of which were:

1) To remain in Ashraf according to the applicable international law. In this case, the GOI would recognize the refugee and residency rights of the Ashraf population whose entry and 25 years' residence in Iraq was fully compliant with the Iraqi laws then in force. The GoI would also recognize their right to their acquired property and their unhindered access to public utilities and services at their own expense. The agreement between Ambassador Bremer, the Administrator of the Coalition Provisional Authority of Iraq following the 2003 invasion and the then Prime Minister Allawi

provided the legal framework. This agreement was reaffirmed by General Miller to the representative of Ashraf residents, Mr Baraei, in his letter of 25 June 2004.

2) Failing that, the U.S. who had granted the Ashrafis protected person status under the Fourth Geneva Convention to provide protection for Ashraf until the total transfer of its residents to third countries. This plan was based on article 45 of the Fourth Geneva Convention, which stipulates: *"Protected persons may be transferred by the Detaining Power only to a Power which is a party to the present Convention and after the Detaining Power has satisfied itself of the willingness and ability of such transferee Power to apply the present Convention. If protected persons are transferred under such circumstances, responsibility for the application of the present Convention rests on the Power accepting them, while they are in its custody. Nevertheless, if that Power fails to carry out the provisions of the present Convention in any important respect, the Power by which the protected persons were transferred shall, upon being so notified by the Protecting Power, take effective measures to correct the situation or shall request the return of the protected persons. Such request must be complied with"*. Relocation inside Iraq would only be acceptable if the U.S. would assume responsibility for the process, including the removal, with the residents, of all of their movable assets, the protection of the new location, and a

guarantee of the same living standards set while Ashraf was under control of the USF-I.

3) If none of the above is acceptable to the GoI, the residents would be willing to temporarily relocate to a border area inside Jordan under the supervision of the UN or the ICRC, while their final disposition was addressed. In this solution, the movable and immovable assets of Ashraf would be sold under the supervision of the UN/UNAMI or the U.S. The proceeds would be used to meet the cost of the transfer and the preparation of the new location. In case the government of Jordan did not accept this proposal, other countries such as Turkey, Kuwait or Saudi Arabia could be approached with the same plan. If no plan is made workable because of the eventual withdrawal of the USF-I from Iraq, then the last option is the transfer of all residents to a territory under U.S. sovereignty until a lasting solution became available.

### UNAMI Engaging UNHCR, Summer 2011

Considering all the discussions we had had so far with all the parties, SRSG Melkert convened an internal meeting on 1 June 2011, to reflect on next steps. The meeting came to the conclusion that a prerequisite was political support for and financial encouragement of UNHCR. The engagement of UNHCR was indispensable for providing the status of "protected persons" under international law.

Thus far, UNHCR had not been successful in resettling a small number of former residents of Ashraf that it has recognized as refugees. The orthodox and routine procedure undertaken by UNHCR in these cases was not likely to be successful in the foreseeable future. However, the unfortunate events of 8 April and the ensuing international attention on Ashraf had created an opportunity to approach this issue in a non-conventional way, with the political and financial support of the US, the EU and its individual member states and other willing states. Once political support was obtained, UNHCR and other specialized agencies would gradually assume responsibility from UNAMI. The regularity of our monitoring visits should gradually decrease with the focus on political back-up of the overall process with the main parties (GoI, MEK, UNHCR and HCHR). Once the residents were moved out of Iraq and Ashraf Camp was "depopulated", the case would be closed for UNAMI. The SRSG warned that we had to bear in mind that in the absence of a solution, our failure would encourage the GoI to undertake more radical measures of harassment and physical threat, with growing international criticism of both the GoI and of UNAMI.

All of the UNAMI leadership was now fully mobilized in search of a durable solution. The USG, which is the main UNHCR donor, had earmarked a substantial budget for the Refugee Status Determination (RSD) process and was expecting

UNHCR to proceed with that process. The EU's High Representative of the Union for Foreign Affairs and Security Policy, Lady Ashton, had appointed Ambassador Jean de Ruyt as special envoy for Ashraf. Earlier, lawyers representing the population of Camp Ashraf had suggested that since Iraq was not party to the 1951 Convention on Refugees, the participation of UNHCR could provide the legal framework for the refugee status of the residents, which would attract and encourage resettlement countries to take their share of responsibility.

In a letter dated 23 August 2011, considered a breakthrough for both UNAMI and the Ashrafis, the High Commissioner for Refugees wrote to the Iraqi Prime Minister informing him that "his office had been approached by lawyers purporting to represent the Camp inhabitants with the request that their refugee status be actively reviewed". In his letter, the High Commissioner informed the Prime Minister that "the Camp inhabitants were deemed to be asylum-seekers" and that UNHCR was therefore obliged to consider their claims, consistent with the mandate conferred upon the Commission.

UNAMI had, as a matter of priority, mobilized its assets to facilitate UNHCR engagement with the refugee status determination of the Camp population. By September 2011, UNHCR had received some 3,248 applications for asylum and had scheduled visits to the Camp for the first week of November to verify and identify the applicants. A joint UNAMI-UNHCR operational plan for the RSD process was being drafted. However, both agencies realized that realistic planning could not be done without the consent and active participation of the GoI. Based on this reality, UNAMI and UNHCR requested a meeting with the representatives of the Government of Iraq to reflect together on how to facilitate and conduct the RSD process.

A tripartite meeting was convened in Amman on 29 September 2011 between the representatives of the GoI (Faleh al-Fayadh), UNAMI (Acting SRSG/DSRSG for Political Affairs, Jerzy Skuratowicz and me) and UNHCR (Ms Erika Feller, Assistant High Commission for Refugees and Ms Claire Bourgeois UNHCR Country Representative).
Presenting an overview of the situation, the DSRSG underlined the fact that the plight of the Ashraf residents, with its complexities and sensitivities, was an inherited problem. It needed to be addressed, not as an exclusive problem for Iraq, but as a humanitarian issue of shared responsibility, requiring the participation of the international community. The DSRSG added that UNAMI's mandate was to provide advice, support and assistance to the Government of Iraq in its efforts to build a secure, stable, and democratic nation, based on the rule of law and respect for human rights as well as in the delivery of humanitarian assistance and the safe, orderly, and voluntary return of refugees and displaced persons.

The DSRSG requested the re-activation of the "Ashraf Committee" and the nomination of high level members to make it a credible interlocutor. The committee would discuss and adopt a strategy and an operational plan, with a timeframe for delivering results. Such a high-level committee, led by the Iraqis and assisted by the UN, would explore all avenues that would guide the residents to a dignified exit in compliance with Iraqi legislation, international law and the UNHCR mandate. It would meet periodically to follow up on implementation. He proposed that this high-level committee would be assisted by a working group that would follow up the day-to-day business and address any difficulties. The working group would also engage the diplomatic community and report to the high-level committee.

On behalf of UNHCR, Ms Feller focused on the RSD process, highlighting the following: a) UNHCR had recently received from Ashraf residents a significant number of individual requests for refugee status; b) UNHCR was putting in place a process to consider these requests on an individual basis in a fair and efficient procedure; c) the residents, who had submitted requests, were now formally "asylum-seekers" under international law, whose claims require adjudication. International law required that asylum-seekers must be able to benefit from the basic protection of their security and well-being; d) UNHCR considers inappropriate the request for refugee status on *a prima facie* or group basis for the entire population of the Camp; e) residents wishing to return to the Camp after interviews must be able to do so; f) each individual case will be judged on its merits and in accordance with international law; and g) there was no formal requirement for individuals to dissociate themselves from the PMOI/MEK in order to apply for refugee status.

NSA, Al-Fayyad, explained that although the issue of Camp Ashraf was a matter of national sovereignty, he came to the meeting out of respect for the UN. He pointed out that some were stirring up the issue for political reasons and questioned why those calling for the protection of the MEK were not willing to admit its members into their respective countries. He underlined the GoI's commitment to safeguard the safety and security of the inhabitants of Camp Ashraf and to honour the principle of *non-refoulement*.

At the same time, the NSA warned that the GoI should not be expected to meet the humanitarian treatment standards of the UN. He questioned the "VIP treatment of members of an organization that committed crimes against the Iraqi people and occupied a part of Iraq". The GoI, he said, "will not compromise about outlawing the organization (MEK/PMOI). Any deals with the so-called Camp 'representatives' or the organization itself would be unacceptable. Any process that would lead to a *prima facie* recognition of the group as refugees is unacceptable". He offered to participate in any process that was likely to lead to the peaceful closure of the Camp, rejecting the UNHCR process, as presented, for fear that it would legitimize the organization's presence in the country.

The NSA said that Iraqis had so far shown patience in implementing the decision to expel the "monafiqin" but this would not last forever. He emphasized that the deadline set by the Council of Ministers for the closure of Ashraf was irreversible. The NSA further explained that the Council of Ministers' decision to close the Camp at the end of the year was related to the departure of USF-I, which had been a deterrent against possible attacks from neighbouring countries. In the absence of USF-I, the Camp would probably face an attack which would undermine Iraq's sovereignty and would place the Government in an untenable position. He emphasised that, as a fortress of the Iranian resistance, the Camp must be brought to an end.

The NSA found it objectionable that the EU had designated a Special Representative on Camp Ashraf issues. He said it would have been better if such a Representative worked, not in Iraq, but in European capitals securing countries willing to take the residents.

Thus, from the GoI point of view, the outcome of the Amman Meeting was an endorsement of the closure of Ashraf, while, from the UN point of view, UNHCR would undertake the process of refugee status determination and thus the prospects for a peaceful relocation of the Ashrafis had increased.

UNAMI's presence in Iraqi was now mortgaged to the closure of Ashraf. The untold story begins here.

# Appointment of the New SRSG, Martin Kobler, Summer 2011

SRSG Melkert was not known for having established the best relationship with Prime Minister al-Maleki. The latter was working to establish a system that would increase his power in the country and in its institutions, particularly the national independent commissions. At that time, he was targeting the Independent High Electoral Commission (IHEC). If he managed to bring it under the control of his office, it would certainly secure him a majority in the parliament, hence, his insistence on undertaking, through the existing Council of Representatives, an evaluation of the performance of the IHEC for its eventual reconstitution before the forthcoming general elections.

The SRSG, however, was worried that if the PM's hegemony extended to the IHEC, there would be no free and fair elections. In a press release of 11 October 2009 the SRSG suggested that "*a thorough evaluation of IHEC's performance in carrying out all electoral activities in Iraq since 2008 should be undertaken by the Council of Representatives once the results of the January 2010 elections have been officially announced. At this stage, however, UNAMI believes that significant changes to the institutional set-up in IHEC would severely disrupt the ongoing electoral preparations to the point that it would not be possible to hold credible elections*". By this statement, SRSG Melkert denied al-Maleki the opportunity to place his men on a new IHEC, thereby denying him control of the outcome of the elections.

After tumultuous negotiations, the elections were held on 7 March 2010 with no change in the IHEC. Unexpectedly, al-Maleki's 'State of Law' coalition won 89 seats, behind the Al-Iraqiya coalition, led by Ayad Allawi, with 91 seats. This prompted protests from the State of Law coalition which asked for a recount of the ballot. After the Supreme Federal Court confirmed the results on 1 June 2010, SRSG Melkert issued a press release to welcome "the decision announced ... by the Federal Supreme Court, certifying the results of the Council of Representatives election, held on 7 March 2010, in accordance with the Constitution of Iraq". He described it as a crucial step towards the formation of a government that would shape the country's future for the next four years. Al-Maleki would never forgive Melkert, ensuring that New York and Washington would not endorse him for a second term.

The SRSG's difficult relations with al-Maleki continued until his departure from Iraq. On 28 August 2011, SRSG Melkert paid the customary farewell visit to PM al-Maleki. The latter exploited the occasion and published on his personal website, that very day, a statement attributing to the SRSG a position on Ashraf that was not his. Nouri al-Maleki claimed that, during the meeting, Melkert embraced the Government of Iraq's efforts to expel the Ashraf residents by the end of 2011. The next day, 29 August 2011, Melkert issued a press release correcting the Prime Minister, saying: "The UN continues to advocate that Camp Ashraf residents be protected from forcible deportation, expulsion or repatriation contrary to the *non-refoulement* principle. UNAMI will continue to assist the GoI in search of a peaceful and lasting solution to the issues of Camp Ashraf in line with international humanitarian and human rights law and seeks the support of the international community in these efforts". The Associated Press describe the SRSG reaction as unprecedented in diplomatic relations.

The weakness in the UN HQ's approach towards al-Maleki could only be explained by the US expectation that the UN support the man they left in power so as to maintain the narrative that the US, having invaded Iraq, had established a stable, strong government through a democratic process. Hence, the next SRSG to be appointed was tasked with establishing a 'love relationship' between UNAMI and al-Maleki. The man selected to replace SRSG Melkert was Martin Kobler. His mission was to win the approval of al-Maleki, a task that could not be achieved without compromising democracy and human rights and alienating al-Iraqiya, the Iraqi coalition that had won the highest number of seats in the parliament.

Martin Kobler was officially appointed by the UN Secretary General as his Special Representative for Iraq and Head of UNAMI on 11 August 2011. He arrived at the mission in Baghdad on 8 October and, to the surprise of all the staff, announced that his priority was to close down Camp Ashraf. To do so, he effectively brought the whole mission to a standstill. The UN specialized agencies working in Iraq depend upon the security support provided by UNAMI. From the day Kobler arrived at the mission, the UN's specialised agencies in Iraq found themselves grounded in the Green Zone incapable of doing anything of substance. He mobilized all UNAMI's assets to one single objective: the closure of Ashraf and the relocation of its population. He was determined to revive Buttler's failed plan of internal relocation, when the idea seemed to have been abandoned by USG. David Lindwall, the US representative who had replaced Butler had specifically told Madam Parsaei in September 2011 that relocation in Iraq is a dead plan.

Kobler's authoritarian and dishonest behaviour lead most senior staff at the Mission to look for opportunities to leave. The first to depart was the DSRSG for Political Affairs, Jerzy Skuratowicz; the second was DSRSG Christine McNab for the Development and Humanitarian Support component of the UNAMI mission and the United Nations Resident Humanitarian Coordinator for Iraq; the third to leave was the UNAMI Political Director, Madhu Asharya and the fourth was me. Still others followed. Kobler's obsession with Ashraf exhausted everyone. All previous SRSGs had made an attempt to set a strategic vision and a work plan for Iraq, prioritizing education, rehabilitation, reconciliation, reconstruction, institution building, and the consolidation of democracy. Kobler's vision and work plan were PM al-Maleki's political wishes and his strategy was 'improvisation'.

Within three days of his arrival, before securing any agreement on the idea of relocation, he instructed the Mission Support Section of UNAMI to secure him two large helicopters within a fortnight in order to start transporting the Ashrafis out of Ashraf. No one, even on the Iraqi side, knew the location to which the helicopters would be flying. There was disbelief in the Mission Support Section of UNAMI. There was no budget and no prospect of getting one. There was no Iraqi air navigation authorization. The Mission Support Section did not rush to implement the request for helicopters as they knew the realities of Iraq would slow him down. Indeed, within three weeks, he forgot about this project. Kobler turned his attention to signing a Memorandum of Understanding (MOU) with the GoI to set the framework for the relocation. The project was supposed to remain top secret, but the rumours abounded, on 'Uniform Charlie' Plaza and elsewhere, not least because he would mistakenly copy in unintended recipients of his e-mails. With a thick skin and no sense of morality, nothing embarrassed him.

An Ashraf Task Force composed of all UNAMI Heads of Sections and a representative of the UNHCR was set up. The task was to draft the MOU and an operational plan, and to coordinate with the Ashraf Committee of the PM's Office. The first challenge we faced was to determine the parties to the MOU. I argued if we were seeking a voluntary relocation and UNAMI was to act as an impartial facilitator, then the parties to the MOU should be the GoI and the representatives of the Ashraf population. UNAMI as a facilitator should only help establish the dialogue, bridge the gaps between the two parties and be a witness to their agreement. SRSG Kobler was of the view that one could not expect the GoI to negotiate with terrorists, so he appointed himself to negotiate on behalf of the 'terrorists'.

Any negotiation is based on a fundamental rule, *pacta sunt servanda,* a basic principle of civil and international law, and, in respect of the latter, codified in Article 26 of the Vienna Convention on the Law of Treaties (1969). In its most common sense, clauses agreed are law between the parties. A negotiated agreement cannot commit those who are not party to it. Furthermore, in both civil law and international law, an agreement procured by coercion-by the threat or use of force- is null and void and has no legal effect. The draft MOU in question would be produced under the threat to use "all means" against the residents in order to evacuate the Camp. The threats directed towards the Ashrafis were to coerce the UN to act. The proposed MOU was thus doubly null and void.

I argued that UNAMI's role should be limited to its mandate as stipulated in paragraph 2 (b) of Security Council Resolution 1770 (2007), and extended by Resolution 2001 (2011), that the Special Representative of the Secretary General and UNAMI, in coordination with the Government shall: *"[p]romote, support, and facilitate, in coordination with the Government of Iraq: (i) ... the safe, orderly, and voluntary return, as appropriate of refugees and displaced persons"*. This provision did not confer on UNAMI/SRSG the power of attorney to negotiate and give up the acquired rights of the residents. It also did not mandate UNAMI/SRSG to promote, support and facilitate illegal or immoral acts by the government, such as the threat or use of force, the denial of acquired rights, hostility towards UNHCR work, the rejection of international humanitarian law, the rejection of 'UN human rights standards', the refusal to establish an independent inquiry into extra-judicial executions, and the denial to Ashrafis of access to the free market for goods and services. If the GoI wished to dispute the existence of the claimed rights, these disputes should be settled before a court of law. Addressing them by the threat and/or the use of force rendered both the position of the GoI and the position of UNAMI/SRSG untenable.

In the circumstances, I advised that if the GoI was not ready to talk directly to the residents' representatives, the interests of the Ashrafis should be represented through a lawyer. At least a lawyer would have questioned the presumption by representatives of the UN that the Ashrafis were terrorists. The Iraqi side argued that a lawyer would only delay the matter while the closure of Ashraf had to take place at the end of the year 'by all means'. Had Iraq been a truly democratic society, the government could have proceeded with the relocation according to due process, requiring the government to secure an eviction order from the competent court, with the court ordering the protection of the legitimately acquired rights of the residents. Had the SRSG acted in good faith, he would have advocated the due process of law rather than signing an MOU to give legitimacy to what is inherently illegitimate.

# Kobler's Memorandum of Understanding and Human Rights Law

By November 2011, the UNAMI Task Force on Ashraf had been struggling to put a draft text together for more than a month. Every draft presented to the Iraqi side was amended to the effect that the Ashrafis have no status or legal rights in Iraq. No matter how long any Ashrafi had lived in Iraq, regularizing that person's residency status was not an option. Iraq is not party to the Geneva Convention on Refugees and would not recognize the refugee status granted to individuals by the UNHCR. The GoI insisted Ashraf residents should be relocated to a temporary transit location (TTL) pending their departure from Iraq. While in the TTL, they would have no right to freedom of movement, no right to income-generating activities, paradoxically, at the very time they were to be left to fend for themselves. The TTL was not to be a refugee camp and could not be declared so. The TTL would not be permitted to be transformed into a mini Camp Ashraf, the NSA vowed, which meant that building any infrastructure to support and improve the residents' life was not to be permitted. In other words, the TTL was to be a detention centre, ironically called 'Camp Liberty'. The SRSG kept compromising, all the while instructing us to be positive and to move on. Time was of the essence, human rights are not important; we have to save life, the SRSG would say. I was never sure whether it was

205

really a question of saving life or a question of being submissive to the dictates of al-Maleki.

By the end of November 2011, we had drafted over 20 versions of the MOU. Each version was discussed internally and then shared with the Iraqi team who would in turn produce a version in Arabic and present it to the UN team. We never managed to produce a matching version in both English and Arabic. There was always some discrepancy in what the two delegations understood by certain words and phrases. Until 27 November, there was in the preamble of the draft the following sentence: "The common objective is to achieve a peaceful and durable solution *acceptable to all concerned*". That meant the MOU would not have been signed if the sentence was maintained as the operative clauses of the draft were unacceptable to the Ashrafis, the main party concerned. Kobler had to get rid of the sentence, so he could sign it whether the Ashrafis agreed or not. After he signed the MOU, I reminded him that the Ashrafis did not agree it, which made it a forcible eviction. He replied, "Although they did not agree, they have consented". The Iraqis insisted on making reference to their constitution in the first paragraph of the MOU. That was problematic for the UN team as the Iraqi transitional constitution contravened international law in a number of provisions. Technically, a Memorandum of Understanding is an operative arrangement completed by the executive. It does not need to be based on the constitution. Reference to international humanitarian law in earlier versions was removed. "[E]asy access" to the temporary transit locations was restricted to the UN. NGOs, parliamentarians and diplomats were denied access. The word 'location' was used in the plural while originally we were talking about one single location. In relation to the UNHCR role, the Iraqis insisted on a "verification process" rather than a "refugee status determination process". Under the fourth clause of the MOU, 'Procedure at Camp Liberty, A, the sentence read: "The Government of the Republic of Iraq shall permit and facilitate UNHCR to conduct interviews with the residents of the Camp to identify their status in accordance with its mandate and its operational rules". A similar sentence had been vigorously rejected by the Iraqis at an earlier stage. Only when they had received guarantees that not all interviewed residents would necessarily be successful in claiming refugee status,(thus removing an obstacle to the eventual arrest of the MEK leadership), did the Iraqis accept the insertion of the sentence referring to UNHCR's "mandate and its operational rules" rather than the RSD process. It demonstrated the determination of the GoI to block any provision that might entail any form of protection for all residents at Camp Liberty.

To make it clear that the GoI would not be obligated by any outcome of the RSD process, the Iraqi team insisted on inserting a reservation clause. In a bilateral meeting between UNHCR and the GoI negotiating team, held on 27 November 2011,

UNHCR suggested a compromise that would allow it to undertake the RSD process with a limited effect on the GoI's obligations. The compromise was to insert a footnote under the fourth clause of the draft MOU (Procedure at Transit Location). The footnote would read: *"Determination of refugee status by UNHCR in accordance with its mandate does not necessarily entail conferral of refugee status by the Iraqi government. However, in relation to those recognized as refugees by UNHCR, the Iraqi government will protect them until a durable solution is found. In particular, the Iraqi government will respect the principle of non-refoulement, provide an adequate standard of treatment, as well as cooperate with UNHCR and the international community in the realisation of durable solutions"*. Still, the Iraqis were unhappy with the second and third sentences of the footnote as they committed the GoI to protect those recognized as refugees. Further bilateral meetings with the GoI representatives were held, and by 20 December, UNHCR accepted the deletion of the two sentences disliked by the Iraqis and the incorporation of the footnote as amended into the main text to become clause seven of the final draft MOU which read: *"Determination of refugee status by UNHCR in accordance with its mandate does not necessarily entail conferral of refugee status by the Iraqi government"*. By deleting the two last sentences of the suggested footnote (now clause seven), the GoI left no doubt about its intentions. Nothing would stop it from treating the residents of Camp Ashraf/Liberty as detainees pending their departure from Iraq. The UN argued that relocation gave UNHCR the opportunity to conduct the RSD process as the first step towards resettlement in third countries, in a safe and neutral environment. At UNAMI we know that Camp Liberty was neither safe nor neutral. It was simple an argument used to deceive the Ashrafis and to mislead the international community.

However, it was clear to all that either way, the Ashrafis were on the point of being evicted from a 36 km² modern city and sent to a detention centre referred to as Temporary Transit Location (TTL), in a security zone adjacent to BIAP, of little more than half km², without any serious prospect of resettlement in the near future. Kobler argued that having the Ashraf residents in a detention centre was better than having them killed. This argument from the Special Representative of the UN Secretary General is more than objectionable. It denied defenceless people their fundamental rights, including the right to life, since they were told to choose between going to a detention centre with no right of appeal or die in Ashraf. This uncompromising approach meant that UNAMI had taken an even more radical approach to Ashraf than even the GoI; al-Maleki, known as the most hardliner of Iraqi decision-makers, showed more flexibility than Kobler's "move or die" approach.

Until now the UN has requested that the project remains confidential. By the third week of

November, the UN having maintained secrecy and having kept the press at bay, the SRSG decided to inform the Ashrafis. I went to Ashraf on 19 November 2011 to deliver the message accompanied by a UNHCR delegation lead by Andrew Harper from HQ in Geneva. I was told not to provide anything in writing but to explain the content of the draft MOU verbally. To make sure I would not go beyond what the SRSG wanted to share, he dictated the following points:

- The Government of Iraq has undertaken to close Camp Ashraf and to ensure the safe and secure transfer of the residents to Camp Liberty pending their eventual departure to other countries of their choice. Those residents with passports and links to other countries will be treated as priority cases for transfer to Camp Liberty.

- Those residents who want to be repatriated immediately to Iran may use the current channels for doing so.

- Upon arrival of the residents at Camp Liberty, the United Nations will conduct 24/7 monitoring at the Camp until the last of the residents leaves Iraq.

- UNHCR will start the verification process immediately after the arrival of the residents at Camp Liberty. UNHCR will interview the residents of the Camp to determine their status in accordance with its mandate and its operational rules. UNHCR and the United Nations more generally will continue their efforts to resettle you in third countries. However, the final resettlement decision will be made by the third countries themselves. For this purpose, consular visits to individuals at Camp Liberty will be arranged.

- As "asylum seekers", you will be eligible under international law to enjoy basic protections and well-being. UNHCR is able to accept applications from residents who have not yet submitted applications for refugee status at any point. The Government of Iraq has undertaken to afford you protection against any expulsion or involuntary repatriation to Iran.

- With regard to other issues, such as assets and properties, they will be discussed towards reaching a solution that respects the property rights of the residents in an organized way under Iraqi law.

- The SRSG is acting as an impartial facilitator and would not sign any commitment without the consent of the residents.

Knowing that the message I am carrying was not the whole truth, I opened the meeting stating that the purpose of the visit is to convey a message from SRSG Martin Kobler. By doing so, I wanted to distance myself from what I was about to deliver. I briefed the Ashrafis on recent developments following the 29 September meeting in Amman which agreed to the establishment of a Working Group comprising UNAMI, UNHCR and the GoI to work out a strategy for a safe and dignified exit of the Ashrafis from Iraq. I then read the message point by point. The Ashrafis all looked shocked and strained. Ms Parsaei, usually calm and highly articulate, struggled to control her anger. She requested a five minute recess for the leadership to deliberate. When the meeting reconvened she gave me their reply for the SRSG:

- Please inform the SRSG that we are very shocked and upset by his message. He is supporting a plan for killing Ashraf residents. What the SRSG is doing with al-Maleki is a conspiracy to annihilate the residents. He needs to come in person to Ashraf for a frank discussion.

- Residents are wondering if the SRSG is the Special Representative of the Secretary General of the United Nations or if he is a representative of PM Maleki and his Government.

- The SRSG points as read out were the same ones communicated by the Iraqi Ambassador to Brussels which were rejected by the international community.

- The real issue for the residents is the guarantee of their safety and security, respect of their rights and the principles of international law. The SRSG cannot lead us into prison with guns pointed at our heads and call it voluntary relocation.

- The SRSG is imposing a forced relocation of residents despite existing international law prohibiting that. The persecutor of the residents cannot turn into a protector. Residents will only relocate if protected by the UN blue helmets

- Two massacres occurred on UNAMI's watch; what will prevent the third massacre from happening, more especially now that the SRSG is supporting the whole flawed process the Iraqis have been trying to implement for the past three years or so?

- Since the SRSG is facilitating what the Iraqis are planning for us, he cannot be trusted to be impartial. Residents are not shocked by the position of the Iraqis; their concern is the message from the SRSG. If they are going to be killed, it is better to be killed in Camp Ashraf where the international community might hear about them rather than be tortured and killed at some camp where nobody would know.

- Should they be forcefully relocated, they demand the protection of the UN force/blue helmets and the camp should not be managed by the Iraqis; the notion of protection by the Iraqis is absolutely unacceptable. How can the UN justify entrusting the victims to their murderers?

I returned to Baghdad and immediately delivered the message. Kobler immediately engaged in a series of consultations. He could not go to Ashraf without giving an acceptable explanation to al-Maleki and the NSA al-Fayadh or without testing the reaction of the Iranian Ambassador. They usually opposed the idea of UN officials meeting the MEK leadership. Between 20 November and 12 December 2011, he had three meetings with the Iranian Ambassador, and a number of meetings with the Prime Minister, the NSA, the PM's Chief of Staff, the PM's Political Advisor, the American Ambassador and with the UN HQ in New York through video-conferences and code cables. In a code cable to New York, Kobler reported on 10 December that "PM al-Maleki showed no objection to my intention to visit the Camp to hold meetings with the residents and their leadership in order to seek their agreement. The PM insisted however that only UN involvement is acceptable. He rejected any EU participation in the process".

In his quarterly report to the UN Security Council Kobler informed the members that relocation is the only option. He was indeed pursuing Iraqi's dictated wish while claiming to be impartial facilitator. He omitted to inform the Security Council of the real objectives of relocation inside Iraq. He did not reveal to them that the plan consisted of closing down camp Ashraf and returning its inhabitants to Iran while those who refuse repatriation would be interned in Camp Liberty with leave to remain indefinitely; unless a third country will come forward to resettle them. I knew then that the plan has nothing to do with saving life and I had no means of stopping it while being an employee of the UN organization. It was then that I started thinking of separating from UNAMI. The future events would vindicate my predictions. Returning from New York, Kobler met EU officials in Brussels to gain support for his plan. He also met for the first time with a delegation of the PMOI/MEK in Brussels. They told him what Ms Parsaei had told me on 19 November and reiterated it on 2 December 2011. They asked him to go to Ashraf and talk to the residents and find out the truth.

On 13 December, Kobler lead a UNAMI delegation to Ashraf together with the representative of UNHCR, Claire Bourgeois, and the American Embassy representative, David Lindwalll, who had been handling the Ashraf file since the departure of Ambassador Butler. Kobler was very thankful to Lindwalll as the latter's participation in the visit demonstrated to the residents that Kobler's plan had the backing of the USG and that UNAMI and the international community were 'on the same page'.

Kobler told the Camp residents that time was fast running out; there were but two weeks before the GoI's deadline. He said he recognised that the Ashrafis did not trust the GoI but asked them to trust him and his trust in the GoI. His mission, Kobler said, was purely humanitarian - not of a political nature - and the objective was to save life. The UN would act as an impartial facilitator and he would not sign the MOU without the Ashrafis' agreement. Kobler summarized:

1. Relocation is to take place at the end of the year.
2. UNHCR will not conduct the RSD at Camp Ashraf. It will only take place at the new location (Camp Liberty).
3. The GoI is committed to the deadline and it may consider an extension if there was movement of a few hundred.
4. The responsibility for security falls to the GoI.
5. The UN can only monitor, as previously explained.
6. The UN presence would be 24/7 with unhindered access to the Camp.
7. The UN would not engage in conflicts between the residents and the Iraqi security forces, although it would report to decision-makers.

The residents maintained the position they expressed to me on 19 November. They insisted that if relocation was to take place, there must be credible guarantees for their protection, and only the US or the blue helmets could be trusted to do this. Despite this rejection, the SRSG left the Camp feeling he had achieved something since the residents were no longer rejecting the idea of relocation as such. It was now a question of how to protect them in that relocation. He understood that further discussions in Paris with some pressures from the US Department of States will do the job. Kobler reported on his visit to Ashraf that same day to Ambassador Dan Fried,

Secretary Clinton's advisor on Ashraf, and told him he intended to go to Paris the following week and needed US support for that visit. Ambassador Fried promised full support.

On 14 December 2011, the SRSG met with the diplomatic community in Baghdad. On 16 and 17 December, the SRSG met in Paris with Mrs Maryam Rajavi, and the following day with her and the MEK lawyers. In these meetings he discussed the general framework of the MOU but, as I expected, he had refused to provide them with the text and had promised that he would not sign it without their consent. On 19 December, the SRSG undertook his second mission to Ashraf, conducted a teleconference with Lady Ashton's Envoy for Ashraf, Ambassador Jean de Ruyt and held a meeting with George Bakoos, Political Advisor to the PM. On 21December, the SRSG met Deputy Prime Minister, Saleh Mutlaq, and the following day, Prime Minister al-Maleki. In the meantime he had several telephone conversations with the representatives of the residents in Paris and reiterated that he would not sign the MoU without their agreement. On Christmas Day, the SRSG signed the MOU and instantly reported to US Ambassador Jeffrey. At mid night of 25 December, after signing the MOU he called the residents' representative and said I have just signed the MOU. The latter protested vigorously as he and the residents were betrayed and blackmailed. He said to them "otherwise there would be a bloodbath". The resident's representative asked him to immediately send him the MOU but he refused saying he had to first send it to New York. Knowing that New York had already received every single draft and gave legal advice on what should be agreed to, I founding it objectionable that the SRSG keeps hiding the truth. He had already issued a press release and shared the document with a large number of recipients in America and Europe except with the people concerned in Paris and Ashraf. The representative of the residents Mohammad Mohaddessin received copy only hours before Kobler met him in Paris on 26 December. Following that meeting, he immediately reported from Paris the outcome of the meeting to Ali Dabagh, Iraqi Government spokesman by phone. On 28 December he wrote a lengthy letter to the residents and the following day visited Ashraf. This letter was the result of Paris discussion and aimed to make up for the short comings of the MOU but again was far from what he had promised in Paris.

Kobler kept telling Paris and the residents that Camp Liberty is ready and is waiting their readiness. He said only some minor repairs may be needed and promised that it can be done within three days, from 26 to 30 December. He insisted that the first group of 400 must leave on 31 December, otherwise violence would be unpreventable. He knew that Camp Liberty was not ready and he knew well that the Iraqis are incapable of regenerating Camp Liberty and make it habitable within three days. As we later saw, the first group could only move on 17 February 2012 because the Iraqis could not deliver even after the transfer of the first group.

On 14 December 2011, the SRSG met with the diplomatic community in Baghdad. On 16December, the SRSG met in Paris with an MEK delegation lead by Mrs Maryam Rajavi, and then with her and MEK lawyers the following day. On 19 December, the SRSG undertook his second mission to Ashraf, as well as conducting a teleconference with Lady Ashton's Envoy for Ashraf, Ambassador Jean de Ruyt, and holding a meeting with George Bakoos, Political Advisor to the PM. On 21December, the SRSG met Deputy Prime Minister, Saleh Mutlaq, and, the following day, Prime Minister al-Maleki. On Christmas Day, the SRSG signed the MOU and reported to US Ambassador Jeffrey. The following day, he met with the MEK leadership in Paris and reported the meeting by telephone to Ali al-Dabagh, a GoI spokesperson. On 28 December, the SRSG wrote an open letter to the residents, visiting Ashraf the following day. This hectic schedule created a sense of momentum and gave the impression that the GoI was committed to providing protection and to treating the Ashrafis according to international humanitarian standards. The residents' representatives were fed incorrect information and treated as if they had voluntarily accepted the relocation under the terms of an MOU which they had not even seen. The international community was made to believe that the UN had done everything possible to ensure the safety and security of the residents and that the MEK had been difficult, unnecessarily delaying the process. Kobler's tactics were to move fast, create the *fait accompli* and leave the Ashrafis and the MEK trailing behind.

At Ashraf on 29 December, Kobler asserted to the Camp's leadership that "you have accepted in principle the relocation of the residents to the transitional location at Camp Liberty where they will stay until their departure from Iraq". He conceded that:

- The nature of Camp Liberty would be different from Camp Ashraf and that the current structure of Camp Ashraf would not be reproduced.
- The Memorandum of Understanding gives those residents affiliated to third countries priority for transfer to Camp Liberty. This formula was agreed with the MEK Leadership in Paris.
- Cooperation between the residents and the Iraqi side would be essential to address problems related to living conditions that may surface.
- The United Nations will monitor the situation around the clock in Camp Liberty. Monitoring does not entail taking responsibility. This was clearly explained to Mrs Rajavi. [In fact this was on advice of the UN Office for Legal Affairs in New York of 9 December provided on request from the SRSG, which recommended pushing all the

> obligations on to the GoI. The UN should not assume any responsibility.]

- The MOU stands for voluntary and peaceful relocation not forcible relocation. This was clear in statements made by the various parties including the UNSG, US, EU, and others.
- The MOU was agreed between the GoI and the UN but not the GoI and the MEK. Time was limited; it was not possible to address all problems. Many issues remain open to be discussed bilaterally between the residents and the Iraqis.
- The security position at Camp Liberty can be discussed again bilaterally. The interest of the GoI was that the residents leave the country as soon as possible and as peacefully as possible. It has no interest in causing problems.
- The issue of movable property can be addressed at a later date.
- The residents should have the same rights and restrictions in terms of communications as Iraqi citizens. They would have the right to cell phones, computers, television and internet.

The SRSG reassured the residents that the aim of all sides was the relocation of the Ashrafis outside Iraq and that no side had an interest in a violent solution. He again urged the residents to work with a new mentality once at Camp Liberty. It was important to sit together with the Iraqi authorities to address problems in terms of camp management; the fewer problems at the camp, the lower the visibility of security. The issue of respect for the privacy of women would be taken up with the Iraqi side. Issues related to vehicles and property would be dealt with according to the applicable domestic law. The Iraqi authorities were concerned that there were unlicensed vehicles in the Camp and this issue needed to be resolved. The UN would not interfere in conflicts or camp management; it will only monitor and report incidents to the SRSG and the relevant UN authorities. The SRSG added that the UN was in touch with the Iraqi side in order to prepare Camp Liberty and to ensure minimum standards were met. The UN was ready to play its monitoring role.

The UNHCR representative, Claire Bourgeois, reiterated that the interviews would be conducted in a safe and secure place. It would be essential that each individual cooperated in those interviews. Legal representation would be allowed for those who wished it, provided that legal representatives respect confidentiality and did not intervene during the interviews. At any stage of the process, a person could request return to Iran, and the ICRC would continue to monitor those who wished to do so. It was the duty of the residents to cooperate positively during the interview and to respect Iraqi law and regulations. UNHCR would conduct protection monitoring in the camp.

David Lindwall, representing the US Embassy, told the residents' representatives that the US was committed to working with the UN and the GoI and to find a place for the residents as quickly as possible. The US was committed to observation at both Camp Ashraf and at Camp Liberty. The MOU achieved much than the US had expected. The Secretary of State, Mrs Clinton, endorsed it because she believed it was a fair agreement. The US wished to see it implemented as quickly as possible. Iraq had changed tremendously over the last two weeks, and this would have a huge impact on what the international community could do for the Ashrafis. It was clear that Liberty was not like Ashraf, but Liberty should be seen as an important step in achieving the ultimate goal of relocation outside Iraq.

In response, Ms Parsaei said that the MOU gave the GoI a free hand in the fate of the residents. The GoI was implementing the relocation at the request of the Iranian regime. This was an Iranian project. The relocation was neither the demand of the residents nor of the UN. Initially it was agreed that the UNHCR process would be done at Ashraf not at a transit location. Relocation would not expedite their exit to other countries. The intention of al-Maleki was clear. Missiles had hit Ashraf for three consecutive nights that week. They were launched after the MOU was signed. The open letter from the SRSG explaining the MOU had been received the previous night and had been read to the residents. Unfortunately, minimum guarantees had not been provided and the residents had discussed how to relocate without such assurances. Mrs Rajavi had asked that the first 400 residents relocate to Liberty. The residents would comply. However, the firing of missiles into the Camp every night that week had made it a challenge to convince people to relocate. It had destroyed whatever trust had been built. The 400 residents would leave Ashraf as soon as some security guarantees were given and it would help if Ambassador Jeffrey could provide some undertaking to that effect. Ms Parsaei suggested sending six engineers to Camp Liberty to make an assessment of the infrastructure especially essential services.

The SRSG replied that it was not possible to send an advance party both because of time constraints and the fact that all preparations were the prerogative of the GoI. However, the UN would ensure that the Camp was certified by international standards.

On 3 January 2012, I lead a team to verify whether Camp Liberty was in a fit state to accommodate the Ashraf residents. UNHCR sent a team of three protection officers to participate in the assessment of the facilities. On return to UNAMI, the team made the following observations:
- Accommodation needed substantive work - removal of waste, cleaning, fitting with basic furniture and bedding.
- Electricity and water utilities were not functional. Sewerage systems needed servicing. Safety checks needed to be

completed once utilities were working. There were considerable safety issues, including broken cabling. Getting through the check points to reach Camp Liberty was a serious challenge to both UN and UNHCR staff, let alone the contractors to be engaged by the residents. Given that the residents were intending to use contractors for the purpose of making essential repairs and delivering goods, it was likely to create serious problems.

- Outdoor communal toilets were at a distance from the sleeping areas and would represent a challenge to the elderly, disabled or sick.
- There was no public lighting.
- Doors could only be locked from the outside.
- The dining facility was a long distance from the living areas; again, this would be difficult for the sick and disabled, not least because the journey entailed crossing a main road via a yet to be installed over-flying bridge.
- The dining facility and the kitchen had been clearly looted and vandalized and needed to be checked by professionals.

Both the UNAMI and UNHCR teams concurred that there was a huge amount of work to be done. It was doubtful that the camp would be ready for Thursday, 5 January or even soon thereafter. We needed to be prepared for what our messages would be to the GoI, the residents, and the media, if necessary. On the UN's communication strategy, the SRSG had already sent a code cable to New York on 28 November to warn that "it is important that we counterbalance the MEK's media campaign by developing our own active communication strategy to engage international public opinion". UNAMI's Public Information Office had already prepared draft press releases for a number of possible scenarios. In each, the MEK was to carry the blame.

SRSG Kobler decided to start leading the visits to Camp Liberty and to ensure matters are reported "correctly". He instructed the team to take photographs of the most appealing aspects of the Camp. The SRSG personally made the selection of the pictures to present to the Ashrafis, their representatives in Paris and the diplomatic community in Baghdad. I remembered his asking the Ashrafis to trust him.

To complete the 'communications strategy', SRSG Kobler, together with UNHCR, commissioned a shelter management specialist working for UNHCR in Ethiopia, Martin Zirn, to assess conditions in Camp Liberty and to certify them according to international standards. Zirn's mission was ill defined and misleading. The standard he would be applying were those pertaining to the care of refugees in emergency situations, where, due to armed conflict or natural disaster, people are fleeing for their life and the choices are few. The situation of the Ashrafis was totally different. In the latter case, we were dealing with a community that was simply facing eviction from a site where they had lived for over 26 years. It was not a situation of emergency. They were not fleeing a civil war or a natural disaster. They were going to be forcibly evicted from their homes and to be interned in Camp Liberty simply to make their life "unbearable". This was an abuse of power which the UN was endorsing. For the two weeks that Zirn conducted his assessment of Camp Liberty, daily meetings took place between him and the UNAMI/UNHCR Ashraf Task Force. At a meeting on Wednesday, 18 January 2012, Zirn delivered his verdict. It was a disappointment to the SRSG who insisted, in response, that the Ashrafis were soldiers trained to live in worse conditions than those at Liberty. He expected Zirn to certify the Camp as compliant with international standards. After the meeting, Zirn and I went to my office to continue the discussion and I made my views clear in terms of the incomparability of the conditions residents could expect following a forcible eviction with the conditions refugees would expect in the immediate aftermath of natural disasters or armed conflicts. Zirn tried to compare the situation of Camp Liberty with the situation of the Somali refugees in Ethiopia. I laughed at the absurdity of the comparison. He was clearly faced with a moral dilemma. All of a sudden, he stood up and began hitting his head and tearing out his hair.

By Sunday, 22 January, Martin Zirn had recovered enough composure to send out his draft report on the assessment of the TTL (Camp Liberty) to members of Ashraf Task Force. Given the importance of the document and since it is now in the public domain, I reproduce its content below and attach a copy of the original in the annex[12].

**19 January 2012**
**DRAFT**
Temporary Transit Location for ex-Ashraf residents in Camp Liberty
General

**Based on the Technical Assessment of Sector 1 on WED 18 January, UNHCR can**

1) Complete further assessment if the GoU permits.
2) Advise and recommend regarding the camp setup, taking the Shelter and Camp Standards for Refugees in Emergencies into Account;

*The Ashraf caseload may have other and additional demands and requirements.*

Advise and recommend in particular on
Superstructures such as accommodation, prefabs, office structures, sanitary units, etc...

**It is essential that the GoI permits Ashraf Contractors to enter the TTL 3-5 days prior to relocation of the caseload**

**From the technical point of view, UNHCR cannot**

3) Certify and/or verify that the above location meets Humanitarian Standards according to many existing standard books, i.e. UNHCR Handbook, SPHERE, WHO and others, bearing in mind that these are thought for Refugees in Emergencies.
4) UNHCR cannot certify and/or verify the functionality of infrastructures and/or utilities that are buried.

---

[12] See copy of the original document in the annex

<u>5)</u>    UNHCR cannot certify and /or verify the functionality of infrastructures, such as

The document clearly underlines what UNHCR can do and what the UNHCR cannot do. According to the expert, UNHCR cannot    "certify and/or verify that the above location meets Humanitarian Standards according to the many existing standard books, i.e. UNHCR Handbook, SPHERE, WHO and others, bearing in mind that these are thought for Refugees in Emergencies".

This assessment came as a serious blow to the SRSG's hope of using a third party to certify compliance with international standards. The pressure put on the expert not only failed to produce the expected results, but led to a serious challenge to the SRSG. He knew his own certification of conditions would lack credibility, so he had to force the hand of Claire Bourgeois, the UNHCR representative in Iraq and Francesco Motta, Chief of the UNAMI Human Rights Office. It was decided that a press release would be drafted in such a way as to make the MOU the reference document for international standards.  On 31 January 2012, the press release was issued to announce that "[t]he United Nations High Commissioner for Refugees (UNHCR) and UNAMI Human Rights Office have now confirmed that the infrastructure and facilities at Camp Liberty are in accordance with international humanitarian standards stipulated in the MOU". What a paradox. A so called MOU signed by NSA

Faleh al-Fayadh and SRSG Kobler became a source of international humanitarian law overriding the UNHCR mandate and the humanitarian standards books such as UNHCR handbook, SPHERE[13] and the World Health Organization (WHO) . Let us not forget that the former, in his capacity of chair of Ashraf Committee, the institution with the mission to make Ashrafis' life "unbearable" and to expel them from Iraq, had vowed in Amman meeting on 28 September 2011not to apply the UN humanitarian standards to the terrorists of Ashraf, while the latter took it upon himself to mobilize all UNAMI assets in support of the GoI to free Ashraf from the MEK terrorists!

It is worth noting that the UNAMI press release issued on 31 January 2012 was drafted in such a way that:

1. The High Commissioner for Human Rights Office is not mentioned in the process as they had distanced themselves from the certification issue.

2. Reference to the two weeks work of the shelter management expert, Martin Zirn, was deliberately omitted. Kobler expressed his gratitude to those who cooperated in the process and omitted to mention the work of the expert hired at high cost to the UN, simply because he refused to certify.

---

[13] For details visit http://www.spherehandbook.org/en/what-is-sphere

3. Reference to the UNHCR Handbook, SPHERE and the WHO standard books was omitted. Reference was made instead to the stipulations of the MOU, as dictated by those who in the first place oppose the application of UN humanitarian standards to the case.

In the Second report of the Secretary-General to the Security Council, pursuant to resolution 2001 (2011), Martin Kobler wrote, "On 31 January, the Office of the United Nations High Commissioner for Refugees (UNHCR) determined that the infrastructure and facilities at Camp Hurriya [Camp Liberty] were in accordance with basic international humanitarian standards, as required by the memorandum of understanding"[14]. The UNHCR document reproduced above shows the contrary and I have witnessed all the pressure and even intimidation exerted against the shelter expert commissioned by the UNHCR. Despite such pressure and intimidation, the shelter expert did not certify and did not give in to pressure. Kobler had indeed misled the Ashrafis, the international community and most dangerously he lied at the Security Council.

The whole process envisaged in the MOU was a highly manipulative and deliberately misleading exercise at a time the international community was

---

[14] Security Council Document S/2012/185, 29 March 2012, para. 38

prevented from undertaking any independent verification of the Camp. Again, I remembered the meetings in Camp Ashraf where Kobler was desperately asking the Ashrafis to trust him. When the realities came to the open and the truth was revealed, Ashrafis and their supporters all over the world went on chanting "shame on you Kobler".

Camp Ashraf Mosque built by residents while the camp was under US military control

Camp Ashraf – A view from above

Camp Liberty - Trailers protected by 17,500 concrete T-walls when American soldiers were there

Camp Liberty - Trailers after removal of T-walls by Iraq when Ashrafis were moved in, leaving the residents without any protection against rocket attacks

Camp Liberty - Appalling state of infrastructure

Camp Liberty flooded after rainfall mixed with black water making the environment completely uninhabitable

# MEK Victim of UNAMI Violation
# of the Presumption of Innocence

The presumption of innocence is a norm of general international law applicable at all times in all circumstances. This norm has developed to become a peremptory norm of international law (*jus cogens*) from which no derogation is possible even in situations of emergency and armed conflicts. This very norm, also embodied in the International Covenant on Civil and Political Rights (ICCPR) to which Iraq is a member, has been systematically ignored by the GoI under the leadership of Nouri al-Maleki. Most intriguing in this is the conduct of the Special Representative of the Secretary-General of the United Nations in Iraq, Martin Kobler, who has done everything possible to pervert the due process of law and to consecrate the presumption of guilt of Ashraf residents of unspecified crimes. Based on such a presumption, SRSG Kobler signed, on 25 December 2011, a bizarre text he called a 'memorandum of understanding' with the ultimate objective of legitimizing the acts of the GoI against Ashraf residents in violation of its international commitments.

A close look at the MOU reveals cynical objectives wrapped up in a language that appears to those unfamiliar with the issue to be completely benign. But having participated in the drafting of the text, I know about its true meanings. For example, in the preamble it was said "In view of the Government of the Republic of Iraq's decision to find a peaceful and durable solution by transferring the individuals of Camp New Iraq [Ashraf] to the temporary transitional location (Camp Liberty), in preparation for their departure from the territory of the Republic of Iraq". The reality is that the decision[15] of the GoI referred to in this sentence provides for the closure of Camp Ashraf, the expulsion of its residents from Iraq, the arrest of those who have bogus arrest warrants issued against them in Iran or Iraq, and the prosecution of any individual or organization that deals with the Ashrafis. There is no where to find in the government's literature related to Ashraf words such as "peaceful and durable solution". These words in the MOU were recommended by UNAMI to help the GoI hide their true intentions. The most objectionable clause contained in the MOU is the one under number seven which reads: "Determination of refugee status by UNHCR in accordance with its mandate does not necessarily entail conferral of refugee status by the Government of the Republic of Iraq". This sentence was inserted, as explained earlier, to strip the Ashrafis of any benefit of the outcome of the UNHCR refugee status determination process. Furthermore, an attentive observer would not miss the fact that the MOU had deliberately omitted addressing a number of issues related to the residents' rights including

---

[15] Council of Ministers Decision of 17 June 2008 referred to above, page 8.

237

compensation and property rights. The GoI had always contended that the Ashrafis as "terrorists" have no rights whatsoever.

The MOU signed on behalf of the United Nations violates each and every article of the Universal Declaration of Human Rights and the corresponding provisions of the ICCPR, including:

Article 2 "Everyone is entitled to all the rights and freedoms set forth in this Declaration...";
Article 3 "Everyone has the right to life, liberty and security of person";
Article 5 "No one shall be subjected to torture or to cruel, inhuman or degrading treatment or punishment";
Article 9 "No one shall be subjected to arbitrary arrest, detention or exile";
Article 10 "Everyone is entitled in full equality to a fair and public hearing by an independent and impartial tribunal, in the determination of his rights and obligations and of any criminal charge against him";
Article 11 "(1) Everyone charged with a penal offence has the right to be presumed innocent until proved guilty according to law in a public trial at which he has had all the guarantees necessary for his defence";
Article 12 "No one shall be subjected to arbitrary interference with his privacy, family, home or correspondence, nor to attacks upon his honour and reputation. Everyone has the right to the protection of the law against such interference or attacks";

Article 13 "(1) Everyone has the right to freedom of movement and residence within the borders of each state";

Article 14 "(1) Everyone has the right to seek and to enjoy in other countries asylum from persecution".

As UNAMI Chief of the Human Rights Office and the lead person on Ashraf-related matters and advisor to the SRSG from 2009 to 2012, I had monitored the situation of Ashraf residents for more than three years and had witnessed their persecution to the extent they were stripped of their humanity. Since the arrival of SRSG Kobler in Iraq, the UN mission has been turned from a mission mandated by the UN Security Council to assist the people of Iraq in the reconciliation and reconstruction process into an instrument for helping Prime Minister al-Maleki in his vengeful actions against the residents of Ashraf and their Iraqi sympathizers. The UNAMI led by SRSG Martin Kobler has facilitated their forcible eviction from Ashraf, their place of residence for 26 years, to Camp Liberty, a camp assessed in December 2011 as unsafe and failing to meet the required humanitarian standards. Camp Liberty deprived the residents of dignity, safety and security, while the GoI deprived them of freedom of movement, activities that would improve their living conditions, and visits from families, lawyers, NGOs, diplomats and parliamentarians. In doing so, Kobler had on behalf of the United Nations assisted the GoI to implement measures against Ashraf residents that are contrary to the letter and spirit of the Universal Declaration of Human Rights and the ICCPR.

In stunning contrast, the United Nations Human Rights Council Working Group on Arbitrary Detention (WGAD) in its deliberations of 4 May and 30 August 2012 on communications lodged by a number of Ashraf residents made the following findings:

1. Residents of Camp Liberty have the status of "protected persons" under the Fourth Geneva Convention;
2. They are asylum seekers;
3. They have neither been charged with or tried for any offence;
4. The conditions in Camp Liberty are synonymous with those in a detention centre;
5. Residents have no freedom of movement, nor interaction with the outside world;
6. The situation of the residents of Camp Liberty is tantamount to that of detainees or prisoners;
7. That there is no legal justification for holding people in Camp Liberty;
8. That such detention is not in conformity with the standards and principles of international human rights law;
9. Their detention in Camp Liberty violates article 9 of the Universal Declaration of Human Rights and articles 9 and 10 of the International Covenant on Civil and Political Rights.

Consequently, the Working Group requested the Government to take all necessary steps to remedy the situation and bring it in conformity with the standards and principles set forth in the UDHR and ICCPR. *"The Working Group considers that taking into account all the circumstances of the case, an adequate remedy would be the immediate release and lifting of all restraints upon the free movement of these persons and providing them with the enforceable right to compensation in accordance with article 9(5) of the ICCPR"*.

Instead of taking the appropriate measures to remedy the situation, SRSG Kobler together with the Iraqi authorities embarked upon a disinformation campaign aimed at pressurizing the Working Group to change its position. Kobler's persistence in misleading the international community is resulting in the loss of life of protected persons and asylum seekers. It warrants a thorough investigation; but the silence of the UN HQ in both Geneva and New York amounts to complicity.

# MEK Adherence to the Rule of Law and the Due Process

Regardless of any political consideration, the MEK insisted on nothing but the implementation of international human rights law and international humanitarian law regarding its members in Ashraf. But, beyond international law, other political considerations were affecting the plight of its members.

They argued against relocation as they genuinely and rightly believed that after 26 years living in Ashraf they have acquired rights protected under international law. They also argued that even if they are to be forcibly displaced, eviction has its rules and regulations and they expected, as a minimum, UNAMI to observe the UN Guiding Principles on Internal Displacement[16]. But both the UN and the

---

[16] Principle 6 of the Guiding Principles on Internal Displacement (E/CN.4/1998/53/Add.2)
1. Every human being shall have the right to be protected against being arbitrarily displaced from his or her home or place of habitual residence.
2. The prohibition of arbitrary displacement includes displacement:
(a) When it is based on policies of apartheid, "ethnic cleansing" or similar practices aimed at/or resulting in altering the ethnic, religious or racial composition of the affected population;

western powers (members of the coalition that invaded Iraq) preferred to ignore the UN Guiding Principles under the pretext of "sovereignty" in a country where the situation in discussion was the outcome of foreign occupation to Iraq. Moreover, Martin Kobler acted on the presumption that they are terrorists and denied them all rights for political expediency and opportunism. Personally, I believed that the process in which UNAMI was engaged was immoral and unlawful. My conscience dictated that not only I must distance myself from it but I have to denounce it in line with the rules of conduct of the United Nations Staff.

The MEK, had on its part, shown exemplary conduct in respect of the rule of law and the due process. The Mujahedin fought with all patience and resilience for more than a decade in lengthy and time consuming judicial proceedings before different jurisdictions in different countries, under different legal systems. Despite the hostility of certain governments, motivated by national interests and 'raison d'état',

---

(b) In situations of armed conflict, unless the security of the civilians involved or imperative military reasons so demand;

(c) In cases of large-scale development projects, which are not justified by compelling and overriding public interests;

(d) In cases of disasters, unless the safety and health of those affected requires their evacuation; and

(e) When it is used as a collective punishment.

3. Displacement shall last no longer than required by the circumstances.

the MEK had never lost a case before an independent court of law. Unlike the UN Secretariat that had encouraged impunity by endorsing doctored reports and unsubstantiated allegations, the courts of member states of the UN family looked into facts and hard supporting evidence, and exercised vigorous control over the ill-founded designations made by the executive branches of their respective governments.

## *The United Kingdom*

The Proscribed Organizations Appeal Commission (POAC), a superior court of record created by the Terrorism Act 2000 for appeals in cases where the Secretary of State for the Home Office refuses to de-proscribe organisations, ruled on 30 November 2007, that in deciding to maintain the PMOI/MEK on the list of the proscribed organizations, the Home Secretary had misinterpreted the law, ignored important facts and reached a "perverse decision". Courts rarely call government decisions 'perverse'. In this instance, the panel after examining the secret material said: "the decision at the First Stage was flawed and must be set aside. Further, having carefully considered all the material before us, we have concluded that the decision at the First Stage is properly characterised as perverse. We recognise that a finding of perversity is uncommon. We believe, however, that this Commission is in the (perhaps unusual) position of having before it all of the material that is relevant to this decision".

Having found the proscription of the PMOI a perverse decision, the POAC ordered the Secretary of State to lay before Parliament the draft of an Order under section 3(3)(b) of the 2000 Act, removing the PMOI from the list of proscribed organisations in Schedule 2 of the Act. The Secretary of State sought leave to appeal the order, but the POAC, judging the government's chances of success slim, did not grant it. The government then renewed its appeal before the Supreme Court of Appeal.

The Court of Appeal[17] noted that two requirements set out in Rule 12(1) of the Proscribed Organisations Appeal Commission Rules 2007 must be met in listing an organization. The first requirement is that the Secretary of State must explain the reasons for the proscription of the organisation concerned in terrorism and provide a summary of the evidence that is relied on. The second requirement is that the Secretary of State must adduce such evidence as he or she relies upon in opposition to the particular points raised in the appeal. The court stated that it had considered the closed material available to the applicant [the Home Secretary]. This material had reinforced its conclusion that the decision-making process in this case had signally fallen short of the standards set by British public law. The Court

---

[17] *The Secretary of State for the Home Department (Applicant) and Lord Alton of Liverpool and Others (Respondent)*, [2008] EWCA Civ 443 Case No: 2007/9516.

recalled that, following extensive investigations by the Coalition Forces, the United States' military had accorded the residents of Camp Ashraf *"Protected Persons"* status under the Fourth Geneva Convention on 2 July 2004. The court ruled that "this status was wholly incompatible with any of the Protected Persons thereafter being treated as terrorists." The Court of Appeal on 7 May 2008 endorsed the findings of the Proscribed Organizations Appeal Commission (POAC) and ordered the government to lay an order before Parliament to remove the PMOI from the list of the proscribed organizations. The government laid that order which was unanimously approved by both Houses of Parliament on 23 June 2008.

## *The European Communities*

The Court of First Instance (CFI) of the European Communities in its first judgment (*PMOI-I*), annulled Council Decision 2005/930/EC, which had placed the PMOI on the EU proscribed organizations list[18].

In its second judgment, (*PMOI- II*)[19], the CFI annulled another decision because the Council had

---

[18] Case T-228/02, People's Mojahedin Org. of Iran v. Council of the European Union [*PMOI I*], 2006 E.C.R., II-4665,1.

[19] Case T-228/02, People's Mojahedin Org. of Iran v. Council of the European Union [*PMOI I*], 2006 E.C.R. 2008 WL 4657820 (Oct. 23, 2008).

failed to give sufficient reasons as to why it had not taken into account the judgment of the British Proscribed Organizations Appeals Commission (POAC), a superior British court that deals with the appeals of organizations believed to be involved in terrorism. On 30 November 2007, the POAC allowed an appeal against the Home Secretary's decision that refused de-listing the PMOI as an organization concerned in terrorism. The POAC described the decision as "perverse" and unreasonable. The European Council was informed of the decision of the POAC but nevertheless adopted Decision 2007/868/EC and updated the list keeping the PMOI's name in it. The CFI ordered removal.

In its third judgment, PMOI v. Council of the European Union, supported by the French Republic and by the Commission of the European Communities (*PMOI III*), the Court found that continued freezing of the applicant's funds by the contested decision 2007/868/EC was the result of a procedure that did not respect the applicant's rights of the defence and annulled such a decision in so far as it concerns the People's Mojahedin Organization of Iran"[20].

---

[20] Case T-284/08, People's Mojahedin Org. of Iran v. Council of the European Union [*PMOI III*], 2008 WL 5082977 (Dec. 4, 2008).

## The United States of America

In the case *"People's Mojahedin Organization of Iran (petitioner) v. United States Department of State and Hillary Rodham Clinton, in her capacity as Secretary of State (respondents)"*[21] PMOI/MEK, 30 month after the Court ordered to review PMOI's designation and the failure of the Secretary of State to do so, sought a writ of mandamus ordering the setting aside of its Foreign Terrorists Organizations (FTO) designation. The United States Court of Appeals for the District of Columbia Circuit was of the view that according to the anti-terrorist Act (PATRIOT) as amended, to hold as unlawful and set aside a designation, the court must satisfy itself that the designation is:

(A) arbitrary, capricious, an abuse of discretion, or otherwise not in accordance with law;

(B) contrary to constitutional right, power, privilege, or immunity;

(C) in excess of statutory jurisdiction, authority, or limitation, or short of statutory right;

(D) lacking substantial support in the administrative record taken as a whole or in

classified information submitted to the court under paragraph (2), or

(E) not in accord with the procedures required by law.

---

[21] United States Court of Appeals for the District of Columbia Circuit, Case No. 12-1118, decided June 1, 2012

Applying the tests of unlawful designation above, the United States Court of Appeals found that the PMOI's designation as a foreign terrorist organization lacked substantial support in the administrative record and that the Secretary's procedures did not provide it due process. The Court concluded that "the Secretary failed to accord the PMOI the due process protections" and ordered the Secretary of State to either deny or grant the PMOI's petition not later than four months from the date this opinion was issued. If the Secretary of State failed to take action within that period, the petition for a writ of mandamus setting aside the FTO designation would be granted by the Court.

In a letter addressed to the United States Court of Appeals for the District of Columbia Circuit on 28 September 2012, three days before the end of the four months deadline, the U.S. Department of Justice wrote: "We hereby notify the Court that the Secretary has, after the required notification of Congress, revoked PMOI's designation, effective today".

## *Spain*

On 7 September 2009, attorney Anibal Bordallo Huidobro, representing Seyed Morteza Komarizadehasl and Mohammad Reza Mohade, filed before the Central Investigation Court No Four [National Court], Madrid, a criminal complaint against Lieutenant General, Abdol Hossein Al Shemmari, the Iraqi Officer who ordered and supervised the 28-29 July 2009 attack against Camp Ashraf, for crimes against the International Community described and punished in articles 607 bis, 608 to 614 bis and 615 bis of the Spanish Criminal Code in conjunction with eleven crimes of murder (arts. 139, 1 and 3 of the Criminal Code), 480 crimes of serious injury (art. 174 et seq. of the Criminal Code), 36 crimes of illegal detention (art. 163 et seq. of the Criminal Code) and torture (art. 174 et seq. of the Criminal Code) as well as the crime of damage (art. 263 of the Criminal Code) all in connection with and by violation of the IV$^{th}$ Geneva Convention of August 12, 1949, ratified by Spain and Iraq and its protocol I, of June 8, 1977.

To establish competence under the universal jurisdiction, the Central Investigation Court decided to send out an International Letter Rogatory to the competent judicial authorities of the Republic of Iraq so that they would indicate whether there exists, or has previously existed, any legal procedure for the investigation of the facts set out in the complaint and, if applicable, its outcome, and that, until such information was received, the closing of the case requested by the Prosecutor's Office should not take place.

On 31 May 2010, the Ministry of Foreign Affairs of the Republic of Iraq replied to the Letters Rogatory stating that Iraq had already carried out a legal investigation into the matter and was committed to finding "a solution for the residents of Camp Ashraf according to the international law". In light of this response, the Prosecutor's Office asked on 15 December 2010 that the proceeding continue.

According to article 147 of the Fourth Geneva Convention, each High Contracting Party is under the obligation to search for persons alleged to have committed, or to have ordered to be committed, such grave breaches, and shall bring such persons, regardless of their nationality, before its own courts. As a number of UN reports confirmed the Plaintiffs' allegation that there was no actual investigation and prosecution of the facts at hand, the Court issued an International Letter Rogatory to the competent authorities of the Republic of Iraq in order to serve it on the defendant, and to summon him in order to give a declaration on the facts alleged.

The attorney, Aníbal Bordallo Huidobro, filed a supplement to his complaint of 7 September 2009 regarding a continuance of and increased severity in the breaches of the Fourth Geneva Convention and asked for the complaint to be deemed extended to the following persons: Ali al-Yasseri and Sadeq Mohammad Kazem; Lieutenant Colonel Nezar; and Lieutenant Haydar Azab Mashi. On 3 March 2011, the Prosecution Service extended the complaint as requested and asked for testimony from the UN Special Representative of the Secretary-General, Ad Melkert, as a witness. The UN Secretary General declined to authorize his representative to testify before the Spanish Court.

On 14 July 2011, on request from the Plaintiffs'
attorney, the Prosecution Service again agreed to
amend the charges to extend to General Ali Ghaidan
Majad, Lieutenant Colonel Abdol-Latif al-Anabi and
Major Jasem Mohammad Aleive al Tamami who
were requested to appear in the courtroom on 3
October 2011.The Prosecution Service submitted a
Letter Rogatory to the competent authorities in Iraq
to this effect. This new extension took into account
the new attack by the Iraqi armed forces on the
Ashraf Camp on 8 April 2011, which, according to
the UN, caused 36 deaths and hundreds of injuries.
The summoned men have so far failed to appear
before the Judge and the case is still pending.

### *France*
On June 17, 2003, at 6:00 am, some 1,300 heavily-
armed police attacked the offices of the National
Council of Resistance of Iran and 12 other homes of
Iranian refugees in the suburbs of Paris, Auvers-sur-
Oise. French media described the attack as
unprecedented and politically motivated. Twenty
four (24) people were indicted for alleged terrorism
charges.

On 11 May 2011, the Investigative Magistrate of
Paris, Antiterrorism Department, issued an order
dropping all charges of terrorism and financing of
terrorism against the 24 members of the National
Council of Resistance of Iran. The Investigative
Judge concluded that after ten years of thorough

investigation no evidence was found to support the allegation of terrorism against the People's Mojahedin Organization of Iran. The lack of evidence was also acknowledged by the Paris Prosecutor's office which had submitted its views that there should be a dismissal of the charges.

France was the only member state of the EU who appealed against the findings of the judgment of the Court of First Instance of the European Communities in *PMOI v. the Council of the European Union,* 4 December 2008. The Court dismissed the appeal and ordered the French Republic to pay the costs.

## *Canada*
Under the influence of judicial developments in Europe and the United States regarding the status of the MEK, in December 2012 Canada removed the PMOI from its terrorist organizations list and replaced it with the Iranian Islamic Revolutionary Guard Corps' Quds Force.

Thus, outside the United Nations system, justice had prevailed.

# ANNEXES

# ANNEXES

1.  Proclamation by the Commander, MNF-I, recognizing the status of Ashraf residents as "Protected Persons" under the Fourth Geneva Convention – 2 July 2004

2.  MNF-I letter giving Ashraf residents the Iraqi Government assurances for public services - 25 June 2004

3.  MNF-I congratulate Ashraf residents for their new status as protected persons – 21 July 2004

4.  Agreement for the Individuals of the People's Mujahedin Organization Of Iran (PMOI)

5.  Letter by MNF-I Command outlining the rights of Ashraf residents – 7 Oct 2005

6.  US Embassy Statement on Transfer of Security Responsibility for Camp Ashraf – 28 Dec 2008

7.  UN Human Rights Commissioner Pillay condemns Iraqi operation that led to 34 deaths, calls for inquiry – 15 April 2011

8.  US State Department email to MEK leadership prior to April 8, 2011 attack

9.  Senator John Kerry condemns April 8 attack on Camp Ashraf – 14 April 2011

10. Martin Kobler letter to Ashraf residents on signing MOU – 28 December 2011

11. Text of Memorandum of Understanding (MOU)

12. UNHCR shelter expert report about Camp Liberty standard – 19 January 2012

13. Opinions adopted by the UN Working Group on Arbitrary Detention on Camp Liberty at its sixty-fourth session, 30 April–4 May 2012

14. Opinions adopted by the UN Working Group on Arbitrary Detention on Camp Liberty at its sixty-fourth session, 27–31 August 2012

15. Report on visit to Iraq by Senator Robert Torricelli and Steven Schneebaum – 1-4 January 2013

16. Tahar Boumdera testimony, US House of Representatives Committee on Foreign Affairs – 13 September 2012

17. Tahar Boumedra, British Parliament – 29 January 2013

18. Tahar Boumedra, United Nations Headquarters in Geneva – 28 February 2013

19. Tahar Boumedra, Formal session of the European Parliament Delegation for Relations with Iraq – 27 March 2013

Proclamation by the Commander, Multi-National Forces – Iraq, on the Signing of the "Agreement for the Individuals of the People's Mujahedin Organization of Iran (PMOI)" at Ashraf, Iraq

To the residents of Ashraf

The United States has confirmed your status as "protected persons" under the Fourth Geneva Convention and has communicated that determination to the International Committee of the Red Cross in Geneva. The acknowledgement of this determination will assist in expediting the efforts of the International Committee of the Red Cross and the United Nations High Commissioner for Refugees in your disposition as individuals in accordance with applicable international law.

2 July, 2004

**HEADQUARTERS**
MULTI-NATIONAL FORCE – IRAQ
BAGHDAD, IRAQ
APO AE 09342-1400

25 June 2004

MNFI DCG

Mr. Baraii
Ashraf, Iraq

Dear Mr. Baraii,

Prime Minister Allawi of the Interim Iraqi Government (IIG) has given Ambassador Bremer, of the Coalition Provisional Authority, his assurances that the provision of essential services to the individuals living at Camp Ashraf will continue after sovereignty is transferred on 30 June, 2004. These services will be commensurate with the level of service at the quantities and prices as those received by Iraqi citizens living in Diyala' Province and will remain in effect until the final disposition of the individuals living at Camp Ashraf is determined. Prime Minister Allawi said that the IIG would agree to allow the MeK to purchase commodities and services (including oil/fuel, electricity, commerce, agriculture, and health) thus enabling them to remain self-sustaining at Camp Ashraf.

After the transfer of sovereignty, Multi-National Forces Iraq will facilitate transportation for those who need to discuss individual issues with the relevant IIG entities.

Very Respectfully,

Geoffrey D. Miller
Major General, U.S. Army
Deputy Commanding General

**HEADQUARTERS**
MULTI-NATIONAL FORCE – IRAQ
BAGHDAD, IRAQ
APO AE 09342-1400

July 21, 2004

Deputy Commander

People of Ashraf
Ashraf, Iraq

I am writing to congratulate each individual living in Camp Ashraf on their recognition as protected persons under the Fourth Geneva Convention. This determination will assist in expediting the efforts of international organizations in your disposition as individuals in accordance with applicable international law.

You have signed an Agreement rejecting violence and terrorism. This sends a strong signal and is a powerful first step on the road to your final individual disposition.

In our efforts to reach a peaceful future for the people of Camp Ashraf, we will continue to seek the best disposition for each individual and commend you all for your patience and cooperation during this lengthy process.

Very Respectfully,

Geoffrey D. Miller
Major General, US Army
Deputy Commanding General

## AGREEMENT FOR THE INDIVIDUALS OF THE PEOPLE'S MUJAHEDIN ORGANIZATION OF IRAN (PMOI)

You are being offered your release from control and protection in exchange for your promise to comply with certain conditions. In exchange for your promises, you will be released from Multi-National Forces-Iraq control and protection as soon as reasonably practicable.

Please read the Agreement below. If you agree to abide by these terms, then sign your name at the bottom of the page.

### AGREEMENT

I, _____, knowingly, willingly, and voluntarily enter into this Agreement with Multi-National Forces-Iraq. I agree to the following:

a. I reject participation in, or support for terrorism.

b. I have delivered all military equipment and weapons under my control or responsibility.

c. I reject violence and I will not unlawfully take up arms or engage in any hostile act. I will obey the laws of Iraq and relevant United Nations mandates while residing in this country.

I understand that I will be free to leave and to return home when viable disposition options become available. I understand that some of these disposition options include: return to my nation of origin; admission to a third country; application to the Ministry of Displacement and Migration for continued residency in Iraq, or application to international organizations such as the United Nations High Commissioner for Refugees. I agree to cooperate with Multi-National Forces-Iraq while these disposition options are pursued. I agree to remain under the protection of Multi-National Forces-Iraq at Camp Ashraf until these options are completed. If I violate any terms of this Agreement, I may be subject to prosecution or internment, and administrative sanctions. I promise to scrupulously comply with my Agreement.

| | | |
|---|---|---|
| _____ | _____ | _____ |
| SIGNATURE | NAME (PRINTED) | IDENTITY NUMBER |

| | | |
|---|---|---|
| _____ | _____ | _____ |
| MNF-Iraq Representative | PRINTED NAME, RANK | DATE |

**HEADQUARTERS**
MULTI-NATIONAL FORCE – IRAQ
BAGHDAD, IRAQ
APO AE 09342-1400

October 7, 2005

MNFI-DCG

Ashraf, Iraq

To The PMOI General Secretary, Madame Sedigheh Hoseini and The Residents of Camp Ashraf

In June of 2004, the residents of Camp Ashraf were determined to be protected by the provisions of the Fourth Geneva Convention covering alien civilians in a territory of conflict.

Since that date, we believe that Coalition Forces and the residents of Camp Ashraf have greatly benefited from working together to ensure that the rights and protections provided by the Fourth Geneva Convention are enjoyed by the residents of Camp Ashraf, in the spirit of common humanitarism.

As we approach the first anniversary of this legal determination, I would like to take this opportunity to review important rights and protections under international law that this determination provides to the residents of Camp Ashraf.

> i. The residents of Camp Ashraf have the right to protection from danger, violence, coersion, and intimidation, and to special protection for the dignity and rights of women;
>
> ii. They have the right to help in contacting their families outside Camp Ashraf, and their families have the right to help in contacting them;
>
> iii. They have the right to seek assistance from the International Committee of the Red Cross, the United Nations High Commissioner for Refugees, and from other international humanitarian organizations;
>
> iv. They have the right to freedom of thought, religion, expression, intra-community association, and political opinion; they also have the right to freedom from persecution and forced unpaid labor;
>
> v. They have the right to food, health care, and a quality of living which meets the standards of local residents of the territory in which they are protected;

vi.  They have the right to fair treatment under the law, in accordance with Iraqi domestic law and international standards;

vii.  They have the right to pursue employment opportunities and profit-making activities which are consistent with local laws and can be taken without compromising their overriding right to personal safety;

viii.  They have the right to speak with representatives of the Coalition, the Protecting Power, privately and with confidence in the Coalition's humanitarian interest in their situation;

ix.  They have the right to refuse to return to their country of nationality, regardless of their legal status in the country in which they are protected;

x.  They have the right to depart the territory of conflict at any time for their country of nationality or for any other country for which they possess valid travel documentation.

All of these rights are essential for the protection of the residents of Camp Ashraf, and under the terms of the Fourth Geneva Convention, and they cannot be renounced, either by the residents of Camp Ashraf or by Coalition Forces.

It is important that the residents of Camp Ashraf are aware of the rights they enjoy, and of the ways in which they are able to exercise those rights. It is also important that all residents of Camp Ashraf understand that they are free to depart Iraq at any time, and that Coalition Forces and international and humanitarian organizations stand ready and willing to assist them.

All residents of Camp Ashraf wishing to return to the country of their nationality are eligible for assistance from Coalition Forces, the Iraqi Ministry of Human Rights, and the International Committee of the Red Cross (ICRC), which have helped nearly 300 people return to Iran and other countries in recent months.

All residents of Camp Ashraf who do not wish to return to their country of nationality and instead wish to seek an individual or family refugee status determination, and individual or family claims for resettlement in a third country, can request that their cases be referred to the United Nations High Commissioner for Refugees (UNHCR).

Coalition Forces remain committed to fulfilling the humanitarian mission of ensuring that the important rights provided by the Geneva Conventions – to safety and security, to freedom of thought, to food and shelter – are respected at Camp Ashraf.

Please do not hesitate to contact the JIATF Commander, or to speak to any of the men and women under my command who work alongside them at Camp Ashraf, if you have any questions or concerns about your situation.

Communication is one of the most important tools we have in ensuring that the rights provided to the residents of Camp Ashraf are enjoyed equally by all. We welcome conversation with all of the people of Ashraf, and the men and women under my command look forward to hearing your thoughts and concerns.

Very Respectfully,

William H. Brandenburg
Major General, US Army
Commanding

**US Embassy Statement on Transfer of Security Responsibility for Camp Ashraf**

**US Embassy- Iraq**

**Dec 28, 2008**

**With the end of the UNSCR mandate for the Coalition Forces in Iraq, the Government of Iraq will assume** security responsibility for Camp Ashraf and its residents as of January 1, 2009. In that context, the transfer of security responsibility from Coalition Forces to the Iraqi Security Forces will take effect January 1, 2009. U.S. forces will maintain a presence at Camp Ashraf and will continue to assist the Government of Iraq in carrying out its assurances of humane treatment of the residents of Camp Ashraf.

The Government of Iraq has provided the US Government written assurances of humane treatment of the Camp Ashraf residents in accordance with Iraq's Constitution, laws, and international obligations. As recently as September 2008, the Government of Iraq affirmed publicly that it would treat the residents of Camp Ashraf humanely.

The US Government, through its Embassy in Iraq and the military forces present under the new bilateral security agreement, will continue to work to ensure a smooth transition for the camp residents. The US Government and Government of Iraq will work with appropriate international organizations to assist the camp residents in securing a safe future.

The US Government has designated the MeK a foreign terrorist organization.

## Media centre

**Pillay condemns Iraqi operation that led to 34 deaths, calls for inquiry**

15 April 2011

GENEVA – The UN High Commissioner for Human Rights Navi Pillay on Friday condemned a lethal Iraqi military operation in a camp housing an Iranian exile group that left at least 34 people dead and dozens injured, said there must be an independent inquiry, and called on governments to consider resettlement to third countries as a matter of urgency.

"Full details of what exactly happened on the morning of 8 April are still only beginning to emerge," Pillay said. "But it now seems certain that at least 34 people were killed in Camp Ashraf, including seven or more women. Most were shot, and some appear to have been crushed to death, presumably by vehicles."

Dozens more lie injured in the camp hospital and elsewhere in Iraq, she added.

"The Iraqi military were well aware of the risks attached to launching an operation like this in Ashraf," Pillay said. "There is no possible excuse for this number of casualties. There must be a full, independent and transparent inquiry, and any person found responsible for use of excessive force should be prosecuted."

Pillay also called on other governments to help provide a long-term solution for the residents of the camp, who belong to the group known as the People's Mujahedeen of Iran (PMOI). "Everyone had beenfearing a tragedy like this for a long time," Pillay said. "I am well aware that this is a contentious group, with a complicated history, but leaving them to fester in Camp Ashraf was never going to be a solution. Clearly, since they are unable to go back to Iran, and are in danger in Iraq, the solution is most likely to involve moving them to third countries. I urge governments to take the necessary pragmatic and generous steps to resolve what is an untenable situation."

ENDS

OHCHR Country Page – Iraq:
http://www.ohchr.org/EN/Countries/MENARegion/Pages/IQIndex.aspx

For more information or interviews, please contact spokesperson Rupert Colville (+41 22 917 9767 or rcolville@ohchr.org ) or press officers: RavinaShamdasani (+ 41 22 917 9310 or rshamdasani@ohchr.org )

From
"TaharBoumedra" <boumedra@un.org>
Subject:
Fw: Ashraf meetings
Date:
04/07/11 16:03:02
To:
"BehzadSaffari"<saffarib@ashraf-ir.org>, "BehzadSaffari"<saffarib@ashraf-ir.org>

----- Forwarded by TaharBoumedra/UNAMI on 07/04/2011 11:02 PM -----

From:      "Hanks, Russell J (Baghdad)" <HanksRJ@state.gov&gt;
To:        "TaharBoumedra" <boumedra@un.org&gt;
Date:      07/04/2011 10:40 PM
Subject:   RE: Ashraf meetings

Please pass to the MEK leadership. Thank you.

General Ali Ghaydan has ordered the ISF on the ground at Ashraf to only take unoccupied land there and not molest the MeK members.

Maliki has ordered that the ISF take only unoccupied land and that they must not use violence.

The PM is asking the MeK and urge them to be reasonable and not create hindrances.  The GOI's goal is to find a peaceful solution to this and hopes to work to find a humanitarian solution to this situation..."To help, and not hinder," the pm reportedly said.

This email is UNCLASSIFIED.

**U.S. Senate Committee on Foreign Relations**

Press Release

# Chairman Kerry On The Violence At Camp Ashraf In Iraq

*Thursday, April 14, 2011*
**SFRC Communications, 202-224-3468**

**Washington, DC** – Last Friday, Iraqi Security Forces forcefully entered Camp Ashraf in Eastern Iraq. Members of the Mujahedin-e Khalq or MEK are housed at the camp. Earlier today, United Nations officials confirmed that the incursion by Iraqi Security Forces had resulted in scores of dead and injured MEK members. Senate Foreign Relations Committee Chairman John Kerry (D-MA) issued the following statement:

"United Nations confirmation of the scope of last week's tragedy at Camp Ashraf is deeply disturbing and the Iraqi military action is simply unacceptable. Corrective action is imperative. First, the Iraqis must stop the bleeding and refrain from any further military action against Camp Ashraf. Second, the Iraqi government has announced a full investigation into the massacre and it must be thorough and serious. The investigation must hold accountable the responsible parties and ensure that there will be no sequel to these horrific events. Third, the current situation at the camp is untenable. The United States must redouble efforts with all the relevant parties – including the Iraqi government, the United Nations, the European Union, and the Mujahedin-e Khalq itself – to seek a peaceful and durable solution, and to find permanent homes for the residents of Camp Ashraf."

**United Nations Assistance Mission for Iraq (UNAMI)**
بعـثـة الأمـم المتـحـدة لمساعدة العـراق (يـونـامي)
Telephone No. +1 917 36 73614 / +39 0831 23 2700
Fax No. +1 917 36 73615 / +39 0831 23 2705

28 December 2011

*Dear residents of any belief,*

You have all heard by now that I signed a Memorandum of Understanding (MoU) with the Government of the Republic of Iraq on the safe and secure relocation of the residents of Camp Ashraf to a new temporary location. I took this step with your security and safety uppermost in mind. You might have received the MoU by now. Meanwhile I attach a copy for your reference.

Representatives of the United Nations Assistance Mission of Iraq (UNAMI), together with representatives of UNHCR and OHCHR, have conducted weekly visits to Camp Ashraf. I myself have visited Camp Ashraf twice, have spoken with many of you. I can imagine how difficult it could be to leave a place where you have spent many years of your lives.

Moving the camp residents to a new temporary site, known as Camp Liberty, would enable UNHCR to conduct refugee status determination. This is a necessary and indispensible first step towards a long-term solution. It is then up to Member States to accept you in their countries. Once you arrive at Camp Liberty, UNHCR can begin with the verification of your papers immediately after your arrival there and subsequently will start the interviews.

I have understood from the many discussions that I have had with you that most of you are willing in principle to leave Camp Ashraf, relocate to a temporary site in Iraq and finally find a permanent home where you can live in peace and security in the future.

I was involved in these negotiations as an impartial facilitator. For the UN and myself, it is a humanitarian imperative. It is about seeking to prevent violence and confrontation. It is also about respecting your human rights. Respect for human rights is at the core of the values of the United Nations.

The success of the implementation of the MoU depends on your cooperation. The MoU is an offer to you which provides you with an opportunity to live in peace and security.

You will have noticed that many of your requests were met. The MoU is a good start. It outlines the process of relocation to Camp Liberty, which will take place exclusively under the security responsibility of the Government of the Republic of Iraq. The United Nations will be monitoring throughout. The Government of the Republic of Iraq, at the highest levels, has given its assurances to the United Nations that it will ensure your safety and security both during the transportation from Camp Ashraf to Camp Liberty and in Camp Liberty itself until the time comes when you leave Iraq.

Given the short time available, it was not possible to address all your requests. Many issues will have to be arranged between you and the representatives of the Government of the Republic of Iraq in Camp Liberty. It requires sincere cooperation between you and the Government of the Republic of Iraq. We will monitor all stages of the process. I explained to you the concept of monitoring during my visits to Camp Ashraf.

I want to clarify some of the provisions that were agreed in the MoU in order to give you a better understanding:

1.     According to the MoU, the residents of the Camp will be transferred directly from Camp Ashraf to Camp Liberty, which will be a temporary transit location until the resettlement process to other countries is completed.

2.     Those Camp Ashraf residents who want to be repatriated immediately to Iran may use the current channels for doing so.

3.     The Government of the Republic of Iraq has undertaken to ensure the safe and secure transfer of the residents of Camp Ashraf to Camp Liberty and from Camp Liberty to other countries. Those residents with passports and links to other countries will be treated as priority cases for transfer to Camp Liberty.

4. Upon arrival of the residents at Camp Liberty, the United Nations will conduct 24/7 monitoring at the Camp until the last of the residents leaves Iraq. Communication procedures will be established to facilitate this monitoring.

2

5. UNHCR will start the verification process immediately after the arrival of the residents at Camp Liberty. UNHCR will interview the residents of the Camp to identify their status in accordance with its mandate and its operational rules. UNHCR and the United Nations more generally will continue their efforts to resettle you in third countries. However, the final resettlement decision will be made by the countries themselves. For this purpose, consular visits to individuals at Camp Liberty will be arranged.

6. As "asylum seekers", you will be eligible under international law to enjoy basic protections and well-being. UNHCR is able to accept applications from residents who have not yet submitted applications for refugee status at any point. The Government of the Republic of Iraq has undertaken in the MoU to afford you protection against any expulsion or involuntary repatriation to Iran (the principle of *non-refoulement*).

7. As you may have seen in the press, the Government of the United States has also committed itself to visit Camp Liberty regularly and frequently.

8. I am aware of your request for respect for your privacy, in particular regarding women. I will continue my efforts with the Government of the Republic of Iraq in this regard to establish the appropriate arrangements, with the agreement of the Government of the Republic of Iraq, which would respect the sovereignty of Iraq.

9. With regard to other issues, such as assets and properties, we will continue the discussions towards reaching a solution that respects the property rights of the residents in an organized way under Iraqi law.

Martin Kobler
Special Representative of the Secretary General

3

# Memorandum of Understanding

## between the Government of the Republic of Iraq

## and the United Nations

In accordance with the principle of the sovereignty of the Republic of Iraq and based on its Constitution; and

In compliance with its commitments under the rules of International Human Rights Law, and

In view of the Government of the Republic Iraq's decision to find a peaceful and durable solution by transferring the individuals of Camp New Iraq to the temporary transitional location (Camp Liberty), in preparation for their departure from the territory of the Republic of Iraq, and

In order to facilitate the repatriation to the home countries of those wishing to do so voluntarily or resettlement in other countries, and

Considering the impartial and facilitating role of the United Nations,

The Government of the Republic of Iraq and the United Nations agree to the following:

### First: Mechanisms for Transport to the (Temporary) Transit Locations

A. The Government of the Republic of Iraq shall ensure the following:
   1. The safety and security of the temporary transit location in the Yamama Hotel at Abu Nousass Street.
   2. The safety and security of Camp Liberty.
   3. Easy access for the UN to the temporary transit locations.
   4. Safe transportation for the movement of individuals of Camp New Iraq to the temporary transit locations.

B. The Government of the Republic of Iraq shall facilitate the performance by United Nations of the following tasks:
   1. Conduct of security assessments of Grizzly Base, security units' location outside the Lion's Gate, the temporary transit location in Abu Al-Nuwwas Street and in Camp Liberty (the final temporary transit location).

1

2. Monitor the transit process from Camp New Iraq to the temporary transit locations, including the departure of the residents from Camp New Iraq, their arrival and entry into Camp Liberty.
3. Monitor the temporary transit locations.

C. Those Camp New Iraq residents with passports and links to other countries will be treated as priority cases for the transfer to Camp Liberty.

### Second: Verification Processes in Camp Liberty:

A. the UNHCR Verification processes aims at:

1. Identifying and recording the wishes of individuals (individuals of Camp New Iraq) either to return voluntarily to the Islamic Republic of Iran or to depart to other countries.
2. Verifying the identification papers of the individuals of Camp New Iraq and registering them in its data base.
3. The verification process will be completed within a period not exceeding 3 weeks from the date that all necessary equipment for the conduct of the verification process is installed at Camp Liberty.

B. The Government of the Republic of Iraq agrees that UNHCR may carry out the verification process at Camp Liberty and shall facilitate its doing so.

### Third: Management of the Temporary Transit Locations

A. The Government of the Republic of Iraq shall undertake the management of the temporary transit locations, and shall ensure the following:
1. The transit locations meet humanitarian and human rights standards.
2. The security of those accommodated at the transit locations and of United Nations personnel carrying out their duties at or near those locations, to be ensured through officers trained for this purpose with the assistance of the United Nations.
3. Accommodation infrastructure, hygiene facilities, medical care and facilities for religious observance while taking into consideration the "separation between the sexes" in Camp Liberty. The Government shall allow internal and external communication in accordance with the Iraqi laws.
4. The Government shall facilitate and allow the residents, at their own expense, to enter into bilateral contact with contractors for provision of life support and utilities such as water, food, communications, sanitation, and maintenance and rehabilitation equipment. The Government shall allow residents to move their individual movable assets from Camp New Iraq into Camp Liberty. The Government of the Republic of Iraq shall allow the entry of an adequate number of vehicles for transportation within the camp.

B. The Government of the Republic of Iraq shall permit the United Nations to carry out monitoring of the human rights and humanitarian situation in the temporary transit locations and shall establish procedures for the reporting of complaints.

**Fourth: Procedures at Camp Liberty**

A. The Government of the Republic of Iraq shall permit and facilitate UNHCR to conduct interviews with the residents of the Camp to identify their status in accordance with its mandate and its operational rules.
B. The Government of the Republic of Iraq shall facilitate consular visits to the individuals of Camp New Iraq at Camp Liberty.

**Fifth: The Repatriation or Resettlement of the individuals of Camp New Iraq**

A. The Government of the Republic of Iraq, with the assistance of the United Nations shall:
    1. Request the Islamic Republic of Iran to provide assurances to returnees
    2. Facilitate the safe return to the Islamic Republic of Iran of those voluntarily wishing to return there at any time.
    3. Encourage diplomatic missions to repatriate individuals to the countries with which they are affiliated.
    4. Mobilize the international community to accept the individuals of Camp New Iraq in other countries.
    5. Identify persons from the Government of the Republic of Iraq who can be contacted in cases of emergency and who can be reached at anytime.

B. The Government of the Republic of Iraq shall:
    1. Accompany departing individuals of Camp New Iraq to the departure points or borders.
    2. Protect the security of United Nations personnel.
    3. Commit to *non-refoulement* of the individuals of Camp New Iraq to Iran.

**Sixth:** The Government of the Republic of Iraq shall ensure the substantial involvement of its Ministry of Human Rights in the process including the provision of a liaison officer from the Ministry of Human Rights 24/7 for referral of incidents to the Government of the Republic of Iraq for appropriate action.

**Seventh:** Determination of refugee status by UNHCR in accordance with its mandate does not necessarily entail conferral of refugee status by the Government of the Republic of Iraq.

3

**Eighth**: The Government of the Republic of Iraq and the United Nations shall consult with each other, at the request of either of them, on any difficulties, problems or matters of concern that may arise in the course of the implementation of this memorandum of understanding.

**Ninth:** This memorandum of understanding shall enter into force as of the date of its signature.

**Tenth:** This memorandum of understanding is concluded in two original copies in Arabic and English, each text being equally authentic.

DONE at Baghdad this $\underline{21}$ day of December,     2011 AD/ this _____ day of -
_____, _____ AH

First Party
The Government of the Republic of Iraq
Represented by

Falih Al-Fayyadh
National Security Advsior

Second Party
The United Nations
Represented by

Martin Kobler
Special Representative
of the Secretary-General for Iraq

United Nations High Commissioner for Refugees
Haut Commissariat des Nations Unies pour les réfugiés

Representation in Ethiopia
P. O. Box 1076

Tel.: +251 11 6612822
Fax: +251 11 6611666
Email: ethad@unhcr.org

19 January 2012

Notre/Our code:

# DRAFT

## Temporary Transit Location for ex-Ashraf residents in Camp Liberty

### General

**Based on the Technical Assessment of Sector 1 on WED 18 January, <u>UNHCR can</u>**

1) Complete further assessments if the GoI permits.
2) Advise and recommend regarding the camp setup, taking the Shelter and Camp Standards for Refugees in Emergencies into account;

*The Ashraf caseload may have other and additional demands and requirements.*

Advise and recommend in particular on

- Superstructures such as accommodation prefabs, office structures, sanitary units, etc.
- Site planning figures in terms of
  - ➤ Land
  - ➤ Shelter space
  - ➤ Fire break space
  - ➤ Roads and walkways
  - ➤ Open space and public facilities
  - ➤ Environmental sanitation
  - ➤ Water
  - ➤ Tap stands
  - ➤ Warehouse space

**It is essential that the GoI permits Ashraf Contractors to enter the TTL 3-5 days prior to relocation of the caseload**

### From the technical point of view, <u>UNHCR cannot</u>

3) Certify and/or verify that the above location meets Humanitarian Standards according to the many existing standard books, i.e. UNHCR Handbook, SPHERE, WHO and others, bearing in mind that these are thought for Refugees in Emergencies.
4) UNHCR cannot certify and/or verify the functionality of infrastructures and/or utilities that are buried.
5) UNHCR cannot certify and/or verify the functionality of infrastructures, such as
   - ➤ Generator sets
   - ➤ Water pumps
   - ➤ Water supply
   - ➤ Water tanks
   - ➤ Waste water disposal (pipes, tanks and pumps)
   - ➤ Electrical / IT supply and distribution etc.

# DRAFT

Baghdad, 19 Jan 2012

**General Assembly**

Distr.: General
17 July 2012

Original: English

Human Rights Council
Working Group on Arbitrary Detention

### Opinions adopted by the Working Group on Arbitrary Detention at its sixty-third session, 30 April–4 May 2012

### No. 16/2012 (Iraq)

Communication addressed to the Government on 2 March 2012

Concerning Hossein Dadkhah, Farichehr Nekogegan, Zinat Pairawi, Mahrash Alimadadi, Hossein Farsy, Hassan Ashrafian, Hassan Sadeghi, Hossein Kaghazian, Reza Veisy and Mohammad Motiee

No response has been received from the Government.

The State is a party to the International Covenant on Civil and Political Rights.

1.     The Working Group on Arbitrary Detention was established in resolution 1991/42 of the former Commission on Human Rights, which extended and clarified the Working Group's mandate in its resolution 1997/50. The Human Rights Council assumed the mandate in its decision 2006/102 and extended it for a three-year period in its resolution 15/18 of 30 September 2010. In accordance with its Methods of Work, the Working Group transmitted the above-mentioned communication to the Government.

2.     The Working Group regards deprivation of liberty as arbitrary in the following cases:

       (a)     When it is clearly impossible to invoke any legal basis justifying the deprivation of liberty (as when a person is kept in detention after the completion of his or her sentence or despite an amnesty law applicable to the detainee) (category I);

       (b)     When the deprivation of liberty results from the exercise of the rights or freedoms guaranteed by articles 7, 13, 14, 18, 19, 20 and 21 of the Universal Declaration of Human Rights and, insofar as States parties are concerned, by articles 12, 18, 19, 21, 22, 25, 26 and 27 of the International Covenant on Civil and Political Rights (category II);

       (c)     When the total or partial non-observance of the international norms relating to the right to a fair trial, established in the Universal Declaration of Human Rights and in the relevant international instruments accepted by the States concerned, is of such gravity as to give the deprivation of liberty an arbitrary character (category III);

(d)     When asylum seekers, immigrants or refugees are subjected to prolonged administrative custody without the possibility of administrative or judicial review or remedy (category IV);

(e)     When the deprivation of liberty constitutes a violation of international law for reasons of discrimination based on birth; national, ethnic or social origin; language; religion; economic condition; political or other opinion; gender; sexual orientation; or disability or other status, and which aims towards or can result in ignoring the equality of human rights (category V).

Submission

*Communication from the source*

3.      The case summarized hereinafter was reported by the source to the Working Group on Arbitrary Detention as follows:

     (a)     Hossein Dadkhah;

     (b)     Farichehr Nekogegan;

     (c)     Zinat Pairawi;

     (d)     Mahrash Alimadadi;

     (e)     Hossein Farsy;

     (f)     Hassan Ashrafian;

     (g)     Hassan Sadeghi;

     (h)     Hossein Kaghazian;

     (i)     Reza Veisy; and

     (j)     Mohammad Motiee.

4.      According to the source, these 10 persons of Iranian nationality are part of a group of 400 dissident members of the National Council of Resistance of Iran (NCRI) who accepted relocation from Camp Ashraf to Camp Liberty, a former United States of America military base near Baghdad international airport, in order to begin the process of having their refugee status reconfirmed. Before being transferred to Camp Liberty, these persons and their belongings were processed for 11 hours by security forces, under similar procedures to those for admitting inmates to prisons. Many belongings, such as wheelchairs, communication and video equipment, personal photographs, medicine, heaters and sanitary equipment were not allowed and were confiscated.

5.      On their arrival at Camp Liberty, the relocated people were ordered to line up for a headcount, and told by the commanding officer that he would assign them their rooms. They felt as if they were in a prison. They then found themselves in a situation of deprivation of liberty, with no possibility of obtaining authorization to go out of the camp without being accompanied by the security forces. They could not receive visits either from relatives or legal counsels. The source reports that one lawyer, Hamid Jalil, was refused entry to the camp on 21 February 2012, when he was supposed to meet with one of the relocated persons.

6.      According to the source, Camp Liberty is surrounded by a four-metre high concrete wall, and residents are not allowed to go out. Armed Iraqi police agents guard checkpoints inside the camp. A police headquarters is located adjacent to Section One where residents are housed, and police stations are located at the north and south gates and at the northeast

end of camp. Police patrols regularly enter the residents' resting area, just as prison guards would inspect the cells of inmates.

7. The source describes the conditions in Camp Liberty as inhumane and appalling. Rather than a relocation centre conforming to international standards, Camp Liberty is said to be an open-air detention centre. The health of persons held in Camp Liberty is at risk. The camp allegedly lacks the most basic infrastructure and sanitary conditions, electricity is only intermittent and running water supplies are insufficient. The residential area is surrounded by layers of sand bags and a concrete wall. Surveillance cameras and sound bugs are installed all around the camp. The private life of the residents is constantly under surveillance.

8. The source adds that residents are not allowed to leave the camp without military or police escort and that they are subjected to headcounts, heavy police presence and invasions of privacy, similar to conditions in a prison. The residents suffer from the lack of adequate living conditions; restrictions on transfer of assets and restrictions to freedom of movement. The source also reports that the Government is not allowing international monitors or visitors access to Camp Liberty.

9. The source recalls that persons held in Camp Liberty have "Protected Person" status under the Fourth Geneva Convention. They are asylum seekers and have not been charged with or found guilty of any offence. Indeed, they have all been living in Iraq for over 25 years.

10. Furthermore, the source expresses fear for the physical and psychological integrity of these persons, as they are facing unnecessary suffering and trauma, as well as being subjected to degrading and humiliating treatment. It recalls that Camp Ashraf, from where they were transferred, had twice been attacked by Iraqi military forces since the Iraqi Government took control of the camp from the United States military in 2009.

11. The source submits that the detention of the 10 above-mentioned persons is arbitrary and contrary to article 9 of the Universal Declaration of Human Rights, and articles 9, paragraph 1, and 10, paragraph 1, of the International Covenant on Civil and Political Rights to which the Republic of Iraq is a State party.

## Response from the Government

12. The Working Group transmitted the above allegations to the Government of Iraq, requesting it to provide detailed information about the current situation of Hossein Dadkhah, Farichehr Nekogegan, Zinat Pairawi, Mahrash Alimadadi, Hossein Farsy, Hassan Ashrafian, Hassan Sadeghi, Hossein Kaghazian, Reza Veisy and Mohammad Motiee, and to clarify the legal provisions justifying their continued detention. The Working Group regrets that it has not received a response from the Government.

## Discussion

13. In the absence of a response from the Government and further to its Methods of work, the Working Group can render an opinion on the basis of the information submitted to it by the source. The Government has not rebutted this information, although it had the opportunity to do so.

14. The Working Group is not unfamiliar with the situation of the residents of Camp Ashraf from which the above-mentioned persons were transferred to Camp Liberty, a

former military base of the United States of America in Baghdad. It had already issued opinion No.11/2010 (Iraq)[1] concerning the detention of Camp Ashraf residents.

15.    Residents of Camp Liberty have the status of "protected persons" under the Fourth Geneva Convention; they are asylum seekers and have neither been charged with or tried for any offence.

16.    The conditions in Camp Liberty are synonymous with those in a detention centre, as residents have no freedom of movement, nor interaction with the outside world, nor do they have freedom of movement and the semblance of a free life within the Camp. The situation of the residents of Camp Liberty is tantamount to that of detainees or prisoners.

17.    The Working Group considers that there is no legal justification for holding the above-mentioned persons and other individuals in Camp Liberty, and that such detention is not in conformity with the standards and principles of international human rights law, and more specifically violates article 9 of the Universal Declaration of Human Rights and articles 9 and 10 of the International Covenant on Civil and Political Rights.

### Disposition

18.    In the light of the preceding, the Working Group on Arbitrary Detention renders the following Opinion:

> The detention of Hossein Dadkhah, Farichehr Nekogegan, Zinat Pairawi, Mahrash Alimadadi, Hossein Farsy, Hassan Ashrafian, Hassan Sadeghi, Hossein Kaghazian, Reza Veisy and Mohammad Motiee is arbitrary, being in contravention of article 9 of the Universal Declaration of Human Rights and articles 9, paragraph 1, and 10, paragraph 1, of the International Covenant on Civil and Political Rights, and falling under category IV of the categories applicable to cases submitted for consideration to the Working Group.

19.    Consequent upon the opinion rendered, the Working Group requests the Government to take the necessary steps to remedy the situation of these 10 persons and bring it into conformity with the standards and principles set forth in the Universal Declaration of Human Rights and the International Covenant on Civil and Political Rights.

20.    Taking into account all the circumstances of the case, the Working Group considers that adequate remedy would be immediate release and lifting of all restraints on the free movement of these persons as well as an enforceable right to compensation, in accordance with article 9, paragraph 5, of the International Covenant on Civil and Political Rights.

*[Adopted on 4 May 2012]*

---

[1]    Adopted on 7 May 2010 and concerning Jalil Gholamzadeh Golmarzi Hossein and 36 other persons.

United Nations

**General Assembly**

A/HRC/WGAD/2012/32

Distr.: General
2012
Original: English

ADVANCE UNEDITED
VERSION

Human Rights Council
Working Group on Arbitrary Detention

## Opinions adopted by the Working Group on Arbitrary Detention at its sixty-fourth session, 27–31 August 2012

## No. 32/2012 (Iraq)

### Communication addressed to the Government on 25 June 2012

Concerning Mehdi Abedi, Akram Abedini, Bahman Abedy, Aliasghar Babakan, Mohammad Reza Bagherzadeh, Sahar Bayat, Fatemeh Effati, Farhad Eshraghi, Maryam Eslami, Manijeh Farmany (residents of Camp Ashraf); and Asghar Abzari, Ali Reza Arab Najafi, Homaun Dayhim, Fatemeh Faghihi, Zahra Faiazi, Ahmad Fakhr-Attar, Effat Fattahi Massom, Jafar Ghanbari, Habib Ghorab, Robabeh Haghguo (residents of Camp Liberty)

The Government has not replied to the communication within the delay of sixty days.

The State is a party to the International Covenant on Civil and Political Rights.

1.    The Working Group on Arbitrary Detention was established in resolution 1991/42 of the former Commission on Human Rights, which extended and clarified the Working Group's mandate in its resolution 1997/50. The Human Rights Council assumed that mandate in its decision 2006/102 and extended it for a three-year period in its resolution 15/18 of 30 September 2010. In accordance with its working methods, the Working Group transmitted the above-mentioned communication to the Government.

2.    The Working Group regards deprivation of liberty as arbitrary in the following cases:

(a)    When it is clearly impossible to invoke any legal basis justifying the deprivation of liberty (as when a person is kept in detention after the completion of his or her sentence or despite an amnesty law applicable to the detainee) (Category I);

(b)    When the deprivation of liberty results from the exercise of the rights or freedoms guaranteed by articles 7, 13, 14, 18, 19, 20 and 21 of the Universal Declaration of Human Rights and, insofar as States parties are concerned, by articles 12, 18, 19, 21, 22, 25, 26 and 27 of the International Covenant on Civil and Political Rights (Category II);

(c)    When the total or partial non-observance of the international norms relating to the right to a fair trial, established in the Universal Declaration of Human Rights and in the relevant international instruments accepted by the States concerned, is of such gravity as to give the deprivation of liberty an arbitrary character (Category III);

(d)     When asylum-seekers, immigrants or refugees are subjected to prolonged administrative custody without the possibility of administrative or judicial review or remedy (Category IV);

(e)     When the deprivation of liberty constitutes a violation of international law for reasons of discrimination based on birth; national, ethnic or social origin; language; religion; economic condition; political or other opinion; gender; sexual orientation; or disability or other status, and which aims towards or can result in ignoring the equality of human rights (Category V).

## Submissions

### Communication from the source

3.      According to the source, for over a quarter century, the Iranian group known as the People's Mojahedin Organization of Iran (PMOI), also known as the Mujahedin-e Khalq (MEK), has legally lived in Iraq in accordance with Iraq's laws at Camp Ashraf. In 2003, as part of Operation Iraqi Freedom, Coalition Forces took control of Camp Ashraf and subsequently designated all the members of the PMOI as protected persons under the Fourth Geneva Convention. On 1 January 2009, control of camp Ashraf was transferred to the Iraqi Government as part of the U.S.-Iraq Status of Forces Agreement. From this point onwards, the safety and well-being the residents at camp Ashraf deteriorated.

4.      It was alleged that once in control of the camp, the Government began to block the free flow of food, maintenance and medical supplies, and denied the camp residents' freedom of movement in and out of Camp Ashraf, and access to their lawyers. In 2009 and 2011, Iraqi security forces carried out two unprovoked attacks on Camp Ashraf, resulting in dozens of deaths and injuries among the camp residents. The Government then declared its intention to close Camp Ashraf by the end of 2011, threatening to *refouler* the camp residents to the Islamic Republic of Iran.

5.      This series of events resulted in the UN High Commissioner for Refugees (UNHCR) declaring the camp residents to be asylum-seekers on 13 September 2011, having committed to working with the Government of Iraq to extend Iraq's deadline for camp Ashraf's closure. On 25 December 2011, the United Nations and the Iraqi Government signed a Memorandum of Understanding that provided for the voluntary and safe transfer of camp Ashraf residents to camp Liberty, at which point their identities would be confirmed, their refugee status would be determined, and then they could voluntarily resettle in third countries. As part of this process, the Memorandum of Understanding states that the Iraqi Government will ensure camp Liberty meets humanitarian and human rights standards, has proper infrastructure and accommodation facilities, and allows for camp residents to work with outside vendors for the provision of life support and utilities.

6.      On 18 February 2012, the first group of camp residents was transferred from Camp Ashraf to Camp Liberty. The residents immediately discovered that the conditions at Camp Liberty fell short of what they expected and what is required under the Memorandum of Understanding and international law. The residents lacked prompt access to medical treatment; adequate housing space, water, sanitation, electricity, and cooling mechanisms; proper facilities for the disabled; the opportunity to receive visits from family, friends, and supporters; and the means to communicate regularly and freely with the outside world. In addition, they soon learned that they would be prohibited from leaving Camp Liberty, in alleged violation of their rights as asylum-seekers. The source states that while the residents of Camp Ashraf were also detained illegally since 2009, they were at least in a safe

2                                                                                                      GE.12

environment with proper infrastructure, which they had built in the course of more than a quarter century of living there. On Camp Liberty, the first group learned that they had been moved to a small prison under harsh conditions.

7.    Moreover, the camp residents found their due process rights being violated because their detention has never been authorized by law; their lawyers are prohibited from entering Camp Liberty and thus are unable to communicate and consult with camp residents; there is no grievance mechanism or complaints procedure to address their conditions; and the residents are unable to challenge their detention in a court of law.

8.    As of 27 May 2012, approximately 781 of the almost 2,000 residents of camp Liberty have completed the verification process of re-establishing their identity. Thus far, only 361 of the residents of Camp Liberty have been interviewed by UNHCR. Since arrival at Camp Liberty on 18 February 2012, not a single individual has left for third countries.

9.    On 13 September 2011, after receiving applications from all Ashraf residents for asylum, UNHCR declared the residents to be "asylum seekers under international law" which entitled them "to benefit from basic protection of their security and well-being." Furthermore, UNHCR stated, "[it] . . . would work together with the Government of Iraq and the United Nations Assistance Mission in Iraq (UNAMI) and other concerned actors to identify a location [for asylum processing] that ensures the safety and respects the rights of all individual applicants." As part of this, UNHCR also committed to "putting in place a process to consider these requests on an individual basis in a fair and efficient procedure."

10.    On 21 December 2011, Iraq agreed to extend its deadline for the Camp Ashraf closure to April 2012. On 25 December 2011, the United Nations and the Government of Iraq signed a Memorandum of Understanding (MOU) aimed at securing a humanitarian and peaceful resolution for the residents of Camp Ashraf. The residents of Camp Ashraf were initially consulted as part of this process but an agreement was signed without them having been given the opportunity to review or approve the final text. In short, the MOU allowed for the safe transfer of Camp Ashraf residents to Camp Liberty, at which point their refugee status would be determined before they voluntarily resettle in either the Islamic Republic of Iran or other third countries.

11.    As of 1 June 2012, approximately 1,949 residents have been transferred from camp Ashraf to camp Liberty, 611 of whom are women and nine minors under the age of 18. However, the conditions in the camp have not met the expectations of Ashraf residents, the requirements set out in the MOU, or relevant provisions of international law. Camp Liberty is 658,000 square meters [or 254 square miles/7,082,653 square feet] in size, which is significantly smaller than camp Ashraf. Residents are living in housing units that contain six people per unit. Each unit is approximately 12x3.60 square meters [or 465 square feet.]. Each person has 7.2 square meters [or 77.5 sq. ft.].

12.    Prior to moving between the camps, Camp Ashraf residents demanded a commitment that no Iraqi police would remain inside Camp Liberty given the prior attacks on Camp Ashraf by Iraqi security forces. The residents report, however, that there exist several police posts inside the camp, with a 24-hour presence by 150 police guards armed with heavy machine guns. The residents also report that Camp Liberty is significantly smaller than they were told it would be. Men and women are living in separate living quarters. However, the Iraqi forces have encroached 70 meters into the female section of Camp Liberty and settled there. This has caused tension and is a source of harassment for the women in the camp. The female residents of the camp have repeatedly, both written and verbally, protested against this situation to UNAMI.

13.    Additionally, camp residents have reported circumstances that directly violate conditions set out in the MOU. They report major inadequacies in camp conditions including problems with drinking water, electricity, and a proper sewage system, and that

they are being denied free movement and access to medical services. As such, residents report that Camp Liberty is a prison rather than a temporary transit location. The provision of water and electricity are of particular concern. Because Camp Liberty is not connected to a central water source, the residents must procure their water with outside tanker trucks and from a broken internal water system.

14. The private companies bringing in water to the camp, however, are faced with numerous impediments by the Iraqi security forces and are frequently prohibited from entering. Moreover, due to obstructions by the Iraqi Government, the residents of Liberty have been unable to transfer their lift trucks and mechanical material needed to carry out repairs and unload supplies for daily living. The residents must purchase their food from outside contractors who face challenges getting the food inside Camp Liberty. In some cases, it is reported that the Iraqis prohibit the food from being delivered, in other cases the Iraqi police threaten the drivers of the contractors, or the food is held outside for days and is no longer suitable for consumption.

15. Reliable and accessible electricity is also in short supply. Generators deliver all the power, as Camp Liberty is not connected to Baghdad's power grid. This supply problem is exacerbated by high fuel needs and costs.

16. Access to medical care, while available, is not prompt. There is a medical centre in Camp Liberty's vicinity, but those with serious medical problems must be taken to an outside hospital. However, there are delays of hours, and in some cases days, to transfer those seriously ill to a hospital.

17. Moreover, residents are prohibited from leaving the camp, thus denying them freedom of movement.

18. In the source's view, in addition to these challenging conditions, there are serious due process violations. The Government has prohibited all lawyers from accessing the camp; the Iraqi lawyers representing the residents who have gone to the camp entrance were threatened and turned away.

19. According to the source, the deprivation of the camp residents' freedom falls within Category IV of the Working Group's classification of cases because they are asylum-seekers subjected to prolonged detention without the possibility of administrative or judicial review or remedy. Specifically, the detention of the residents results from the deprivation of freedoms under the International Covenant on Civil and Political Rights (ICCPR), the UN Body of Principles Regarding Persons under Any Form of Detention or Imprisonment (Body of Principles), and the UN Standard Minimum Rules for the Treatment of Prisoners (Minimum Rules of Treatment). In addition, the deprivation of freedom arises under violations of international refugee law including UNHCR Revised Guidelines on Applicable Criteria and Standards relating to the Detention of Asylum-Seekers and the UN Working Group on Arbitrary Detention's Deliberation No. 5 Regarding the Situation of Immigrants and Asylum Seekers.

20. The source adds that this is a straightforward situation in which the camp residents are asylum-seekers that are being held arbitrarily in violation of their due process rights and the conditions under which they are being detained are in breach of minimum standards recognized under international law.

21. The source requests the Working Group to extend its prior Opinion regarding the detention of ten residents of Camp Liberty to all the residents of Camp Liberty and Camp Ashraf, *in toto*, as their situation is either identical to or fundamentally the same as that addressed in Opinion No. 16/2012. In that Opinion, the Working Group found the detention of ten camp residents to be in contravention of Iraq's obligations under Articles 9(1) and

10(1) of the ICCPR and Article 9 of the UDHR, falling under Category IV of the Working Group's Methods of Work.

22.    The source adds that, as asylum-seekers, the camp residents must be afforded protection under ICCPR Article 9(1). However, for the following reasons they are being detained arbitrarily in violation of Article 9(1):

First, their detention has not been authorized by domestic law. At no time has the Government issued legal documents authorizing the detention. Even if it had, such detention would be inconsistent with international law because, as discussed below, this would engender other human rights violations and thus would be in contravention of Article 9.

Second, the detention is both unreasonable and unnecessary. The camp residents pose no flight risk and have committed no crime. As demonstrated by their over quarter century stay in Iraq, the camp residents are perfectly able and willing to live in Iraq in conditions similar to those found previously at Camp Ashraf before the Coalition Forces' invasion of Iraq while their asylum claims are processed. Moreover, there is no indication that the Iraqi Government has considered a less invasive means of detention.

Third, there has been no judicial or periodic review of the detention. Even if Iraq had given legal justification for the initial detention, such authorization would now be immaterial because for 42 months there has been no periodic judicial review of the camp residents' detention.

Finally, Camp Liberty contains no grievance procedure or complaint mechanism, making it impossible for the residents to challenge their detention. As such, the camp residents are being detained arbitrarily.

23.    The first camp residents legally entered Iraq 26 years ago and have since lived in the country in compliance with its laws. On 13 September 2011, UNHCR declared all camp residents to be asylum-seekers. For these two reasons, the camp residents are considered to be "lawfully within the territory" of Iraq and thus afforded additional protection under Article 12(1). Moreover, the Government of Iraq has had full control of camp residents since re-acquiring control of Camp Ashraf from the United States on 1 January 2009. The Government of Iraq has never provided any justification as to why such a process could only take place in the context of the camp residents' ongoing detention. Because the residents are prohibited from leaving Camp Liberty, the source submits that their right to freedom of movement under Article 12(1) is being violated.

24.    According to the source, the conditions in both camps are in breach of the Body of Principles and Minimum Rules of Treatment due process protections. Additional violations exist under Principles 17(1), 18(1), and 18(2) because the camp residents' counsel are prohibited from entering Camp Liberty, thus denying the residents the possibility to communicate and consult with their counsel. The camp residents are also unable to challenge their detention in a court of law, in violation of Principles 11 and 32.

25.    The deprivation of the camp residents' freedom further violates the guarantees under Deliberation No. 5 of the Working Group. Where the Working Group determines whether the custody of an asylum-seeker is arbitrary, there is also an assessment of whether certain due process guarantees contained in Deliberation No. 5 have been met. Asylum-seekers in custody should be brought before a judicial authority.

26. In the source's view, residents are not permitted to leave Camps Ashraf or Liberty, which constitutes detention. Established alternatives have not been considered by the Iraqi Government.

27. The source concludes that these persons are being held in detention arbitrarily. They are being denied freedom of movement in violation of the International Covenant on Civil and Political Rights (ICCPR). Their detention conditions violate the ICCPR and the Body of Principles and Minimum Rules of Treatment.

### *Response from the Government*

28. The Working Group regrets that the Government has not responded to the allegations transmitted by the Group within the sixty days in accordance with paragraph 15 of the Working Group's Methods of Work.

29. Despite the absence of any information from the Government, the Working Group considers it is in the position to render its Opinion on the detention of the 20 persons, subject to this case, in conformity with paragraph 16 of its Methods of Work.

### Discussion

30. In its previous Opinion, concerning Camp Liberty (Opinion No. 16/2012 (Iraq), para. 31), the Working Group found that conditions in Camp Liberty "are synonymous with that of a detention centre as there is no possibility of freedom of movement and interaction with the outside world. There is no free movement and life within the camp as well rendering residents as detainees or prisoners." The Working Group also considered that "there is no legal justification for holding the (...) individuals in Camp Liberty and such detention lies beyond the pale of domestic and international human rights law (articles 9 of the Universal Declaration of Human Rights (UDHR) and 9 and 10 of the International Covenant on Civil and Political Rights (ICCPR) (*ibid.*, para. 32).

31. The Working Group reaffirms this rationale and considers that the same applies to the residents of Camp Ashraf. The Government chose not to rebut the fact that the 20 residents of the two camps, on whose behalf the communication was submitted, are prohibited from leaving the camp and the opportunity to receive visits from family, friends, and supporters; and the means to communicate regularly and freely with the outside world is restricted. Indeed, the residents of both Camp Liberty and Camp Ashraf are effectively deprived their liberty without any legal justification.

32. The residents of camps who have submitted requests for refugee status are formally asylum-seekers under international law (see, for instance, UN High Commissioner for Refugees, UNHCR calls for cooperation and solidarity amid efforts to find solutions for the residents of camp "New Iraq", 26 July 2012).

33. The Working Group recalls that in its resolution 1997/50, the Commission on Human Rights requested the Working Group to devote all necessary attention to reports concerning the situation of asylum-seekers allegedly being held in prolonged administrative custody without the possibility of administrative or judicial remedy.

34. The Working Group reiterates that in order to determine the arbitrary character or otherwise of the custody of an asylum seeker, it considers whether or not the person is able to enjoy, *inter alia*, the following guarantees: (a) to be entitled to have the decision involving administrative custody reviewed by a higher court or an equivalent competent, independent and impartial body; (b) to have possibility of communicating by an effective medium such as the telephone, fax or electronic mail, from the place of custody, in particular with a lawyer and relatives; (c) to be assisted by counsel both through visits in the place of custody and at any hearing; (d) to have possibility to benefit from alternatives

to administrative custody (Report of the Working Group on Arbitrary Detention, E/CN.4/1999/63, Situation regarding immigrants and asylum seekers, 18 December 1998, para. 69).

35. In the case under consideration, none of aforementioned guarantees are met by the authorities, which leads the Working Group to conclude that the custody of these individuals is arbitrary in violation of articles 9 of the Universal Declaration of Human Rights and 9 and 10 of the International Covenant on Civil and Political Rights.

Disposition

36. In light of the foregoing, the Working Group on Arbitrary Detention renders the following opinion:

The detention of Mehdi Abedi, Akram Abedini, Bahman Abedy, Aliasghar Babakan, Mohammad Reza Bagherzadeh, Sahar Bayat, Fatemeh Effati, Farhad Eshraghi, Maryam Eslami, Manijeh Farmany (residents of Camp Ashraf); and Asghar Abzari, Ali Reza Arab Najafi, Homaun Dayhim, Fatemeh Faghihi, Zahra Faiazi, Ahmad Fakhr-Attar, Effat Fattahi Massom, Jafar Ghanbari, Habib Ghorab, Robabeh Haghguo (residents of Camp Liberty) is arbitrary, being in contravention of article 9 of the Universal Declaration of Human Rights and articles 9 (1) and 10 (1) of the International Covenant on Civil and Political Rights, falling under category IV of the categories of the Working Group's Methods of Work.

37. As a result of the Opinion rendered, the Working Group requests the Government to take all necessary steps to remedy the situation of these 20 persons and bring it in conformity with the standards and principles set forth in the UDHR and ICCPR.

38. The Working Group considers that taking into account all the circumstances of the case, an adequate remedy would be the immediate release and lifting of all restraints upon the free movement of these persons and providing them with the enforceable right to compensation in accordance with article 9(5) of the ICCPR.

39. The Working Group urges the Government to consider alternatives to the detention of the asylum seekers in Camps Ashraf and Liberty.

40. In accordance with Article 33(a) of its Methods of Work, the Working Group considers it appropriate to refer the allegations concerning conditions in Camps Ashraf and Liberty to the relevant human rights mechanisms for appropriate action.

[*Adopted on 30 August 2012*]

**Fox Rothschild** LLP
ATTORNEYS AT LAW

1030 15ᵗʰ Street, N.W. Suite 380 Washington, DC 20005
Tel 202.461.3100 Fax 202.461.3102 www.foxrothschild.com

## REPORT ON VISIT TO IRAQ

1-4 January 2013

Robert G. Torricelli
Steven M. Schneebaum

1.      The two of us visited Iraq from 1 through 4 January 2013. As planned, the agenda for the trip
was to include the following elements: identifying, interviewing, and retaining Iraqi counsel to
advise on Iraqi law issues; liaison with senior staff of UNAMI; meeting with Iraqi Government
officials to discuss resolution of outstanding issues, most notably including the demand for
compensation for **all** property (moveable and immoveable) of the MEK left behind at Camp Ashraf;
and visits to the residents of Camps Liberty and Ashraf.

2.      The trip turned out rather differently from what had been expected. No Iraqi Government
agent would meet with us, and we were denied permission to visit Camp Ashraf or Camp Liberty.
Our meeting with the people of Camp Liberty was conducted off-site, and attendance was limited to
seven designated representatives of the residents.

3.      Still, it was and remains our conclusion that it was the right decision to proceed with the trip,
even if we had to travel over New Year's Eve, to demonstrate our and the residents' desire to reach a
fair solution.

### I. Interactions with UNAMI

4.      The Special Representative of the Secretary General, Martin Kobler, was on home leave
during our visit. We were attended to by his deputy, Ambassador Gyorgy Busztin, and two staff
officers, Mohammad Al-Najjar and Marija Ignjatovic.

5.      On a personal level, we were deeply impressed by the competence and professionalism of the
UNAMI personnel, including the security officials responsible for keeping us safe.

6.      UNAMI has concluded that the future development of Iraq is dependent upon the survival of
the current government of Nouri Al-Maliki. Shoring up Maliki, and protecting him from any
potentially avoidable disruption, seem to UNAMI to be the only alternative to watching Iraq descend
into civil war along ethnic (Arab/Kurd) and sectarian (Sunni/Shiite) lines. Sadly, this pessimistic
prediction of the future of the country may well be accurate. Contrary to UNAMI's analysis, many
observers consider Maliki to be the problem, not the solution.

1

7. In our view, much of the attitude of UNAMI toward the MEK file can be explained in light of this premise. We were explicitly told, for example, that the Maliki Government would literally not survive a decision to pay the MEK for its immovable property. In our view that is a preposterous leap of logic, but it is highly instructive that it reflects the position of UNAMI at the highest levels: the outcome of the MEK negotiations controls the survival, or not, of what UNAMI sees as the last bulwark against chaos.

8. We spent many hours with the UNAMI team. Their constant refrain was to ask us to understand the positions of the Iraqi Government. They would not join in any kind of reciprocal request for understanding of the MEK's situation. There was some criticism of the most outlandish and gratuitous insults directed at the MEK, or for that matter at us (*e.g.*, the ridiculous limitation on the number of Camp Liberty residents we were allowed to meet), but they were apparently not communicated to the Government.

9. We did, of course, make our positions very clear. With respect to the property issue, we said that this was a straightforward case of expropriation, which international law permits only if it is accompanied by fair, effective, and prompt compensation.

10. We are concerned – and we said this to Amb. Busztin many times – that the focus of the Iraqi Government on our nomination of local counsel suggests that what the Government intends is simply to task our Iraqi lawyers with performing an inventory of moveable property, and then selling it (probably under severe constraints). The Government's concept is that the 100 residents will depart Camp Ashraf after assembling the moveable property and preparing it for gradual sale, leaving for later (or for never) the disposition of immoveable assets. This is the essence of the "six-point plan" that seems to have been agreed by UNAMI and the Government (but not by the MEK). We reiterated constantly that the "six-point plan" cannot and will not be the basis for moving forward, as it would deny the residents their basic rights.

11. Over a number of separate conversations, UNAMI helpfully presented to us the outline of the Government's legal arguments, which struck us as hastily put together, likely with little input from actual lawyers. We do not consider any of them to constitute a serious obstacle to our success as a matter of law. The arguments include: (a) there is no general obligation of compensation under Iraqi law[1]; (b) the MEK does not have standing as an entity in Iraq[2]; (b) the improvements made by the MEK at Ashraf were built with funds supplied by Saddam Hussein, which were stolen from the Iraqi people[3]; (c) any value added by the MEK at Ashraf is more than offset by the rental value of the real estate (which the MEK never paid and was never asked to pay)[4]; (d) the improvements were made

---

[1] Iraqi law most certainly does recognizes the need for compensation in cases of expropriation. The residents are entirely willing to put this question to an international arbitration in order to settle the dispute.

[2] We have been shown numerous precedents of Iraqi courts recognizing the status of the MEK as an entity with its own legal personality.

[3] No evidence in support of this allegation has ever been produced, in the nine years since the previous Government was toppled. In any event, this is purely political and not a legal claim, which is inconsistent with such principles as the law of state succession. Moreover, as a matter of fact, some 50% of the improvements at Ashraf were created since 2003, after the fall of the Hussein regime and while Diyala Province was under the jurisdiction of the United States.

[4] There was never an express or implied undertaking to pay rent.

without permission and are therefore illegal[5]; and (e) the claimed value of the property is grossly inflated.

12.     In addition, we were given the following suggestions regarding political considerations that the Government will need to take into account: (f) there is severe resentment against the MEK at all levels of the Iraqi Government, because of various misdeeds its members are alleged to have committed since 1986; (g) it would be impossible for Maliki to use Government funds to pay the MEK when there are so many more pressing demands on those funds; (h) under no circumstances can the Government make any kind of direct payment to what it considers to be a terrorist organization; and (i) the real agenda of the MEK is not to leave Iraq, but rather to stay indefinitely, and the Government is unalterably opposed to that. These arguments too can readily be deflected, rebutted, or where appropriate accommodated.

13.     We fully understand that the Iraqi Government will erect all kinds of barriers to a legally correct and fair outcome. We are concerned that UNAMI must not act in a way to legitimize or to support baseless arguments. Rather, we expect UNAMI to take an impartial position, consistent with international law principles that have long been part of the United Nations system. If international and domestic law requires that the residents should be compensated for their property, saying so should be entirely consistent with UNAMI's mandate.

## II. The Meetings with the Iraqi Lawyers

14.     We met twice with the team of three Iraqi lawyers who are prepared to undertake the assignment of advising us in property negotiations with the Government. For purposes of this Memorandum, we will not identify them further, except to note that one is Sunni, one Shiite, and the other a Kurd. All three are experienced and competent. We were quite impressed with their knowledge, their courage, and their conviction.

15.     Starting from the premise that the residents are entitled to be paid for the value of all of their property at Ashraf, whether moveable or not, the lawyers explained to us that Iraqi law provides a two-stage process for addressing claims of expropriation. The first step is a non-adversarial procedure for determining the value of the property at issue. This is typically handled by local trial courts, and results are not generally appealable. In a normal case, this stage may not involve any controversy at all, beyond whatever disagreement there might be of how the market would value the assets that the owner claims were taken from him. Only the second stage, in which the question of entitlement to compensation is before the court, is confrontational. In this case, political factors and possible pressure from the Government must also be taken into consideration.

16.     The Iraqi lawyers, although willing to undertake this representation and committed to the principle of providing the best possible legal services to their clients, are concerned about the possible impact of this work on their practices. They recognize that they are likely to come under extreme pressure from the Government to capitulate on the immoveable property, and to agree to withdraw the 100 people from Ashraf. They are also painfully aware of the lack of confidence in the

---

[5] The former Government of Iraq had recognized the rights of the MEK to build at Ashraf, and was aware of the extensive construction, never raising any objection. Moreover, as was said earlier, at least half of the development was done under U.S. oversight.

independence of the judiciary in Iraq, which has been widely reported in the media and has been discussed in Parliament.

17.    To reduce the likelihood of this unacceptable outcome, we designed a retainer agreement in which the Iraqi lawyers are granted no authority to enter into negotiations, much less agreements, that would bind the MEK or its members, without our express written approval. In other words, the retainer agreement makes us, not the MEK, the lawyers' clients: the lawyers are consultants to us in the context of seeking a comprehensive solution to the property dispute.

18.    The lawyers were appreciative of our efforts in this regard, and realized that our solution protects them as well as the MEK and its members. They agreed to sign the retainer agreement, which is to be sent to them from the U.S. on our return. Financial arrangements will be made directly with the residents.

### III. Legal Proceedings Outside Iraq

19.    It does not follow, however, that we are without other legal strategies and tactics to deploy. The fact that the Iraqi Government's intentions are so clearly illegal in international law – as expropriation without compensation – gives rise to the possibility of identifying a forum in which its sovereign immunity can be overcome and the legality of the measures tested. In such circumstances, not only might the MEK (or its membership, or a subset of the membership with local ties) initiate a legal action against the Iraqi state, but it might be able to secure a judgment by way of execution on local property belonging to Iraq. Some legal systems provide the possibility of execution even before judgment under certain circumstances.

20.    We shall explore this option as a matter of high priority. One of us (SMS) will begin that work right away. The Iraqi lawyers agreed that the pressure represented by such an initiative might help domestically. And UNAMI obliquely hinted at the same view: that Maliki might be prepared to take certain actions that would otherwise be politically difficult if he could make the credible argument that they were legally compelled.

### IV. The Aborted Contacts with the Iraqi Government

21.    We had been told before leaving the United States that we would meet with high Iraqi officials, most likely Fayad or his deputy Baqoos, to discuss the property issue. When we arrived, we learned from UNAMI that Fayad would not meet with anyone representing the MEK except Iraqi lawyers, and that Baqoos was out of the country. We consider this something of a betrayal, and of course the distinction drawn by Fayad makes no sense. Various thoughts occur to us on why Fayad will not meet with anyone not of Iraqi nationality. None of these explanations reflects credit on Fayad, his boss, or the Government. The insistence of the Government of Iraq to deal only with Iraqi lawyers is a matter of grave concern. We certainly hope that UNAMI and the United States will suggest that such condition is unacceptable, and should be dropped.

22.    The idea of our going to Iraq had been initiated by UNAMI to representatives of the residents outside Iraq. In several exchanges of correspondence before our trip the framework of the visit had

4

been agreed. There was absolutely no ambiguity: we were to meet GoI officials, and all of the MEK's property (including the immoveable property) would be discussed.

23.    Still, we take some comfort in knowing that it will be made clear to the Government that a final resolution of this matter will have to be agreed directly with representatives of the MEK: *i.e.*, us. Government representatives will be told that by the Iraqi lawyers, and by UNAMI and the U.S. Embassy.

## V. The Meeting with the Camp Liberty Representatives

24.    Although under absurdly constrained conditions – off-site, at a UNHCR facility, with participation limited to seven residents – we met with the people of Camp Liberty for a couple of hours. They were in remarkably good spirits, and were well-dressed, focused, and alert. They brought us gifts, including some extraordinary handicrafts made by residents of Liberty with scarce resources. And they provided a wonderful and ample Persian lunch (which they also offered to the U.N. staff). Nevertheless, the fact that we were not permitted to meet our clients in Liberty corroborates the view expressed by the UN Working Group on Arbitrary Detention that Camp Liberty is equivalent to a detention center.

25.    The substance of our discussions was exactly what would be expected. They recounted some of the indignities and violations occurring at Camp Liberty, while we explained to them the legal theories and the strategies that we intend to deploy in order to achieve a fair solution to the property issue. They reiterated their commitment to timely relocation of all of the residents, and expressed regret for the timing issues that had recently undone efforts to move a few residents to Finland. In addition, of course, everyone understands that the unsettled and even volatile political atmosphere in Iraq puts the residents at risk.

26.    In keeping with our position that communications with our clients are privileged, we will not summarize here the remainder of our conversation, including the questions and answers that took up a large part of our meeting. We did discuss the logistics for optimizing the expropriation case to present either in Iraq or elsewhere, including the need to marshal and to preserve the key evidence.

## VI. The Canceled Visit to Ashraf

27.    Right up until the last minute, we thought that the Iraqi Government would make it possible for us to visit Camp Ashraf, where one of us (RGT) has never been. No reason was given for the apparent change of position. Amb. Busztin did volunteer that he thought the trip would be dangerous. The residents were quite obviously disappointed, and prepared and sent to us a video showing the welcome that we missed. We considered the visit to Ashraf to be critical to our mission. There was no good reason to deny us, or the residents, that opportunity

## VII. The Conversation with the U.S. Ambassador

28.    We spent two hours with Steve Beecroft, the U.S. Ambassador to Baghdad. He was accompanied only by Melissa Sweeney, a political officer not well-versed in the file. Her superiors who are more current were both on holiday leave.

29.     The Ambassador began the meeting by presenting the point of view on the MEK file related to him by the Iraqi Government. When we tried to lay out the MEK position, we were told that we should not argue, that he is not an advocate for either side.

30.     He began to see that our posture was measured, and that we were really trying to find room for compromise. By the end of the meeting, he was willing to express some criticism of Iraqi intransigence. He did not offer to act as intermediary, nor did we ask him to play such a role. But he is clearly in regular contact with Fayad, and we are certain that our views will be relayed in a rather different tone after our meeting.

31.     Beecroft was strongly of the view that Kobler is not the villain in this drama, and suggested that, were he to leave, there is no guarantee that his replacement would not be far worse. He also argued that the Maliki Government has been taking a number of measures that put it at odds with the regime in Tehran. We spent quite awhile discussing the Ambassador's views and observations on the Middle East generally, and we both came away seeing him as thoughtful and astute. Beecroft's perceptions of the future of Iraq and also Iran are surely being channeled to Secretary Clinton and to President Obama. He believes that the Iranian regime is in extreme distress, with far-reaching consequences.

32.     One key point that the Ambassador made sure to repeat to us emphatically is the need for substantial progress in resettling the MEK members outside Iraq. He urged us to use our influence in Washington to overcome resistance to acceptance of a substantial number in the U.S. His view is that the resistance is not principled, but comes from mid-level bureaucrats in the Departments of Justice and Homeland Security. He felt that our visible involvement in promoting resettlement in the U.S. would serve two objectives: it would prime the pump for other countries to begin to agree to accept substantial numbers, and it would provide evidence for the Iraqi Government that, in fact, the MEK wants to leave Iraq as soon as proper arrangements can be made. In his view, Maliki simply does not believe that the MEK is committed to an orderly departure in real time. We assured the Ambassador that we and other friends of the MEK in Washington will do what we can on this issue. We both observed the irony here: just a few months ago the State Department was calling the MEK a terrorist organization, and now its principal representative in Iraq is proposing a strategy to prevail on his own Government to make room for several hundred MEK members to enter the United States.

## VIII. Conclusion

33.     There is obviously a great deal of work yet to do to bring the property issue to an acceptable resolution. The crux of the matter is to reach an agreement on compensation for the immoveable property. Given UNAMI's current position, it is vital for the United State to play its crucial role in order to resolve this problem.

34.     As far as we are concerned, the next steps seem clear enough. The Iraqi lawyers are in principle ready to introduce themselves to their Government, indicating our desire to move forward. However, it must be recognized that a final agreement will include compensation for all of the property of the MEK at Ashraf, including the immoveable property. There will be considerable pressure on them to consider the "six-point plan" to be the roadmap to follow, but the Government

will be told that the lawyers' principals will not accept that. The residents have made it clear that such a solution is not acceptable to them either.

35.   Since returning to the U.S., we have identified the Iraqi lawyers to Martin Kobler, and have asked him to inform us in writing that he has obtained Iraqi Government assurances of three things before we can move forward: (i) no retaliation or retribution for their activities; (ii) an understanding that negotiations are to be with us as principals and not with the lawyers; and (iii) acceptance that those negotiations, when they do occur, will be with respect to all property and not just the moveable assets. Before we move forward, we must have assurances on these points. Its willingness or unwillingness to agree will indicate whether the Government of Iraq really wants a solution.

36.   What we are asking now is minimal. Everyone is aware of Iraqi law that criminalizes cooperation with the MEK. Protestations that such law does not apply to lawyers are simply indefensible: we have documents showing that Iraqi Government officials have applied that very law to the MEK's legal counsel in the past. Those documents have been provided to Kobler.

37.   It is unfair to the Iraqi lawyers to ask them to argue to the Government for the terms of their own engagement. Yet to the extent that Fayad sees the lawyers' role as simply taking an inventory of cars and construction equipment, and then selling that material at a deep discount to some straw-man buyer, thus facilitating the voluntary withdrawal of the remaining MEK personnel at Ashraf, it is critical that he be disabused of the notion immediately.

38.   At the same time, we come back from this trip very concerned about the vulnerable position of the people still at Ashraf. We understand their resolve, and we deeply respect it. We believe that initiation of the legal strategy outlined here helps to protect them. But we will not be content until a solution is reached that respects the rights of the MEK members, who have invested 26 years of life and labor in Ashraf, and which will permit them to leave with their heads held high, to resettle in other places where they can work to achieve the objectives of their organization in peace and freedom.

**January 10, 2013**

United States House of Representatives
Committee on Foreign Affairs
Sub-committee on Oversight and Investigations
13 September 2012

# Conditions at Camp Liberty: U.S. and Iraqi failure

**Chairman Rohrabacher:**

...We are talking about conditions at Camp Liberty in Iraq and what the United Nations has been telling us about those conditions, whether the reports are accurate, and why the United Nations and the United States has been spinning the reports and downplaying Iraqi harassment of Camp Ashraf residents who are being moved to Camp Liberty.

Camp Ashraf has been the home for decades to the MEK, a group of Iranian exiles who are the enemy of the mullah's dictatorship in Tehran. Under pressure from and in sympathy with Iran the government of Prime Minister Maliki and Tehran ordered camp Ashraf closed by the end of last year. The objective and I agree with Mr. Boumedra...

So, here the objective and I agree with Mr. Boumedra on this, was to move the Iranian exiles not only out of camp Ashraf but out of Iraq itself and perhaps back to Iran where they would be imprisoned, tortured or killed.

So, I hope Mr. Boumedra will explain to us why processing of the MEK for relocation to other countries was not done in Camp Ashraf itself. The 3400 residents are being moved to the new site within Iraq called Camp Liberty. The new camp does not have the facilities of the old camp which had been built up for over several decades by residents; nor have the residents been allowed to bring all their possessions to the new camp. Just like other doomed souls on their way to the end, a humanitarian crisis was created where there never should have been one. Camp Ashraf was subjected to extreme harassment under the Maliki regime loudspeakers surrounded the camp bombarded the residents with death threats. The camp itself was attacked in 2009 and 2011 by Iraqi security forces. With 9 civilians killed in 2009 and 34 people, unarmed people, killed in 20011 and hundreds more wounded. An American military unit was ordered away from the camp only hours before that attack began. Someone in our government then must have known about the attack and that it was coming and ordered our troops out of the way thus violating an American pledge to protect the camp. I have never been able to find out who that was and who gave the orders not to even investigate the situation.

There are still those in the government who think we must get along with the Maliki regime despite Mr. Maliki's misdeeds and his grab for authoritarian power as well as his alignment with the mullah dictatorship in Iran. I am not among them. Maliki has proven that he cannot be trusted and must be dealt with accordingly. Perhaps that's why he kicked me out of his country last time I was there.

The most recently, the sixth convoy of residents being... as being moved from Camp Ashraf to Camp Liberty, over 20 of those people were beaten by Iraqi security forces who were also stealing personal possessions owned by those residents.

Many of those attacked had broken bones and required hospital care. The US state department put out a statement after this on august 27th that despite these beating, hailing that mission as the safe arrival of the sixth convoy of approximately 400 Camp Ashraf residents and no mention was made of the violence inflicted on the residents. Indeed, the State Department claimed the government of Iraq has made considerable efforts to achieve a peaceful resolution for residents of camp Ashraf.

The United Nations and the US, it appears, are misleading the public about what the heck is happening in Iraq. And it's time we get to the truth and that's why we are trying to have this briefing and hearing today and hopefully find out what the truth is and who is accountable for their actions.

Thank you very much. And now, Congresswoman Chu is not a member of this subcommittee but you are certainly welcome to offer the opening statement and join us in this briefing and hearing.

**Congresswoman Chu:**

Thank you so much Mr. chairman.

First I want to thank you Mr. Boumedra for being here today. It takes so much courage to quit your job, because of your belief that your employer is not doing what is right and it takes even more courage to come before us and before the rest of the world to talk publically about it.

I have to admit that I was shocked when I read your op-ed in the Hill last month. For months we've been hearing from both the UN and from US officials about the conditions at camp Liberty. We've heard them say that it was adequate. So to hear a different story from you, an outsider, who's been there and visited is very critical to our understanding about this extremely important issue and it makes me extremely disappointed in the conduct of the US officials who have been telling a very different story.

I am here today because I strongly believe that we must do all that we can to protect the people of Camp Ashraf from harm after two deadly attacks at camp Ashraf, I do not have faith that the violence is behind us. Reports of interference and misconduct at Camp Liberty only further shape my belief that we will find peaceful resolution to this problem. Like you, I am committed to ensuring the well being of residents at Camp Liberty. So thank you again for being here and I hope that by doing that we will have a better outcome in the months ahead.

**Chairman Rohrabacher:**

Thank you very much. It was good to have you with us today.

Do you have an opening statement? Now and for the opening of the actual hearing itself you are welcome to proceed.

**Congressman Ted Poe:**

Thank you Mr. chairman I will take the opportunity to speak twice, then, since you just gave it to me. Thank you for being here. Two issues are involved, I think, today. One is the treatment of people and how they are being treated and who is to blame for their mistreatment? The Maliki government? The United States? The UN? All of the above? None of the above, or a combination? The other issue is more far reaching: the designation of the MEK as a foreign terrorist organization. And I hope we are able to talk about both of those today.

The first one: I was with you Mr. Chairman last year when you and I both were evicted from Iraq. We were evicted from Iraq because we had the audacity, the nerve, to go and ask Mr. Maliki "we would like to see the people in Camp Ashraf," and he said "no way will you see those people".

So, of course, he had something to hide. He had the truth to hide about how these people, real people, were being treated by the Maliki government and the United States complicit, in my opinion. And he was so infuriated with your request that we go visit these people, that he just told us to leave his country, which we eventually did on our own.

Now those folks are being moved to Camp Liberty and we hear the same song and dance: all is well here in Iraq with the residents of camp Ashraf and Camp Liberty. That is just not true. Conditions at Camp Ashraf, as bad as they were, and the fact that people were murdered there, the camp issue and conditions at camp Liberty are worse.

You know, I was a judge for a long time. I sent people to prison who actually did bad things and while in prison, those individuals got to visit with their families, they got running water, they got to visit with their lawyers. Those things are not occurring in Camp Liberty and these people are not criminals. These people are not in a prison. They were supposed to be taken to this staging area so they can be removed from the country on their own. But they're not being treated even as we treat criminals. They're actually in my opinion in a concentration camp and being treated worse than they were in Camp Ashraf. That ought not to be.

Mr. Chairman I am asking you if you would, I am volunteering to go with you to Camp Liberty. I can request to go and see what it's like, let us in to see these people and make our own determination and tell the world about it. However we do that? I don't know, but you do know people, we can get in. I am making that request through you Mr. Chairman.

The other issue since there is no liberty in Camp Liberty is the designation of the MEK. Maliki told us the reason that he was treating the people at Camp Ashraf the way he was treating them, was because this country labels those folks as a foreign terrorist organization and he is treating them as armed terrorists. And that's why he is treating them so poorly. We have to address that issue and hope that the State Department will remove that designation which we will talk about later. Thank you for being here and thank you for spreading a little truth on the situation in Camp Liberty.

**Chairman Rohrabacher:**

Thank you very much your honor. If someone committed a crime against my family I want them tried in your court!

We do have with us for the briefing, and then we will proceed with our official hearing, Mr. Boumedra, ok I am going to get that right! He became chief of the United Nations UNAMI Human Rights Office in Iraq in January of 2009. His work was to monitor the human rights and humanitarian situation of Camp Ashraf. He was also an advisor to the the UN Secretary General Special Representative to Iraq. He resigned these posts earlier this year because of what he believes as being a UN failure to protect the human rights and humanitarian conditions of the Ashraf residents. The argument, he laid out in the issue of the Hill newspaper August 22nd and which he will elaborate today. He's graduated from the University of London in United Kingdom where he worked as the editor of the African Journal for International and Comparative Law. And deputy Secretary General of the African Society for International and Comparative Law. In 2004, he served as regional director for the Plenary Reform for International which is based in Oman, Jordan and from there, he moved to United Nations. I would like to echo my colleagues' praise for your moral stand and if you are willing to leave a position in order to maintain own personal standards of morality, and that speaks very well of you. We are here to hear, I know you have some things to tell us today, that will help us understand that situation in Camp Ashraf and you may proceed with your testimony.

**Tahar Boumedra:**

Thank you very much, Mr. Chairman.

Thank you very much, members of this sub-committee for giving me the honor and the opportunity to be here to share with you my experience of three years and half being in charge of Ashraf file at the United Nations Assistance Mission for Iraq.

First, Mr. Chairman, I would like to put on record, the fact that during these three years and half, I worked very closely with the young men and women, the American soldiers and officers who were in Camp Ashraf. And I would like to bring to your attention that there would be no opportunity where I would not commend their highly professional and humanitarian attitudes.

From 2003 to 2009, we do not have at UNAMI, the United Nations Mission in Iraq, any record of any complaint against any of their behavior in Camp Ashraf. I was close to them, I received all the support, and at very short notice, they were always there to accompany me, to help me, to protect me, they made available helicopters to me at very short notice and I am here to testify and rather commend that kind of humanitarian conduct they have shown during those years I worked with them.

Mr. Chairman, I would like first put the whole situation of Camp Ashraf in this context, it's legal context. First I have to say that from the time the Camp was handed over to the Iraqi authorities, and let me be clear, because when we say Iraqi authorities, we are generalizing. Because in fact this file is run by the office of the Prime Minister.

So the file was handed over in 2009, and from the first day the Prime Minister's office took over this file, we started receiving complaints. We started receiving complaints about serious violations of human rights, serious violation of humanitarian standards, and when we asked why you are not keeping the standards set by American forces, they will tell to me that these people do not deserve any human rights or humanitarian treatments, they are terrorists.

My mission, Mr. Chairman was to watch human rights and humanitarian situation of Camp Ashraf, and for me, everyone in Camp Ashraf is presumed innocent until they are duly condemned by court of law.

Unfortunately Mr. Chairman, the United Nations has dealt with this file in reversing the fundamental principal of presumption of innocence. We have dealt and I sat with, including myself, because I was the lead person on this file. We have dealt with bad faith and we have presumed guilt and we expect these people to prove their innocence. This is fundamentally against the main and the fundamental values of the United Nations.

Mr. Chairman, in 17 July of 2008, the Council of Ministers met and decided to close Camp Ashraf. This decision is the official policy of the Government of Iraq. So, I am not going to add to it or diminish it. This is what the Council of Ministers set as an official policy: first, to close down the Camp. Second, to revive arrest warrants against the members of the residents of Camp Ashraf. Third, to make it a criminal offence for anybody or any organization that deals with residents of Camp Ashraf. Any organization or individual is banned from visiting Camp Ashraf. And that explains everything when we, the United Nations reported that everybody is welcomed and the United Nations and the Government of Iraq are meeting their international obligations, at the time the Iraqi Government itself decided and reiterated every year, including in July 2011, reiterated this policy of treating them as terrorists, meeting with them is a criminal offence, nobody is allowed to visit them and all the treatments that followed, which I do not have time to go into details and I will answer your questions on any details you want to know. With this policy, the United Nations periodically issues reports that the Iraqi government is meeting its international human rights obligations. I will not make any comments and leave it to you to draw your own conclusions.

The way things are conducted, the Iraqi government themselves are saying we are not respecting the human rights of these people, and the UN is reporting that they are respecting. That speaks for itself.

So, Mr. Chairman, when we started talking about relocating from Camp Ashraf to Camp Liberty, it was the Chair of the so-called Ashraf Committee who met with UNAMI and the representatives of the High Commission of Refugees. And he did warn us very clearly, he said: United Nations can do whatever it wants, but we will not implement the human rights and humanitarian standards the United Nations is advocating for. So that is part of the Iraqi policy. It's not hidden, it's on the record. But again we at the United Nations, we reported that Iraqi government meets its international obligations.

I would like to move to the conduct of UNAMI, how we dealt with the situation since I was appointed in charge of this file in January 2009. I worked for three special representatives of the Secretary General of the United Nations.

Initially, we were working as mandated by the Security Council resolution 1770, which gives UNAMI the authority to monitor and report. So, the two SRSG's, two Special Representatives of the Secretary General I worked with, worked on this monitoring and reporting.

Then came the third Special Representative of Secretary General, last October. From the very first day, he turned UNAMI --- this is --- internally we used to say UNAMI has been turned into UNAMA, the UNAMA is United Nations Mission for closing camp Ashraf. So this sudden change of policy made UNAMI devout its assets and time and personnel, 95% of UNAMI was put towards helping the government of Iraq to close Camp Ashraf.

Serious money was spent on this operation. Serious taxpayers' money was spent on this operation to assist the Prime Minister's office implementing the policy I just stated, which was fundamentally against the principals of the United Nations. So, in a way, we have used taxpayers' money to defeat the fundamental values of the United Nations. I reminded my boss, special representative of the secretary general that what we are doing in unacceptable. I always received the reply "be positive". "Be positive" of course means "close your eyes", work with us. And I tried to be positive in doing my work as dictated by my conscious. But let me explain why UNAMI suddenly changed to such a machinery for violating its values and principles. If we look at Security Council Resolution, 1770, it declares the mandate of UNAMI which makes it an instrument in the hand of government of Iraq to do whatever it is suitable. Now anything done by UNAMI, it must be by the request – this is the language of the Security Council resolution – it has to be by the request of the Government of Iraq. I have to admit that while I was the Chief of the Human Rights Office, I tried to remove, because every year we change the mandate of the UNAMI , we draft the first draft of the resolution in order to Security Council to renew the mandate. I tried to remove this clause of "by the request of Government of Iraq", but I failed.

When we see that the government of Iraq will not tolerate anything that goes against its fundamental policies set on the resolution of the Council of Ministers and also there was an incident it is important to reflect on it. This incident was the elections. The Election where the Al-Iraqiya won 91 seats, Al-Maliki's State of the law coalition won 89.   The coalition of Maliki requested that they have to recount the ballots. The authorities who were overseeing the election, stood for UNAMI, stood for justice and declared that the election was fair and there was no need for the re-count. Al-Maliki never tolerated this and he said to them, representative of Secretary General that his mandate will not be renewed and this is how we ended up with a new representative of Secretary General who came and straight learned the lesson that in order to achieve anything in Iraq, you have to accept whatever  the prime Minister Maliki dictates and from the very first day, UNAMI became an instrument for closing Camp Ashraf and not only that, I do not have the time to duel on other issues that were totally abandoned and were fully part of the mandate of UNAMI. But somehow we became the instrument of the Prime Minister's office policy vis-a-vis Camp Ashraf.

**Chairman Rohrabacher:**

Perhaps you could summarize for the record.

**Tahar Boumedra:**

Very quickly, Mr. Chairman.

I would like to just to briefly tell you how we prepared this relocation! How we prepared this MoU!

I was the first person who drafted the draft of the MoU. And I can assure you Mr. Chairman that the signed document was not the one that we agreed on with the Iraqis. The signed MOU was simply a document that was agreed incommunicado, in camera  between the SRSG, Special Representative of the Secretary General and the Prime Minster himself.

So, there was a fundamental change in the content and the procedure of the MOU.

Camp Liberty -- I was the first person to go and visit Camp Liberty and I reported that Camp Liberty amounts, it looks, it is, a detention center. For UNAMI to reach there, we crossed 7 check points. It's highly fortified military zone with all the headquarters of the military branches of the Iraqi army based in the area. And then all the T-walls, this concrete walls of 3-4 meters to run the cameras and I always address my interlocutors, the Iraqi interlocutress, and tell them "Why do you need all this, these people are asking you we are leaving. We would like to leave Iraq." They are not asking to stay. They gave up their status in Iraq they want to leave. Why are you dealing with them this way? They tell me these people are terrorists, you are defending terrorists. So, thank God at the time I was enjoying certain immunity of the United Nations otherwise I would be subject of their regulations.

Now, my visit to camp liberty, I always said that this is in fact extremely unacceptable, particularly what we know. We talk about relocation, it's not relocation. It's an eviction. It's a forcible eviction. There is a difference between eviction and relocation. Relocation is consensual, it's in accord with an agreement but an eviction is a forcible eviction and the United Nations has standards and rules of conduct on how to implement a forcible eviction. Basic element is that people who are evicted should be compensated with similar standards or better in any circumstances, not less. But Camp Liberty, I was the first one to visit it. I reported that it's absolutely unacceptable. It's a prison-like.

But just not to waste your time, Mr. Chairman, I just want to read to you one paragraph of the working group of the United Nations Council of Human Rights in Geneva, who deals with this issue and their conclusion I read: The working group considers that there are no legal justification for holding the above mentioned persons and I mean Ashrafies, and other individuals in Camp Liberty and that such detention is not in conformity with standards and principals of international human rights law and more specifically, violates article 9 of the universal declaration of Human Rights and article 9 of term of convention of civilian and political rights. The situation, it adds, the situation of the residents of Camp Liberty is tantamount to that of detainees or prisoners. So, this is a document that it would be, you recall that this is united Nations group, they are specialist independent specialist appointed by the council of Human Rights this is their conclusion and I was on 30th of August before this working group testifying that their finding is absolutely correct and absolutely in line with my experience in UMAMI having visited and having worked in Ashraf and Camp Liberty for 3 years and a half. I thank you Mr. President and Mr. chairman and I am prepared to answer any further questions you would like to put to me.

### Chairman Rohrabacher:

Thank you very much we would have to be brief because we have a hearing afterwards. You said that under United Nations Special Representative, the United Nations basically have lost its independence, Mr Kobler lost its independence in Iraq, could you explain how United Nations is able to maintain an independence face of a regime which is obviously is now making more and more demands from Maliki government and do you consider now the United Nations not to be operating independently of that government or now which we would say the stooges of the government.

### Tahar Boumedra:

Yes Mr. Chairman. I do confirm here in front of you that UNAMI has no independence what so ever that is every issue dealt with regarding Ashraf is decided at the Prime Minister's office and sometimes at the Iranian embassy in Baghdad.

### Chairman Rohrabacher:

The Iranian Embassy in Baghdad! I think that it is an important point for us to underscore. Yes let me ask you this while you were operating there in Iraq was there to your knowledge any real effort to perhaps to make sure that the people of Camp Ashraf could go to Jordan or Qatar or Saudi Arabia, Turkey or even United States? Was there a, was this option pursued by the United Nations or by the United States or by Iraq itself?

**Tahar Boumedra:**

Mr. Chairman, it was within my authority to suggest of possible exits for these people and I did suggest after having discussed in length with my counterparts at US embassy. I discussed all kind of exits. Including an exit to Gambia in Africa, in west Africa, we considered Romania, we considered a number of exits but these were always dismissed by my Boss because the end of the relocation is not just a sort of let people disappear in the air. There is a process put in place which is rather cynical, dangerous and I would like you to do your own conclusions because there will be this process the what is refer to as the refugee status determination process (RSD). The refugee status determination process and I have the documents of the high commissioners for refugees. It will actually at the end of the process would be 2 categories of residents in Camp Liberty. One category will benefit eventually from the refugee status and will have some protection. Second category will be denied the refugee status, this second category will be effectively locked up in a detention centre called Camp Liberty and God knows what happens after that!

**Chairman Rohrabacher:**

Your honour

**Judge Ted Poe:**

What do you think is the motive of the United Nations to lie?

**Tahar Boumedra:**

It is very difficult for me to sort of read into the intensions of individuals but as a matter of policy New York wants to hear that everything is fine and everything is smooth and the Secretary General when he came to Baghdad during the Arab League summit in Baghdad he expressed satisfaction of how things are conducted and he said that he is very proud that the Special Representative is holding very friendly relations with the Prime Minister so here there are issues of the policy and also personal ambitions, personal attitudes and I have to testify that from the very first day SRSG Kobler arrive to Baghdad he touched me on the shoulder and said "Hi Mr. Ashraf" meaning I am going to deal with you very soon and in fact he dealt with me in a sense that he reached a point where he removed me from every mailing list of UNAMI as chief of in charge of the leader of team of Ashraf , I had no access to any information, any report , any document that it is circulated related to Ashraf not only that I was banned from visiting Camp Ashraf and Camp Liberty and it was at that stage I decided to resign because I don't deserve my salary any more I was just being kept in an office , very well paid but I did not deserve it so I decided to go.

**Judge Ted Poe:**

One last question. You have mentioned and I just want you to explain a little more behind the scenes of all of this mischief going on with Iraq Prime Minister, the treatment of the people in Camp Liberty and Camp Ashraf you got Iran, what do you think Iran's influence is on Maliki to treat the people in Camp Ashraf so poorly?

**Tahar Boumedra:**

I have to say that I will only talk about meetings that I personally attended. I personally attended about five meetings at the Iranian embassy in Baghdad. The Iranian embassy, when they receive us, they don't want to talk, they want results. In a sort of powerful manner, the minute we sit, they ask what have you done? Tell us about results. And we were in a defensive and apologetic position to say that, sorry, we are working on it, we will let you know.

The powerful man today in Baghdad is the National Security Advisor to Prime Minister Al-Maliki, Fallah Fayaz. He is the decision maker on this file. He does not want to discuss, he just orders and says he wants results. He wants dates, he says we have given the deadline of December and it has passed, we will not tolerate any more delays.

Here, we hear every day about these difficulties about water, access to medicine, access to lawyers and …. I seriously put these questions to my counterparts. You here very much about Colonel Haghi, Colonel Sadeq and I saw them everyday and worked with them. I asked them why are you doing this?

First, I must say that they are not the decision makers, they are executive officers. The main decision makers on this file are Fallah Fayaz and the Prime Minister Maliki. When I asked these executive officers, my counter parts on this file, they said we deal with them the way we want to deal with them and I reminded them that the Spanish Criminal Court has Sadeq on his list, and when I asked Sadeq why you want to be so notorious in your conduct? He said to me I will never travel, they won't get me. He never denied his crime and what he has done. He just told me, with the mentality of a villager, he will not travel and so, they won't be able to get him. These are the kind of people we deal on a daily basis. Sadeq is just the running manager of Camp Liberty. So, the policy is there, it is clear, has been put in place long time ago and is in violation with the fundamental values of the united nations, it is ordered by the office of the Prime Minister, executed by these two officers and we were there to simply to satisfy this person or that and also be reminded that we are Iraq's guests and have to behave. And if the Prime Minister gets upset, we have to pack and go.

**Chairman Rohrabacher:**

When I used to go to college, there was a movie by the name of Z, do you remember it? What you are describing is the real nature of the United Nations, supposedly supposed to protect human rights.

We have been joined by our ranking member, Mr. Carnahan. He, unfortunately, like too many us is running between so many events right now. Do you have anything you would like to ask?

**Congressman Carnahan:**

I just want to thank you for being here. I understand we have another part of hearing coming up, so, I am going to reserve my questions so we can move on again, apologize for going back and forth between two different hearing. I am glad to be here for part of it, thank you.

**Chairman Rohrabacher:**

Congresswoman Chu, do you have a question or two?

**Congresswoman Judy Chu:**

Yes, thank you. Mr. Boumedra, first I would like to ask questions about the condition of Camp Liberty.

You are one of the outsiders who were able to visit camp Liberty and you were there before the residents of Camp Ashraf were transferred there and described the terrible conditions of the mobile units and the prison-like security. Today, the residents are still concerned about the lack of access to water and electricity. The US official say it is Spartan, but livable. When you visited initially, were you able to determine whether there were basic humanitarian necessity such as water, electricity and shade. Have you been there since and have the conditions changed at all and do the existing conditions meet the humanitarian standards?

**Tahar Boumedra:**

Thank you. This is the question I have been waiting to answer.

Since December, where we began preparing the file, we went to take pictures, we had to select pictures that are sellable to the residents of Ashraf and to the international community. We had to make specific selection. We had to take pictures of corners and sceneries. With these pictures, we had to sit down, the whole UNAMI decision makers, and had to go through them one by one. The pictures that were appealing and sellable, we put aside, the pictures that were not suitable, were put at another side. Even when we were there, a delegation of about 8 people, everybody was instructed to take such pictures so when we go back to base, we compare. That is what we did. We compared pictures and only selected a number of pictures.

The camp in December of 2011 was totally vandalized. The Camp was handed over from the US military to Iraqis on December 3rd. At the end of December, when I was there, the Camp was totally vandalized. It was all looted.

I hear some reports here in Washington Post that they have flat TV on the wall. I can show you pictures that the flat TV space was empty because it was stolen. Now that the residents have brought some improvements to the Camp, they are putting it to the account of the Iraqi Government. The Government of Iraq does not spend a penny for the residents of Camp Liberty; it is their own work and their own hardship.

There has been certainly some improvements from December to today, but this is not because of the hospitality of the government of Iraq, it is their own achievements at a very high cost because they pay for everything above the market price.

They are isolated and have no access to outside, so the Iraqis are imposing on them certain merchants and there is a long story that I do not want to open it here, it will take a lot of time, but even these merchants are specially selected by the Prime Minister's office and then you hear about issues of properties. These merchants suddenly turn up and become decision makers of the future of the properties of the residents of Ashraf and Liberty. That is the situation, any improvements, if any, are not because of the government of Iraq or the United Nations, it is thanks to the hardship and entrepreneur spirits of these people.

**Chairman Rohrabacher:**

For the record this witness has testified that the purpose of the activity and rules and policies that were being laid down, when he worked there for the United Nations, the policies and the rules that were being laid down by the Iraqi government and by his United Nations' superiors was that they were trying to make life for the people of camp Ashraf unbearable. Correct? So these people were intentionally creating a suffering of certain of these people. That was the intentional outcome…

**Tahar Boumedra:**

That is my understanding Mr. Chairman.

**Chairman Rohrabacher:**

Your understanding and your vision of that was obtained through your personal actions or personal situations which put you right in the middle of …

**Tahar Boumedra:**

As a little person on Ashraf file, yes this is my understanding.

**Chairman Rohrabacher**:

So, we have government officials and let us know that at the same time there is no way out for this people, because our government has designated these folks as terrorists. So, our government has prevented them from leaving and the other government entities, the United Nations and Iraqis are intentionally creating suffering. Did you at any time ask representatives of the United States government for help, to help you in this situation?

**Tahar Boumedra:**

I was interacting with the officials of the prime minister's office on a daily basis.

**Chairman Rohrabacher:**

What about the United States government?

**Tahar Boumedra:**

The United States government within my official level is not within my job to sort of interact with them. It is the Special Representative of the Secretary General who briefs his counterparts at the …

**Chairman Rohrabacher:**

OK, to your knowledge, was the United States asked for help in preventing the suffering?

**Tahar Boumedra:**

The US embassy always declared that "we are behind UNAMI". "We support whatever UNAMI does".

**Chairman Rohrabacher:**

But you are now testifying that the policy was to create suffering.

**Tahar Boumedra:**

I do confirm that.

**Chairman Rohrabacher:**

So, the United States, the people who laid this down on the part of the United States, supported this policy, were they also aware that the actual policy was not to try and treat these people decently, but instead to create suffering among them?

**Tahar Boumedra:**

At my level, the only people that I dealt with closely are my counterparts of the US embassy and my counterparts of the USFI in camp Ashraf. And I commend their behavior, their conduct. I have nothing to complain about, but it is above my capacity to talk about who would relay this information.

**Chairman Rohrabacher:**

OK, but you did just testify that the US government was to back-up the UN's activities all the way and you are also testifying that the UN as well as the Maliki government, their actual goal was to create suffering among these people.

Someone who has never been there speculate so your observation that the suffering of these people was intentional and created by decisions made by the Maliki government and by the United Nations to go along with it and at the very least our government knew about this and did nothing to stop it. Correct?

**Tahar Boumedra:**

I have no doubt about that

**Chairman Rohrabacher:**

All right, thank you very much for your testimony today.

**Chairman Rohrabacher:**

We are now moving on formal hearing on the United States and Iraq failure in regard to Camp Ashraf and by extension, the strategic situation in Iraq and the region.

I say that behind the attack on Camp Ashraf is Iran through the Maliki government which has aligned it with the dictatorship in Tehran. Ashraf is just one example of this growing threat to American interest in the region and could be very symbolic of what we can expect on this region.

Consider Shiite militias and terrorist groups like Hezbollah that operate in Iraq and are funded by Iran, the Iranian elite squads "Qods" operate in Iraq without interference by Maliki government. President Barak Obama was not able to negotiate a new status of forces agreement with Prime Minister Al-Maliki that would have allowed a small American military presence in Iraq past the end of 2011. He then placed a limit on the size of U.S. embassy staff and CIA.

Maliki government was adamant in US forces leave the country thus removing a check on their actions. Iran was also adamant about United States withdrawal. A day after the last US troops left Iraq, Sunni Vice-President, Hashemi, a long time foe of the Shiite Prime Minister Maliki, was charged with terrorism.

Hashemi fled first to Kurdistan, a province in Iraq, then on to Turkey. On September 9, he was sentenced to death by hanging. Maliki was hailed once as an Iraqi nationalist, has obviously become a sectarian plotting against the Sunnis and the Kurds of his own country. He has provoked a new domestic unrest and violence. The Sunnis were persuaded to turn on to Al-Qaeda in Iraq because we promised they will get a fair share in a democratic country. That promise is fading and the door may open again for the Al- Qaeda to re-build.

An editorial Monday in the British Guardian newspaper raised questions of whether Maliki would become an outright dictator or not. It ended with the statement and I quote: "Maliki's quest for domination could drive his country back into civil war."

Iraq is a conduit of weapons and supplies to the Syrian dictatorship which is trying to crush an uprising of its Sunni majority. The Syrian regime is allied with Iran. I initially supported the invasion of Iraq; I personally did, to overthrow the dictatorship of Saddam Hussein. I thought that was what was the right thing for us, the United States, to do, to oppose dictatorships, and to help people struggling to create democratic societies. In retrospect, I consider this to have been one of the greatest errors I have ever made and certainly the greatest error made by the previous administration, the Bush administration.

We sent an army into Baghdad to get rid of a hostile government which we did. But then, while our troops were still there, what happened but a hostile government came into power. But this new hostile government is a hostile government aligned with the most dangerous regime in the region: Iran, which is a supporter of terrorism and has ambitions to develop nuclear weapons.

Americans need to think about this a long time to figure out what we should be doing in the future and what policies we have. But one thing is sure; we should always be on the side of people who are longing for freedom. And that's where Camp Ashraf comes in. The camp Ashraf story may start about human rights, but is ending up as part of a tragic, an epic tragedy, that ties into how or who lost Iraq. With us today to discuss this tale is Lincoln Bloomfield Jr. We invited Ambassador Daniel Fried to testify on behalf of the State Department but Ambassador Fried is in charge of Camp Ashraf and that issue, but he is out of the country and State Department said that he was the only one who could actually discuss this adequately, so today we have with us Lincoln Bloomfield Jr. instead.

Given that since the withdrawal of US troops from Iraq, the State department is in charge of US policy now our troops are gone, and now it's all up to the State Department. I find it hard to believe that they could not find someone to come up here and tell us what it's all about. So be it.

Mr. Bloomfield is the Chairman of the Simpson Center. He was the special envoy for the Man Portable Air Defense Systems Threat Reduction from 2008 to 2009 and Assistant Secretary of State for Political Military Affairs for 2001 and 2005. Mr. Bloomfield previously served as Deputy Assistant Secretary Of State for Near Eastern Affairs from 1982-93, Deputy Assistant Vice President for National Security Affairs in 91- 92 and Principle Deputy Assistant Secretary of Defense for International Security Affairs from 88 to 89, among other positions. I don't see if I could squeeze any more positions in that resume dating back to 1981. Mr. Bloomfield, if you could try to limit your testimony so we could have a few questions as we expect a vote here, fairly soon. You may proceed.

**Ambassador Bloomfield:**

Thank you Chairman Rohrabacher and thank you for the invitation to appear before this subcommittee. With your permission sir, I prepared some testimony; I would ask that it be introduced into the record of the hearing.

**Chairman Rohrabacher:**

Without objection, so ordered.

**Ambassador Bloomfield:**

I will also be referring I expect to Mr. Boumedra's testimony, and perhaps if it's permissible his testimony, prepared statements and his briefing could be made part of the record if that is permissible.

**Chairman Rohrabacher:**

So ordered without objection.

**Ambassador Bloomfield:`**

Thank you very much. With your permission sir, I take just one minute. I have had five jobs in the State Department and I am going to talk about the State Department.

I like to just say a word of respect and condolence to the four State Department employees who lost their lives in Ben-Ghazi. It's a terrible loss and my condolences to their family and friends and to the State Department community. It just reminds us how tough and how important the work they do is and even though I will be framing a policy issue that is very much of a problem for the State Department it does not imply any disrespect at all for their vital mission or the people who serve.

I have one message and I would ask, I would hope the folks will digest my testimony. There are copies that would be made available through the records. Mr. Boumedra testified as a human rights expert and as a former UN official and it was clear from his testimony, from his briefing, that he is very much concerned that the United Nations uphold its own principles. So the reason he resigned was that he felt he was not being true to the principles of the UN and I respect that. The people in this room and there are constituents to the Subcommittee who have friends and relatives in Camp Liberty and Camp Ashraf and there is no question that they are vitally concerned for the welfare of their relatives in camp Liberty and camp Ashraf I share both of those concerns but my message concerns a third focus which is United States interests and US policy.

Looking at the facts of this case I believe that what Mr. Boumedra has brought to light has serious implications on US policy and Mr. Chairman you talked about this as well and I wanted to amplify the point you were getting at as well. From my perspective what we thought was happening in Iraq was that we were undergoing a process of relocation of 3400 people to a place where UNHCR could process them as potential refugees and the US governments hope is that they will complete the process that most if not all would qualify as refugees and they will find third party countries that are willing to take them in a perfect world all of them will be relocated elsewhere safely securely problem solved.

Secretary Clinton herself testified in February to the House Foreign Affairs Committee that that was United States policy to try to process these people as expeditiously as possible safely and securely and to see them passed along to willing third countries.

What we heard from Mr. Boumedra was something very very different. You heard them mention the Iranian embassy I heard him mention at least five meetings that the Iranian embassy is at the decision table what we heard was that an element of the Iraqi government surrounding the Prime Minister of Iraq is implementing an agenda that is very much Iran's agenda.

I am here today because I don't believe that the scenario that Mr. Boumedra has revealed as the real scenario that UNAMI has been supporting can be squared with the US goal here. I think that they are operating directly across purposes and that poses some serious problems and some serious risks. Some of the implications are that it puts the United States in a horrific position of giving this population at camp Ashraf essentially two choices either move to what you have clearly learned as a detention facility with seven check points guarded by a group that is commanded by Colonel Mohammad Sadeq who lead the 2011 April massacre.

Mr. Boumedra said he was taking orders we had heard that at the Nierenberg trials before he was at the command of security at camp Liberty I pray that no one at the State Department knew that when they consented to a process that would drive people to be put under a man who lead the massacre that alone has to be a human rights violation to be facing the guns of people who wounded you and who killed people amongst you is clearly a problem and so there has been resistance amongst this population not to be put in that position and they had been told again by the Secretary of State in that same testimony that her deliberations on the foreign terrorist organization list her decision to whether to list or delist the MEK will be guided in large part by how much cooperation this population exercises in leaving willingly and going to camp Liberty so look at the choice and I must say we have heard through the appeals court process that the Secretary Clinton herself has been pre occupied by some major crisis in the world and I take them at their word that she is not able to review the file herself but to put the Secretary in a position that she is saying either go to a detention center where you going be unarmed looking at people who have killed people amongst you or plan to be on the terrorism list from now to eternity where you cannot travel your families are separated from folks in the US and all your movements are being tracked by financial investigators FBI and counter terrorism people that is the choice we have given them and I just don't believe that the United States if they knew all the facts that we have now learned would allow the United States to be behind that kind of a Hobson's choice there would have to be a third option that respects the principals of human rights and I think America is better than that I hope that the Secretary of State would become acquainted at least with those facts we should not be coercing the population into an untenable and illegal situation. Secondly, there has been some concern and I have investigated the open source about the MeK history that the Iranian intelligence for years has been planting false information it doesn't mean that MeK was not conducting armed resistance against the mullahs in Iran I could talk about that but my point is that when the last group leaves camp Ashraf what protection do we have that they are not going to plant false evidence that they were planning terrorist activities there by manipulate our counter terrorism policy ,

And some of the residents of camp Ashraf have asked for a third-party independent investigation of camp Ashraf, and have been told "No" and I believe the US government has said it's not necessary. That's a risk.

The third risk is a third massacre. Imagine if Col. Sadeq, who—by the way—did travel -- he went to France this summer to try to brief the European Parliament and was arrested at the door and held for several hours and then put on a plane back to Iraq. But if there's a third massacre, this does implicate the United States law. And as someone who has worked for years on security assistance relationships, this one, we've lost a lot of troops to try to get us to the point where US and Iraqi forces will mentor and will be partners for many years, we have huge programs with jobs lined-up behind them: fighter aircrafts, tanks, their assembly lines that are waiting for these programs to go forward.

If there is a third massacre, the Arms Export Control Act could severely complicate that. It would give the Congress and the administration a terrible choice of either overlooking the law and giving them a pass under those circumstances or interrupting a program for which so many troops fought and died.

There is also the Leahy Human Rights Law and if Colonel Sadeq doesn't qualify as someone who has committed gross human rights violations I don't know who would, but he should be banned under the law from ever receiving training from the United States.

Those are two laws that I helped enforce and wrote the guidance for in some cases, and there is no good outcome here. And I guess I would say as long as this Iranian and Prime Minister Maliki's agenda to do as Mr. Boumedra said, it's an announced policy to make their lives unbearable. So we hear a lot about clean water and air conditioning and private property and these are huge issues but if you look at it strategically as part of a plan to make them lose their will and say "alright, I can't look at this 120 degree container box any more, just let me out of here" and put them out into the open in Iraq where they could be vulnerable to Iraqi elements or to Iranian intelligence and then take the top 200 [or] thereabouts for whom there are arrests warrants out who could never qualify by the way as refugees as long as there is a warrant out. The plan would obviously be turn them over to Iran which violates the non-refoulement principle, which is a cardinal principle of humanitarian law. Do we want to be a party to such things?

I testified last December that I wondered why we didn't try to move the whole enterprise with the UNHCR to a safe harbor somewhere else. I repeat that recommendation today and I redouble my belief that US interests and the State Department's interest would be much better served if Secretary Clinton tried really hard, maybe at the UN general assembly meetings this month, to find a friendly country to take all of these people.

**Chairman Rohrabacher:**

It was pretty hard to miss that. In fact If I remember seeing those photos, did you watch the videos?

Yes Sir.

Was he the fat guy with gun shooting at the people?

**Ambassador Bloomfield:**

I don't know.

You are correct, it was him

**Chairman Rohrabacher:**

So, he was

It is a disgrace. It is a betrayal of everything America believes. We made a deal with these people and now we have someone who has already committed a massacre against them and put that person in charge of their security.

**Ambassador Bloomfield:**

If I could make a comment Mr. Chairman, we can look back and say this was a mistake, that was a mistake, but we could also look forward and say worse things could happen, third massacre could happen, that would be detrimental to America's honour and reputation. One of the things I learned from listening to Mr. Boumedra is that the US forces who provided 4Th Geneva Convention Protected Person status to all residents of Camp Ashraf in 2003 and gave them Protected Person identity card, there is a Rand report we could discuss, I have some issues with the report, which tries to make the case that it should have never been granted, however, in any case, it did not outlive when US troops pulled back from Camp Ashraf. Mr. Boumedra says under article 45 of the 4th Geneva Convention which I have read and try to understand as a non-lawyer, if the party that you give the security over to, namely Iraq does a good job, then you are fine. If the party that you hand security over to does not uphold their security, you continue to have that obligation. So, we have and he wrote this in his column in the Hill that the United States has an international legal obligation that continues to this day, a promise made in 2003 has not expired for those residents. So, it is more than just a moral issue, it is a legal obligation. I dearly say that is why so many senior US former leaders are outspoken on this issue.

**Chairman Rohrabacher:**

It sound like an obligation to fulfill a contract, what we are talking about is the potential massacre of unarmed human beings and if that outcome happens, it will not be because, oh, we did not know that was possible, what a mistake we made by overlooking the fact that the Colonel who last oversaw the massacre is now put in charge of their security. This is not a mistake, this is evil …….. of duty on the part of our people who establish these policies of our government that reflect what I consider to be the moral base of American.

Secretary of State, for example, we have no doubt that the secretary knows exactly what this situation is. I mean this is not "well I'm so busy that I overlooked it, I was just too busy…" no she knows. And it's the policy of this administration; it's the policy that was decided upon by this administration, this secretary of state, this president to make a rotten corrupt deal with the mullah dictatorship in Iran. That's what it's all about. It's not about a mistake, it's about an intentional deal that has been made and kept from the American people. Now how do you verify that that deal actually exists? Well it's sort of like the old thing: quack! Quack! If it looks like a duck, and walks like a duck, and talks like a duck, and flies like a duck, it's probably a duck. And that's what we probably have on our hands here, not a duck but what we have is an immoral deal between our government and the mullah dictatorship, because all the indications are that that's what's driving this bad policy. I will now yield to Judge Poe, who will tell us whether or not what I said is admissible in his court.

**Congressman Ted Poe:**

Thank you Mr. Chairman. Mr. Bloomfield, thank you for your candor. I am surprised, but I do appreciate your candor today.

We have a large group of people that our seated behind you and I see tired eyes in this audience. This are just regular folks. Many of them, as you know, have family in Ashraf or Liberty. Many of them had family in Camp Ashraf. They have friends that have been murdered in Camp Ashraf by the Maliki government. The person in charge is now in charge of Camp Liberty. And these eyes that I see, these tired eyes, they're tired for a lot of reasons. They are tired of being treated not like people but like criminals. Maybe even worse than criminals, they are tired of promises, promises, and promises. They are tired of abuse. They are tired of having their properties being stolen from them. They are tired of being treated as sub-humans. They are tired of the loss of lives of their family and their friends, tired eyes. They are tired of Maliki, they are tired of Iran and they are tired of the United States' promises to keep them safe.

We are, as you know, the human rights country in the world. We have done a pretty good job of spreading that Gospel. We have not done a good job at all with these people, the MEK. They are in the situation they are in because of the United States. We labeled them as a Foreign Terrorist Organization. You do not see eyes of terrorists in this room. They are not terrorist.

And we have it in our power to help this bad situation with the Maleki government, with the Iranian government, with the criminals that are stealing their property and stealing their lives. We have it in our power to fix it. You mentioned that it would be great if we could get them all to some other country. They can not get in another country. They cannot leave Iraq because no country will take them. Because we, the US, have given them a label of a Foreign Terrorist Organization. We remove that label as we should have done a long time ago and they will have hope to go to some other country even the United States. But they can not get out of their concentration camp because of the label, our label. And in the last year the State Department has been stone walling court order in our country telling them to get it together, make up your mind, review the designation! Whether they should keep that designation or not? And by making no decision they are still labeled. So the day of reckoning ought to be the Secretary of State when she goes to the UN in my opinion ought to say: guess what folks we are removing the FTO designation from the MEK. And now we are going to help those people get out of Iraq and actually be free. And then we may no longer see tired eyes. The eyes that believe in Liberty in Camp Liberty.

I have one question. Well, I have a lot of questions. I don't know how much time you are going to let me talk, but I am going to talk till you make me stop.

I understand your position. I understand your position in our government and some of our questions probably should be to others. What can we do to make sure as a nation, us, that Martin Kobler is removed from is removed from and authority in the United Nations?

**Ambassador Bloomfield:**

Judge Poe, as you know, I am speaking as a former official. In my testimony, you will see, I was shocked and disappointed by the statement out of the UN under-secretary for political affairs office on July 28.

The reaction to the news that Mr. Boumedra was launching is going on, I leave that to Mr. Boumedra to talk about, but that was the public statement.

I am not aware that the US government has made an official statement of reaction. I urge them to be very careful and I stated an example that were, when I had 320 people in the state department under my leadership there was an allegation made. I did not know if it was true or false. I did not know if the person was credible or not. I had no choice but to do the right thing, which is had a town hall meeting. Announce that we are going to allow the professional investigators to come in and we are all going to cooperate. It was painful. It slowed us down in our work, but we did the right thing because the minute that you started sending the message that standard and laws and rules can be overlooked, it is a very slippery slope.

So my answer would be: UN should be sending in another envoy, may be they do not want to dismiss Mr. Kobler they should send in a veteran to ride side saddle and watch over what happens from here. That is point one.

Point two is really the US government. I am here to tell you that the Government of Iran ever wants the exiles inside Iraq to leave alive. Because if they do, they will find safe harbor in countries around the world and they will conduct political activities aimed at ending the dictatorship in Tehran. We know that the government of Tehran does not want that to happen. That is clearly now believed to be the operative policy.

I think the state department needs to take a deep breath and say our plan, the one the Secretary testified to, the smooth, processing and onward relocation is going to take years and probably it is not going to happen because the government of Iraq or the Prime Minister office with Iranian Embassy and the regime in Tehran right behind them is going to obstruct this at every turn. It is a losing proposition. We need to think of something different. My due is something perhaps they could be granted refugee status but short of that the UNHCR process could be relocated into a safe facility that they are still under the supervision of the United Nations that they could be interviewed and there would be no coercion; there would no threat to public safety and to the lives of these people and there would be no question of United States being complicit in the violation of international humanitarian standard human rights laws.

**Judge Ted Poe:**

Thanks Mr. Chairman

**Chairman Rohrabacher:**

Well, it is clear that the government of Tehran, the Mullahs Dictatorship is not acting in good faith. After all, what they really want us, as you say, they want this group of people to be squashed like bugs. So they would not be bothered by them. It appears that government of Iraq is not operating in good faith. Any government that places a perpetuator of a massacre, in charge of security over the same group of people, who have been massacred, certainly is not operating in a good faith. There is no doubt these people know what they are doing. Well, that leaves the United States government; are we in a good faith? Is our State Department operating in good faith? Considered the fact that this could be solved we believe at least we know would be very good possibility that we could solve the situation in an acceptable way. If our designation of this group as a terrorist group was taken off, I do not see how we can assume that our government is operating in good faith. That's pretty bad. Well, this is pretty bad. The mullah regime is not acting in good faith. Iraq is not operating in good faith. US State Department is not operating in good faith. I am kind of disappointed from that crowd.

And so let's just note this in 1939 the U.S. St. Louis, a passenger vessel was loaded with Jews in Europe, and it took off for the West. And a whole ship load of Jews who were going to escape the holocaust. You know what happened to that ship, we turned them down, well the US turned them down and a significant number were back in the Europe and died in the holocaust.

A group of people who have already suffered a massacre knowing that they may well be massacred and we are just going to say no we are not going to change that designation and we expect the ship to sail on.

**Ambassador Bloomfield:**

Mr. Chairman I give you my perspective as someone who has served in 5 administrations, I can't get the policy calculus out of my mind. A lot of issues are imperfect, a lot of issues that are hard sometimes too hard. No one can say this is easy for the state Department, I recognized that.

The question is now what should we be doing to rectify the situation, I would say foreign terrorist organization list is not an impediment to living up to our human rights standards and fulfilling our international legal obligations as a super power, anything less is not acceptable. We can do this in the right way, so there is no excuse not to stand up for our principles. If we were to back away from Mr. Maliki's activities, as if to say seeding him the plain field, at a time frankly when Iran is losing its grip in Syria and Lebanon, this is not the time for us to be seeding territory in what is used to be the strongest country in the Arab world to people who are not fulfilling international legal principles. What we should be doing is making an issue of it and urging them and showing them forwards that says if you straighten up we can do this the right way but you need to stop abusing an at risk population. On the issue of foreign terrorist listing, I think the analogy can go a little further. What is foreign terrorist organization listing? What does that mean? It means we have some of the smartest, most patriotic talented people who were good enough to get into the treasury department, the FBI, the national counter-terrorism center, these are the people who are supposed to be tracking terrorist around the world. If you are on that list, they are chasing you through Interpol, they are looking for financial transaction, they are looking for front companies, they are checking airline manifests, that is their job and they are doing it very well. So, if a group is on that list and I am a European government, I am thinking to myself do I really want the treasury department and FBI and all these people tracking, do I want to bring people to be tracked through all this scrutiny and jam up my airline security, do I want all that? I don't think the US government has been honest about the burden the FTO places. Should they be on the list or not, I have never answered that question. I have studies the issue but I left it to people to read the evidence for themselves. Now I am close to completing a very in-depth study of all the allegations including the history, and I cannot find anything that comports with the 2004 law, certainly not within 2 to 5 years that would fall under the definition of terrorism. That doesn't mean it doesn't exist but if you permit me imagine that there is something that is classified, imagine there is a smoking gun piece of intelligence, all I can say if it is a month old, if it is a year or two years old and we haven't released it and I was the British government, I would say you let us have a royal wedding, you let us have the queen's 60th jubilee and we had the Olympic games and you didn't tell us that there is a smoking gun of terrorist activity of people who are running around our country free, that would be issue one and if the answer was actually we did share it with the Brits, then you are going to have a call from the appeals court which we know for a fact hasn't seen it, they are waiting for it, you gave it to a foreign country but you didn't give it here to a court of law.

### Chairman Rohrabacher:

How about you didn't give it to the Oversight and investigation subcommittee of the congress that is supposed to oversee the American foreign policy?

This is outrageous; it is obvious to me, actually obvious to any honest observer that this designation is on there for some corrupt agreement with someone and that someone is likely to be the mullah's regime in Tehran. I don't know what we got for it, probably they wouldn't be supporting terrorist activities as long as we kept this terrorist group on the list. What is the dictatorship of mullahs who have murdered so many people in their country, who think who the terrorist is that is anybody who opposes them,

The world should never forget one organization exposed the Iranian nuclear program. And America should never forget our duty given the role we played in Iraq to make sure that refugees at camp Liberty are treated correctly and the remaining residents of camp Ashraf are treated in a manner consistent with high standards of human rights. I was leading Democrat on a letter with the chairwoman Ileana Ros-Lehtinen last July to press the State Department and the Iraqi government to improve the dire living conditions at camp Liberty. Some 79 members of both political parties in the house of representative joined us in that letter, and now we have to do everything possible to make sure the fundamental rights of the exiles are respected that we see humane living conditions that those who are sick and wounded receive medical attention, and the Iraqi government cannot be left to its own devices. The standards should be what is called for by international law not what does Baghdad want to do in order to put its terror act.

http://www.isdciran.org/index.php?option=com_content&view=article&id=1840:tahar-boumedra-united-states-house-of-representatives&catid=10:conferences&Itemid=25

## United Nations Headquarters - Geneva
Remarks by Tahar Boumedra
28 February 2013

Geneva, February 28, 2013 - Thank you Mr. President. Thank you Madam President. It was really a painful experience for me, three years and a half I spent in Iraq, a very injuring experience. My sister next to me (Ms. Zanjani) was one of the victims that were there personally, in Ashraf, to persuade her to leave and to go look after herself in Canada. And she firmly refused my offer to help sending her for treatment in Canada. But my job in Iraq as chief of human rights was to promote and protect human rights. My job in Iraq, as advisor to the Special Representative of the Secretary General (SRSG) is to advise him on the right path for finding a dignified way for the Ashrafis to get out of that situation and I must admit that I think I failed in both missions, because I did not protect and I did not really change much on the ground in Ashraf. But the reality is that I witnessed a lot and I could tell you that the experience I went through, it is extremely difficult to summarize it in a few minutes but I'll make sure that I won't be too long

First I would like to shed some light on UNAMI's actions vis-a-vis the Ashrafis. We operated always on the presumption of guilt of these people. Everything we did at UNAMI, we presumed that they are terrorists and we dealt with them accordingly. I did advise UNAMI that the fundamental principle in the United Nations is to presume innocence, but unfortunately that was not the case. We worked exactly opposite and in defiance of the fundamental principle of justice, which is the presumption of innocence.

On that ground, we drafted a so-called Memorandum of Understanding for the relocation of the Ashrafis from Camp Ashraf to Camp Liberty. This Memorandum of Understanding is absolutely the content of a letter, addressed by the Ambassador of Iraq in Brussels to the Member States of the EU, telling them what's the plan and the program for the government of Iraq to relocate these people. In this letter, he categorically tells them: "These are a group of dangerous terrorists and the government will take all necessary measures to get them out of Iraq, to expel them out of Iraq." Now again, this letter is drafted on the presumption of guilt and the due process of law was put aside. Because the government of Iraq, the current government of Iraq, when you talk about the process of law it is something completely different. Now, the draft MoU was that it's a shared responsibility between UNAMI and the government of Iraq to close Camp Ashraf. Then, we sent this draft MoU to New York to the department of legal affairs (OLA) to ask for advice. We were told: This is dangerous, you are assuming, UNAMI is taking responsibility. No, we don't want you to take any responsibility. We want you to simply be a facilitator. So, we changed the MoU accordingly. If you look at the MoU, the actually signed MoU. Seven clauses in the MoU, they all give the responsibility to the government of Iraq. The seventh clause of the MoU is related to the work of the UNHCR. It just sort of strips the government of Iraq of its responsibility vis-a-vis the mandate of the UNHCR. It says that, even though the government agrees that the UNHCR will take the refugee status determination process, the RSD, it is not bound by it; it will not recognise the outcome of this process. Meaning, let the UN do whatever they want to do, but we have our own way of handling the situation.

That said, we started preparing, after the signature of this document we started preparing the transfer process. And we had to first make two assessments. And unfortunately, most of you heard about one assessment, the humanitarian assessment in Camp Liberty, but no one ever mentioned the security assessment of Camp Liberty. So, we first made the security assessment of Camp Liberty and we found that the camp is so vulnerable. And then we started talking about how to attenuate the vulnerability of the camp. It was by making sure that we had more Fijians, more soldiers, Fijians are the ones protecting UNAMI, to protect not the Ashrafis but to protect the UN staff. So we were reinforced to the attenuate security situation. But we did not do anything to protect the Ashrafis.

So now we moved to the second assessment of Camp Liberty. Camp Liberty was assessed by a specialist brought from the UNHCR in Addis Ababa, at very high cost. And he was brought to certify whether Camp Liberty meets the international standards or not. He arrives, we met him and he was instructed to certify. Mr. Kobler told him: "You are not here to do anything but to certify." And the man was put in a very difficult position. I was with him, I was the first to visit with him Camp Liberty and we all agreed that this is an unacceptable situation. Particularly, knowing very well Ashraf and knowing that it is not a situation of refugees who are running for their lives, to save their lives in an emergency situation. This is what the shelter expert was looking for. We have people, like now in Syria or elsewhere in Africa when people are actually running away to seek refuge to save their lives from imminent danger. That was not the case in Ashraf. The case of Ashraf was people settled peacefully for twenty-five years in Camp Ashraf and all of a sudden, for political reasons, the government decides to evict them from their homes. So we should not confuse between relocation and eviction. The case of Ashraf it was an eviction. And UNAMI was very well aware of the conditions according to the UN standards of an eviction. An eviction has to be done in accordance with the due process of law by a judicial process.

All this did not happen and we were aware that we were violating the fundamental principles of the United Nations. But yet we had to be positive, according to the instructions of the SRSG. Positive, it means close your eyes. Don't try to, sort of, expose the situation because we are here to save lives. So he claims. To save lives. And we know that Camp Liberty is not a place to save lives and I hear that in this forum. I tell you frankly, through my connections with the Iraqis, they never hide anything concerning the Ashrafis. They always told me: "We will get them." It was not a secret and it is not also a secret that documentation is there. The Council of Ministers decision that says we will use all means, all means, which means including the use of force, to evict them. So we followed this process and we signed at UNAMI the document in order to give some kind of legitimacy to an otherwise illegal operation. So this is why, when you look closely at the MoU, what is the role of the United Nations? There is no role for the United Nations whatsoever except to give some legitimacy to what the government of Iraq, the Prime Minister's office, wants to do. So it was done.

Now, when the ninth of February attack took place I felt that I was vindicated in a sense, that I did warn not only UNAMI, I warned UNHCR and at particularly UNHCR I warned them even after I resigned from the UN. Last summer, I went to the UNHCR and I told them there will be an attack, there will be blood. And you will be accountable for it. And all I got from them was just some smile to say: "Oh, don't worry." So now, here we are. We have covered up all kind of illegal measures, we covered them up and we made lies, blatant lies. We doctored documents, yes we did, and I was the head of the team that doctored the pictures. Now, there is also some cover-up in the human rights report and I'll just give you a very simple example of the kind of cover-up, subtle cover-up. The events of April 2011, I was on the ground and I did a fact finding. I reported that there was extrajudicial killings. When we talk about extrajudicial killings it is different from what you have read in the human rights report where it said there was excessive use of force. Excessive use of force! I mean the police have the right to use force but if they use excessive force that is something that should be called to order. But extrajudicial killing is a crime and in the particular circumstances of Ashraf it was a crime against humanity. So that is the difference. But this report was signed in Baghdad, amended here in Geneva and in New York to come back to us in Baghdad to be presented, before it was made public, to the government of Iraq to agree to it and then we make it public. So this is the kind of procedure for covering up the serious violations of human rights in Iraq.

Mr. President, I beg you to give me some time, just to move now from UNAMI to UNHCR. Yes? Two minutes. The story with the UNHCR: From 2009 I was trying to convince them to get involved in this process and the position of the UNHCR was that: "No, these people are terrorists. We do not deal with them, we don't visit them." And the UNHCR never visited Camp Ashraf until I took them there. Why didn't they want to visit Ashraf? They said they would only deal with defectors. But I said, hold on, defectors are charged with a political kind of meanings, but this is a violation of the International Covenant on Civil and Political Rights. People, whether refugees or not, they have a right to political opinion, they have a right to association and a right to express themselves. So why does the UNHCR only want to deal with defectors? And to be honest to you, what they call defectors... Usually when there are some people that want to leave Ashraf they are taken out of the camp, the Iraqi Army will put them in isolation for up to three months and do the brainwashing and then they bring them to me to interview them to sort of put them stamp of the UN that these people have made declarations, serious, very serious declarations. What are these serious declarations?

I testify here in front of you that all the people I interviewed, none of them told me anything that has been reported in different reports in Iraq and Iran or elsewhere, particularly what was reported in the RAND report and also the Human Rights Watch report of 2005. All that was fake and I testify to that. So UNHCR set this as criteria for dealing with Ashrafis that they have defected, they have to run away and submit themselves to the Iraqi Army. And then the Iraqi Army will take them to the UNHCR. But INHCR always told us that they want to deal with them with total impartiality, neutrality. But still they put them in Hotel [Assohor] and Hotel [Enmuhajad], two hotels, and there the Iranian security people will visit them. It's a long story so let me just stop here on this point.

Now, when I convinced the UNHCR to visit Camp Ashraf, they said: "Yes, we are here to take applications from you. We are ready to address your applications and do the interviews here in Ashraf, inside the camp." A few weeks later they changed their mind because the Iraqis were not happy with that. I said: OK, we will do the interviews outside Ashraf but after the interview people will go back to Ashraf. And that with the agreement with the Ashrafis. The Ashrafis designated a building were the interviews could take place. Then, at the pressure of the government of Iraq, this plan was removed. And then, with the help of Kobler it's decided to do the interviews outside Camp Liberty.

Camp Liberty was known to be a serious threat to the Ashrafis. The UN was aware of that and we did it. Now people have witnessed the attack. We know that it is vulnerable. People died. Whoever is behind this process must be held accountable. I repeat my call that there must be an inquiry, and independent inquiry into the killing, into the attack on Camp Liberty and the killing of seven people and the maiming of over one hundred people. The UN has played a fundamental role in this operation. It must send an independent commission of inquiry.

Let me say one thing, Mr. President, the very final one. It's about why the Ashrafis should be sent back to Ashraf. It's just a question of, and I use the military words used in UNAMI, and which we have in UNAMI, a safe haven. A safe haven is a military preparation where if an attack takes place we just go underground and be protected. In Camp Liberty there is not such a thing, but in Ashraf there are safe havens. And if we want to take the responsibility to protect these people the most fundamental concern is the safety and security of these people. Save them before any other process. Let's forget about refugee status determination process. Let's forget about the relocation process. Imminent danger is there, protect these people! I tell you, I've said this and I repeat this, there is an imminent danger and you will hear, in the few coming weeks that another attack took place, all the people died and people will come to condemn and that will be it. I really would like everybody to believe that the danger is imminent and we need to take actions to protect!

I thank you very much Mr. President

http://www.isdciran.org/index.php?option=com_content&view=article&id=1814:t ahar-boumedra-liberty-serious-threat-to-ashraf-residents&catid=10:conferences&Itemid=25

**European Parliament**
**Formal session of Delegation for Relations with Iraq**
27 March 2013

**Tahar Boumedra**
*Former Chief of the Human Rights Office for the United Nations Assistance Mission for Iraq (UNAMI)*

I am the former adviser of the Special Representative of the Secretary General Mr. Kobler and also the former chief of the human rights office of UNAMI. I resigned from this position in protest of what I witnessed in both preparing people to be relocated from Camp Ashraf to Camp Liberty and also over the situation I witnessed in Camp Liberty.

Let me tell you from the beginning that I was the person who took the lead in drafting the MOU (Memorandum of Understanding) for the closure of Camp Ashraf and the relocation to Camp Liberty. I could assure you that the draft report I took the lead in preparing was not the one actually approved by the Prime Minister Al Maliki. It was redrafted on 25th of December, on Christmas day. It was redrafted between Martin Kobler and Faleh Fayaz the security adviser of the Prime Minister.

But let me also tell you the background of this MOU. We did prepare it with the intention and the ultimate objective of disbanding the MEK or PMOI (Iranian opposition group). That was the ultimate objective to disband the MEK and expel them from Iraq. That was absolutely the policy of the government of Iraq. And UNAMI was there to implement and help the government of Iraq to implement this policy and we did it. Now I came to resign because I found myself as the chief of the human rights misleading the international community and misleading the United Nations.

How? We drafted the MOU and we have not done anything to effectively protect. What we have done was to close Camp Ashraf and relocate the residents to Camp Liberty. Now we made two assessments to Camp Liberty before people were transferred there. We made a humanitarian assessment and a security assessment. And I am afraid to say that nobody ever mentioned the security assessment we made in November of 2011.

That security assessment pointed exactly to vulnerability of the Camp from the air from missile attacks. But we did nothing to protect the residents that will be soon arriving there. On the contrary, the United Nations recruited 62 Fijian soldiers to enforce the security of UN personnel that will be going to Camp Liberty. Nothing was done to reinforce the security or to guarantee safety and security of the residents. That is the security.

In the return assessment, and I was in charge of that assessment, I reported that the Camp was not fit to accommodate 3300 people. The humanitarian situation was appalling. Now, my boss Martin Kobler asked me to lead, in actually doctoring pictures and reports. I was asked to put together "appealing," this is the word he used "appealing pictures" of the Camp and we made a lot of them about 500 pictures of the Camp and he himself had to actually make the selections which pictures are sellable to the international community and to the Ashraf residents. So we did it.

We mislead the international community, we misled the EU delegation which I used to brief every other week. I used to brief them on the human rights situation not only in Camp Liberty but also in Iraq in general. So we misled the international community and I did warn, not only Kobler but also the UN in general, that the situation is not as represented by Kobler to the international community. Unfortunately I found no ear to listen to me and I was about giving up because I felt that I might pass my message better outside of UN than within the UN.

I want to also point out that in preparing this process, we had met with the Iranian embassy and every time we met with the Iranian ambassador we had to prepare to present to him accounts on what have we done so far and they were never happy to the extent that he refused to give a visa to Kobler to go to Iran.

I tell you that Kobler got his visa to go to Iran on the day the first groups of Ashrafis were transferred to Camp Liberty. So that was done. Now we have numerous meetings with the Iraqi authorities and they made public announcement that they will not be bound by the human rights standards of UNAMI and the United Nations and that is on public record.

Every time we discussed the humanitarian situation we were told forget about the UN standards we are not going to give VIP treatment to people who are terrorists. Now when we decided to finally move on and in order to convince the international community that everything is fine, the UN hired a shelter expert they brought him from Ethiopia to visit Camp Liberty and to certify that Camp Liberty has actually the required humanitarian standards.

The shelter expert refused. I was with him we discussed in details the situation on the ground and he issued a draft report saying that he cannot certify. So Kobler decided to do without him, and believe me, this was done at serious money, tax payers money, EU money, US as well. So this serious money was spent just to bring somebody to make a report, and then that report was dismissed and Kobler issued his own report and we finally convinced everybody that things are up to the standards.

Face to face, I asked Kobler how can we do that, we are the UN we have values to live up to. Kobler would tap me on the shoulder and say "be positive." Be positive meaning forget about human rights, forget about humanitarian standards, we need to do the job, we need to close

Camp Ashraf, and we need to relocate these people. That's the mission that is what UNAMI is doing.

Now in my job as a human rights officer I always addressed the Iraqis and I was also advising the Iraqis in my capacity as the chief of human rights office. I always advised them and requested that the humanitarian standard set by the US army before they handed over the Camp to the Iraqis I spoke to them. There is a standard about the medical treatment, about the food, water and electricity. There are these standards set by the US army and we need to keep that standard going because after all the supplies that the Ashraf residents receive, they pay for them they pay for it at a more expensive price than the price in Iraq. Most of the utility needs are imported from Kuwait.

You will ask me why they import from Kuwait, it is because there is legislation in Iraq: to make it a criminal offense to cooperate with Ashraf people. So anybody, organization or individual caught cooperating with the Ashraf residents will be prosecuted under the anti-terrorism act. And this is why they resort to importing things at very high costs.

But yet I hear that the government tried to justify that they are doing all they could in order to facilitate their life. They keep on denying them any improvement in the Camp. When I asked the government why do you do that, the reply was we don't want to make their life comfortable because they will not leave Iraq if we make their life comfortable, so we have to make it "unbearable". So life has to be unbearable and therefore they will be forced to leave.

But let me also mention that there are about 200 arrest warrants against these people. These arrest warrants, some of them issued in Tehran, others issued in Baghdad, target the leadership of the Ashraf. And the whole process of closing Camp Ashraf and sending them to Camp Liberty is in order to actually arrest the leadership. And the whole problem for Iran and Iraq is the leadership; it is not the rest of the population.

So once they transfer them to Camp Liberty. In fact we were expecting that in the process of the transfer there will be a chaotic situation where the normal residents will suddenly just disappear and then in that chaos the government would move in to arrest the leadership. But it did not happen the way the government wished and no Ashraf residents deserted the Camp.

Now I could tell you and I had lengthy discussions with the Iraqis that the security situation is not going to stop there. We witnessed the act of 9th of February and that was not unpredictable. We knew it is going to happen and we also know right now that further attacks will happen and it is organized in Baghdad the government of Al Maliki is responsible for that. I could tell you that I discussed this and I was always told that these people are criminals they are terrorists and those who have blood on their hands they have to be arrested and extradited and those who don't have blood on their hands will just take their way out and disappear in the air, that is the plan.

Now I am really sorry to sort of find myself in this situation where all the values I lived up to when I joined the United Nations I find myself facing exactly the opposite. When as the chief human rights I was advocating that nobody should ever be arrested or held for a crime without the due process of law, the United Nations, the UNAMI in particular did everything indeed so far under the presumption that these people are guilty.

I opposed to this presumption I asked Kobler you cannot do that, he tells me "be positive." Be positive it means just keep your eyes closed.

Now the presumption of innocence the United Nations including the UNHCR presume that these people are guilty therefore they are not eligible for the refugee status and this is what is delaying the process and let me remind you that a similar process took place in Camp Mahmour. You all know Camp Mahmour; it is a place for the PKK refugees.

I have to tell you those who were processed, I think about 1,500, they were not adjudicated as refugees of concern to the international community. Once you are adjudicated as refugee you have the right to freedom of movement, you have the right to travel documents, you have the right to education, you have all the rights of a refugee.

The Ashrafis do not have these rights and yet the UNHCR is keeping quiet on this issue. Worse than that, if you look at the Clause 7 of the MOU signed by Kobler and the government of Iraq, Clause 7 strips the UNHCR from its very mandate. It says that the Iraqi government will allow the UNHCR to undertake the RSD (Refugee Status Determination) process but will not be bound by its outcome, meaning the government of Iraq will not recognize the refugee status of these people even though they are recognized by UNHCR. And yet we do not report on this.

The report to the Security Council by the Secretary General, I tell you how this report was prepared and it is a normal procedure. Every Special Representative of the Secretary General prepares his own chapter to be integrated in the Secretary General's report to the Security Council. So what was quoted in the three chapters about Ashraf, as was presented by Kobler, they were prepared in Baghdad by Kobler himself. So here again misusing the Security Council and this is very dangerous I am afraid.

I thank you very much for your attention.

## UK Parliament
Remarks by Tahar Boumedra
29 January 2013

Thank you Mr. Chairman. Members of this house, the mother of Parliaments, ladies and gentlemen, I received a letter from the Office of the Legal Affairs of the United Nations threatening me, trying to silence me. Because what I'm saying does not fall in their ears, it's rather disturbing. But I replied to the Office of the Legal Affairs of the United Nations that I will stand firm with the United Nations Charter. Maybe they could accuse me of breaching some rules or procedures but I'm not breeching the rules I'm not breeching the fundamentals of the United Nations, I'm standing for the fundamentals of the United Nations.

Now, as a witness for those who probably didn't hear me before, I was the Chief of UNAMI Human Rights Office in Iraq and I was also the advisor of the Special Representative of the Secretary General, Kobler. In that capacity I was taking the lead on the Ashraf file and let me tell you I'm not going to breech anymore the rules of confidentiality of the United Nations. The documents are already in the public domain.

This report that was published in the Sunday Telegraph of the UNHCR that reads in parts that from a technical point of view UNHCR cannot certify and/or verify that the location, meaning Camp Liberty, meets humanitarian standards according to many existing standard books and it meant that UNHCR have book Sphere, the W.H.O etc. This is a document that I witness. It was done by a person who was hired by your tax money. He was hired, he's worked in Adisababa in Ethiopia, and he was brought to Baghdad with your tax money. And he was suppose to assess the situation on the ground and certify or otherwise, that Camp Liberty, whether Camp Liberty meets or doesn't meet the international standards.

Now we commissioned him in December he arrived he worked for two weeks. He visited with me Camp Liberty and previously I had so many visits and I had already reported that Camp Liberty does not meet the international standards. First of all the whole question put to the expert was a misleading question. It was whether Camp Liberty could be comparable to refugee camps in Ethiopia. This is absolutely out of order. It's a question of a population living in the highly organised city of Ashraf, being evicted and taken to a former military base that has been completely vandalized and looted.

Now I said to the UNAMI leadership that this is unacceptable, yet to prove that I'm wrong they brought the expert. The expert was brought in order to certify and nothing else. He was told from the day he arrived you are here to certify. I went with him to Camp Liberty, he saw things, he reported and he reported that he cannot certify. Kobler was outraged! He said to him we want you to certify and he refused. After the meeting 4:00 O'clock, on the 18th December 2012, after the meeting in the SRSG's Office I moved with the expert shelter Martin Zerek from Switzerland, we moved to my office where he collapsed, he collapsed because of the pressure, and he had a nervous breakdown and yet he did not certify. A week later Kobler decided to certify.

So you saw his press release on 31st January 2012 where he said the United Nations High Commissionaire for Refugees and United Nations Human Rights Office have now confirmed that the infrastructure and facilities at Camp Liberty are in accordance with international humanitarian standards stipulated in the MOU. This is very interesting reference to the MOU instead of the UNHCR handbooks. What is stipulated in the MOU, the clause 7 in the MOU said that Iraq will not recognize any outcome of the work of the UNHCR. So those who read carefully, who know also the background of those document of Kobler, they will understand that it is again, once again misleading the United Nations and misleading the international community.

I'm really surprised that the United Nations is keeping quiet despite my repeated alarms, my repeated warnings, I said that in the U.S Congress, I said it in this House and yet nothing has been done to at least verify what I'm saying. At least an independent commission of enquiry looks at these two documents. This is the expert shelter documents and this is the UNAMI documents. Let somebody look at them and hold whoever is misleading the international community accountable. I thank you very much.

http://www.isdciran.org/index.php?option=com_content&view=article&id=1841:tahar-boumedra-uk-parliament-on-martin-koblers-conduct&catid=10:conferences&Itemid=25